EX LIBRIS:

THE
INVISIBLE
ALCOHOLICS

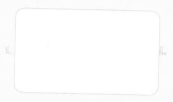

THE
INVISIBLE
ALCOHOLICS

WOMEN AND ALCOHOL
ABUSE IN AMERICA

Marian Sandmaier

McGRAW-HILL BOOK COMPANY

New York   St. Louis   San Francisco
Toronto   Sydney   London   Mexico   Düsseldorf

2 3 4 5 6 7 8 9 B P B P 8 7 6 5 4 3 2 1 0

LIBRARY OF CONGRESS CATALOGING IN PUBLICATION DATA
Sandmaier, Marian.
    The invisible alcoholics.
    1.   Alcohol and women—United States.   I.   Title
HV5137.S25   362.2'92   79–17819
ISBN 0–07–054660–6

Book design by Marsha Picker.

to my mother and my father

CONTENTS

ACKNOWLEDGMENTS

I thought about and talked about writing this book for several months before my friend Jon Landau finally suggested that I stop "not writing" it. I am grateful to him for giving me the push I needed to begin.

Once the work got underway, I was helped and encouraged by literally hundreds of people. I especially want to thank those at my former workplace, the National Clearinghouse for Alcohol Information, who acted as a volunteer clipping service, emergency research staff, and general cheering section during 1977 and early 1978 as I gathered information for the book; I am especially indebted to Dick Bast, Joyce Bartoo, David Doernberg, Bea Hoelle, Sandie Johnson, and Bess Macrae. Terry

Bellicha of the National Institute on Alcohol Abuse and Alcoholism was also tremendously helpful in suggesting information sources and sending needed materials, often before I even thought to request them. Representatives of numerous other alcoholism organizations and institutions generously gave of their time and energy, particularly Jane Armstrong, Head Librarian of the Rutgers Center of Alcohol Studies; E. G. Marcelle of the National Council on Alcoholism's Office on Women; and Nell Wing, Archivist for Alcoholics Anonymous.

I also am grateful to all the recovering alcoholic women I interviewed for their willingness to share experiences that are still often harshly judged and nearly always misunderstood. I also want to thank all those in the alcoholism field whom I interviewed, as well as the dozens of others who informally shared with me their thoughts, research papers, stray clippings, and enthusiastic support along the way. Many members of the growing women's alcoholism movement were particularly helpful, including Toni D'Angelo, Jan DuPlain, Alice Krause, Dale Masi, Joan Volpe, and the CASPAR Women's Alcoholism Program of Cambridge, Mass.

Once the book began to take shape on paper, I was immeasurably helped by Carol Sipe's careful and sensitive reading of the manuscript, and for her rare ability to make me laugh even as we jointly dismembered "final" drafts of chapters. Mary Fillmore, Norma Finkelstein, and Toni Sandmaier also spent many hours reviewing selected chapters and contributing their honest, perceptive appraisals. The instincts for clarity and conciseness of my editor, Peggy Tsukahira, more than once helped me plunge into the heart of the matter when I would otherwise have taken my time getting there, and her unflappable calm and good humor made working with her a genuine pleasure.

I am grateful as well to all those who constantly

encouraged me in the writing of the book and refused to indulge my frequent urges to give it all up and raise tomatoes and petunias in my back yard instead. I count among my most unflagging supporters Tula Demetrakakes, Marian Kratage, Jane Potter, Carolyn and Don Sipe, Alden Todd, Charlotte Vayda, Signe Wilkinson, and my parents. I am particularly indebted to Peggy McManus, who conducted an important interview for me when I had neither the time nor the stamina to do another, and who in countless other ways demonstrated her friendship and her belief in my efforts.

Most of all, I want to thank Dan Sipe, who lived through the book's creation with me and was therefore consigned to two years of missed vacations and movies, daily litanies of the manuscript's progress (or lack thereof), the defusing of periodic anxiety attacks, and the relentless buzzing and clacking of my electric typewriter from morning to night, Sunday to Saturday. He was not only extraordinarily patient and encouraging throughout the process, but contributed importantly to the growth of the book through his incisive, insightful criticism.

MARIAN SANDMAIER

June 1979

INTRODUCTION

Until a few years ago, I honestly never gave much thought to the problems—or even to the existence—of alcoholic women. For one thing, I didn't drink much myself, and as far as I knew, there were no women in my family who ever had had any problems with alcohol. But my obliviousness also stemmed from a more general societal assumption that alcoholism was a "man's disease" to which few women fell prey. In my mind, drinking problems were the province of tortured writers like William Faulkner or Eugene O'Neill, various categories of "ordinary" men, especially traveling salesmen and uncles of my friends, and all inhabitants of skid row. Invariably, my images were male. I knew that alcoholic women existed, of course. I had hazy memories of Janis Joplin rasping out songs onstage between belts of Southern Comfort, the audience egging her on to drink more. Occasionally, I saw tired-looking women sitting in the bars I passed on my way to work in the morning. There were a few movie stars whom I knew had drinking problems, an artist or two, and there were shopping bag ladies. But these were women who lived on the margins in one sense or another, exceptions that only proved the rule. It wasn't that I thought women didn't have reason enough to drink. Not at all. It was just that I envisioned different kinds of escapes for them. I saw unhappy women taking Valium, searching endlessly for the "right" therapist, languishing in mental institutions, trying to kill themselves. I simply didn't imagine them abusing alcohol.

Then, in the spring of 1974, my perspective underwent a swift and radical change. I went to work for the National Clearinghouse for Alcohol Information, a federal information program on alcoholism under the Department of Health, Education and Welfare. I was hired as a writer, not as an alcoholism specialist, so I came to the job almost wholly ignorant of the subject at hand. In the course of a self-imposed crash study program on alcoholism, I came upon a statistic indicating that at least one-third of all alcoholics in the United States were *women*. I was stunned. As someone long active in women's issues, particularly interested in mental health concerns, and at least tolerably well-read, I was at a loss to understand how I had overlooked the reality of literally millions of American women with serious drinking problems. How could my lifelong images of alcoholics have been so overwhelmingly and unquestioningly male?

As I examined the issue more closely, it gradually became clear to me that the problem wasn't my own lack of perceptivity, but rather a bona fide awareness blackout on the subject of alcoholic women. Put another way, most of us can't bear to deal with women who have drinking problems. We sit around at parties and tell anecdotes about our boozing uncle, brother, or occasionally even our father—but how often do we entertain our friends with stories of the time our mother or sister tied one on? Never. Out of the corner of our eye, we see an image cracking, a cherished fantasy disturbed. So we keep the alcoholic woman invisible, guarding her secret. And the woman herself, sensing the unacceptability of her illness even more acutely than those around her, does not protest.

Our culture's need to evade and deny the reality of alcoholic women is so powerful that it permeates the alcoholism field itself. Even in the face of recent pressure from activist groups, some alcoholism treatment centers still refuse to admit women; many others limit the admission of female clients. Efforts of alcoholism programs to identify problem drinking women in the community are often lackadaisical or nonexistent, even as outreach programs for men are energetically pursued. As for alcoholism research, it barely acknowledges the presence of women: by 1970, only twenty-eight of the several hundred English-language alcoholism studies in existence specifically focused on the female sex. Meanwhile, alcoholic men, from skid row derelicts to corporation executives, have been exhaustively studied, with the resulting information used to design case-finding and treatment approaches for *all* alcoholics. So even when problem drinking women are "helped," their real issues and needs are often ignored. As women and as individuals, they still remain invisible.

This book is an attempt to give the alcoholic woman the identity that has always been denied her. It aims first of all to simply bring her into the light of our consciousness, so that her existence and her pain can no longer be misread or ignored. But equally important, it tries to record and interpret women's actual experience in the grip of alcohol. Since alcoholism research has focused almost entirely on men, our current body of knowledge on alcoholism derives almost wholly from male experience. But far from duplicating male reality, the alcoholic woman lives out a nightmare uniquely shaped by her cultural role and status.

On one level, to understand the ways in which women's alcoholism differs from that of men's is to be able to identify, treat, and prevent women's drinking problems more effectively. But from a larger perspective, the interaction between a woman's alcohol problem and her social role underscores the poverty of that role itself. What can be said for a life condition that engenders conflicts so excruciating that an addictive drug is required to quiet them? How can we continue to cherish images of women that make us turn away from real female human beings when they drink too much and need our support most? On what grounds can we defend the forces in women's lives that keep them trapped in an alcoholic vise long after many men have released themselves and recovered?

As alcoholic women are the ultimate authorities on their own experience, I have tried to let them speak for themselves wherever possible. To become acquainted with recovering alcoholic women and record their stories, I visited alcoholism treatment programs in several states; I also met with many women in their homes and occasionally in their workplaces. Altogether I interviewed fifty recovering alcoholic women from every region of the country, their ages ranging from fifteen to sixty-three. They included housewives, women with paying jobs, unemployed women, students, and women on welfare; their annual incomes ranged from under three thousand dollars to more than forty thousand dollars. Most of them had been divorced or separated at some point; a few had never married. Five were lesbians. The majority had children, although several had lost custody of them as a result of their drinking. Many were raising their children alone, on limited incomes. Although most of the women I interviewed were white, I also talked with several black and American Indian women. The majority of all those I interviewed now live in urban areas, although many were originally from small-town or rural backgrounds. At the time the interviews were conducted, they had been sober anywhere from ten days to twenty-five years, with an average of about five years of sobriety. I have changed most of their names to protect their anonymity.

I never attempted to obtain a strictly representative sample of alcoholic women, for my purpose was not to conduct a scientific survey. What I wanted was simply to talk with a reasonably broad cross section of women who were willing to share their personal experiences with drinking problems, in the hopes of discovering some common patterns in their experience, as well as any distinctions that might emerge from factors such as class, race, age, and occupation. And as chapters 5 through 10 illustrate, those differences are often striking, even in the presence of other strong commonalities.

I began my series of interviews in a thoroughly "professional" manner, complete with a prepared set of questions and extra cassettes for the tape recorder. But my reporter's detachment didn't hold up through the first interview. Each woman's story was riveting, full of horror and pain that almost defied belief. At various times during our conversations, I felt anger, shock, guilt, and, a few times, I cried. It was some time before I realized that my emotional involvement in the interviews was rooted not simply in sympathy, but in empathy. It was not the actual drinking experiences that I identified with, nor the specific events surrounding them, but rather the feelings that were described to me: the early, paralyzing inability to express one's needs even when the stakes were high; the lifelong conflict between the person one dreamed of becoming and the "nice girl" one was carefully groomed to be; the chronic, diffuse sense of powerlessness; the bouts of depression that so suddenly and oppressively descended. I didn't have to imagine how it "must have felt"; I knew.

It was through these interviews, not through poring over research studies nor discussing facets of problem drinking with alcoholism specialists, that I came to understand most fully why I had chosen to write a book about women and alcoholism. Not all women suffer drinking problems, but the acute frustration and self-negation that alcohol can temporarily blunt is not the exclusive property of women who drink. In a culture that cuts off women from many of their own possibilities before they barely have had a chance to sense them, that pain belongs to all women. Outlets for coping may vary widely, and may be more or less addictive, more or less self-destructive. But at some level, all women know what it is to lack access to their own power, to live with a piece of themselves unclaimed.

This, then, is not a book about "them," a unique group of women whose problems with alcohol render them inaccessible and ultimately only "interesting" to the rest of us. It is also a book about us: about me, my mother and sister, my female friends, all women. There are no boundaries.

there is a woman in this town

she goes to different bars
sits in the remotest place
watches the other people
drinks til 2 & goes home—alone

some say she is lonely
some say she is an agent
none of us speak to her

Is she our sister?

Pat Parker, "there is a woman in this town."
From *Movement in Black*, Diana Press, 1978.
Reprinted with permission of author.

THE
INVISIBLE
ALCOHOLICS

1

LADIES DON'T GET DRUNK

I was sixteen when I first understood that a woman couldn't get drunk and get away with it. The agent of my education was the Patricia Stevens School of Charm and Personal Development; the time was the summer of 1964. In the company of a dozen other eager young women, my sister Donna and I spent one morning each week in a tiny makeshift classroom on the top floor of a Philadelphia office building, learning the rudiments of refinement, grace, bearing, and other virtues of uncertain utility. On the day of my education on women and drinking, the subject of the class was "Successful Dating."

Our instructor, Miss Drake, a middle-aged woman given to waxy pink makeup and enormous amounts of costume jewelry, didn't take her topic lightly. Her list of dos and don'ts was interminable. Don't kiss a boy on the first date, but do let him know that you like him. Do wear something attractive and eye-catching, but don't be provocative. Do read up on your date's current passions, such as hot-rod racing and Roger Maris, but don't let him think you know more than he does. Donna looked at me from across the room and rolled her eyes at the ceiling. I shifted in my seat impatiently and studied the pattern of my madras skirt. Then, abruptly, Miss Drake cut short her litany and silently surveyed the class for several moments. Somewhat apprehensively, we stared back at her. "How many of you girls," she somberly inquired at last, "have ever seen a drunk woman?"

My hand and Donna's shot up in unison. Here, at least, was something we could relate to. Both of us flashed on the same childhood image: a neighbor woman who passed the evenings drinking straight from a bottle of bourbon which she kept in a cabinet above the kitchen sink. We knew about this nightly ritual because we used to spy on her through her kitchen window on summer evenings when we had nothing better to do. Starting shortly after dinner, about every half hour or so she would sneak into the kitchen, look in both directions to make sure the coast was clear, then take a good snort and lurch out. At the time, we thought it was pretty funny.

It wasn't at all funny, actually, but that day at Patricia Stevens I found out that it was much worse than unfunny. My first clue was the dead silence that enveloped the room as soon as Donna and I raised our hands. The second clue was that we were the only ones who had our hands in the air. Every pair of eyes in the room was on us, and I began to blush without understanding why. Miss Drake cleared her throat. "Girls," she intoned, carefully averting her eyes from Donna and me, "it is important for you to realize that the way you handle alcohol can either enhance your reputation as a lady—or ruin it. Let me be very clear about this. There is nothing quite as disgusting as a woman who is drunk."

I was flabbergasted. My own neighbor, disgusting? The same woman who had faithfully bought our Girl Scout cookies each year, shared with us the proceeds of her vegetable garden, and was endlessly interested in everything we did? She was a little eccentric, maybe, but disgusting? That was hard to swallow. But Miss Drake was armed with evidence. She began to run down a new list, this one of the considerable moral and aesthetic failings of the drunk woman. It all seemed to boil down to a rather intimidating doctrine: If you got drunk, you weren't a lady. And if you weren't a lady, you might just as well take a flying leap into the Delaware River, for as a female human being, your failure was utter and complete. It seemed to be a warning worth remembering.

When the class ended that afternoon and we all crowded into the elevator to go downstairs, I noticed that some of the girls were giving my sister and me funny, sidelong glances. There were a few smirks. I began to feel confused all over again, when suddenly Donna grabbed my arm and whispered in horror, "They must think it's *Mom*!" I felt a pang of fear. How could anyone think anything so revolting about *my* mother?

That was the summer of 1964. Twelve years later, I attended a national conference on alcoholic women where a well-known woman journalist made the keynote address. A recovered alcoholic, she shared with us a gripping and horrifying account of her twenty-year battle with alcohol. When she appeared to have finished her story, the largely female audience was silent, many of us reflecting on the courage and honesty of the woman before us. But as it happened, she wasn't quite through. Leaning over the edge of the podium, our speaker added emphatically, "And one of the things that keeps me sober today, ladies, is the memory of my drinking days. What is more repulsive, after all, than an alcoholic woman?"

A small group of women walked out of the hotel conference room in protest—the only indication that anything had changed since my Patricia Stevens charm school days. The vast majority of the audience, comprised substantially of recovered alcoholic women, neither walked out nor even murmured their displeasure. Instead, they stayed to hear the postscript to the journalist's speech, a narrative of self-castigation and guilt that reflected on all of them as directly as on her. Though the year was 1976 and this was a conference devoted to a new and more compassionate understanding of the alcoholic woman, most of the audience still accepted the insults and the putdowns; in some corner of themselves, they still believed them. On that spring afternoon, they listened to a projection of their own inner voices berating them and pitying them for having sunk so low. There was no point in walking out.

The very words "alcoholic woman" are enough to trigger a visceral response in most people. Few can simply visualize a woman who is seriously ill and in need of medical attention and emotional support. Even when such realities are intellectually understood, they are no match for the often violent feelings that are aroused: anger, revulsion, anxiety, a sense of betrayal. It is felt that she has trespassed on territory beyond her proper sphere, that she has degraded herself in a particularly odious, even unnatural manner.

No alcoholic woman is spared the contempt that follows from such judgments. "If you're a woman and an alcoholic, your culture disowns you," claimed Johnnie Albertson, a recovered alcoholic and outspoken advocate for women with drinking problems. "Nobody wants you, you're isolated from everyone, and you quickly learn to hate yourself. You're simply obliterated as a woman and a person." Susan B. Anthony, great-grandniece of the suffragist and also a recovered alcoholic, put it even more succinctly: "By being a woman and an alcoholic, I became what the Bible calls 'the Anawim,' the lowly one."

It is a bizarre response to a group of people desperately in need of help.

It is also worlds apart from our reaction to the man who drinks too much. Writer Booth Tarkington once noted: "There are two things that will be believed of any man whatsoever, and one of them is that he has taken to drink." A more tolerant attitude toward the man with a drinking problem pervades our history and culture. We have a rich heritage of "favorite" male drunks that reflect and encourage our permissiveness: in fantasy, Dean Martin, the comic drunk; Charlie Chaplin, the whimsical drunk; Andy Capp, the henpecked drunk; in reality, F. Scott Fitzgerald, the romantic drunk; W. C. Fields, the irascible drunk; Edgar Allan Poe, the tortured, half-mad drunk. The excessive drinking of these men, in fiction or in life, has never detracted from their essential characters; in fact, in some cases it has actually enhanced their mystique. In contrast, there is no comparable hard-drinking hall of fame for well-known women who have suffered alcohol problems, such as Dorothy Parker, Edna St. Vincent Millay, Vivien Leigh, or Judy Garland. If we talk about these women at all, it is in lowered voices, murmuring about the "tragedy" of their fall from grace or speculating about their alcohol-related lapses into immorality.

Our differing reactions to recent admissions of alcoholism by two famous and highly respected public figures underscore this double standard. When Betty Ford announced that she was addicted to drugs and alcohol, many people applauded her admission, but others stiffly insisted that Betty's problem was "really only Valium" (an acceptable woman's addiction), while still others angrily cancelled their subscriptions to newspapers that printed news of her alcoholism. And even among those who

admired Mrs. Ford's straightforwardness, many expressed shock
that a woman as respectable and "nice" as the former First Lady
could have a problem with drinking. In contrast, when Wilbur
Mills went public with his alcohol problem, few people either
denied it or were unduly shocked. We were mostly sympathetic,
shaking our heads and clucking about the pressures of high
office. We may have been disappointed in Wilbur, but we tried
to understand: There was the trouble with that woman—and
anyway, who could blame a guy for sowing those last few wild
oats while he was still able? In any case, few people saw a real
contradiction between the respectability or "niceness" of Wilbur
Mills and the reality of his alcoholism.

Our culture's greater disapproval of excessive drinking
among women than among men has been documented by several
studies. A survey of attitudes toward alcohol use and abuse
among four hundred women and men of varying socioeconomic
classes in the United States showed that people of both sexes and
all social classes believed it was "worse" for a woman to be drunk
than a man.[1] A study of drinking attitudes among the primarily
black residents of a midwestern low-income housing project
revealed that half of the men and three-fourths of the women
thought it was all right for a man to get drunk, whereas only
slightly more than a quarter of both sexes would tolerate
drunkenness in a woman.[2] And, although attitudes about
drinking among younger people are changing, a national survey
of teen-age drinking in 1974 showed that a sizable minority of
high school students believed it was less acceptable for a girl to be
drunk than for a boy.[3]

This double standard on drunkenness and problem
drinking is not a case of neat, black-and-white opposites. For
instance, it is not as though alcoholism is condoned in men. In a
society that prizes self-control and productivity as much as ours
does, a serious alcohol problem is generally considered a

symptom of moral and emotional weakness, regardless of the sex of the sufferer. And although both the American Medical Association and the National Institute on Alcohol Abuse and Alcoholism have defined alcoholism as an illness, the image of the alcoholic as a weak-willed loser is shared not only by a majority of lay people, but a good percentage of the medical profession as well.[4]

Further, the attitudes toward drinking and alcohol abuse are not homogeneous; in fact, they vary widely across social class, ethnic group, religion, age, and even type of job or profession. A twenty-five-year-old woman newspaper reporter in New York City, for example, is clearly apt to enjoy more social freedom to drink than a middle-aged Baptist housewife from rural Alabama. And the dual standard on drinking is not a static one. Attitudes toward women's alcohol use are slowly changing, so that in some circles, hard drinking among women—as long as they can hold their liquor—is becoming more respectable. But regardless of generally negative attitudes about alcoholism and diverse and shifting judgments about acceptable female drinking behavior, a very real double standard still exists. Drunkenness and alcoholism are still widely considered "worse"—more scandalous, more contemptible, more degrading—when they occur in a woman than when they occur in a man.

The brutally harsh stigma attached to female alcohol abuse shapes the entire experience of the alcoholic woman, and renders it different—in many ways more painful and obliterating—than that of the male alcoholic. First, a woman is more likely than a man to be driven underground by her drinking problem. To protect herself from public contempt and her own self-castigation for having "sunk so low," she is likely to deny and disguise her alcoholism rather than seek the treatment she needs. "We hid," remembered actress and recovered alcoholic Jan Clayton, testifying at U.S. Senate hearings on women and alcoholism in 1976. "We became closet drinkers, weekend benders, go-to-the-doctor-and-get-pills-for-our-nerves drinkers. Evaders, liars, anything but 'please help me, I have got a screaming tiger on my back' women. We hid behind denials."[5] Betty Ford, in her autobiography, *The Times of My Life*, recalled how she successfully rationalized her drinking problem to herself: "So I forgot a few telephone calls. So I fell in the bathroom and cracked three ribs. But I never drank for a hangover and in fact I used to criticize people who did. At house parties, I would look at friends who knocked back Bloody Marys in the morning, and I would think, isn't that pathetic?"

Those close to the alcoholic woman are likely to join her in her desperate pretense rather than urge her to get help. For if alcohol abuse renders a woman repulsive and disgraceful, how can relatives or friends acknowledge a drinking problem in a woman they care for and respect? Not only would such acknowledgment shatter their entire image of that woman, but it might be seen as a reflection on them as well. Thus the initial response of those close to the alcoholic woman is usually to deny the problem right along with her. Relatives and friends commonly insist that she just "likes to drink," or that her drinking is a temporary response to short-term stress, or they call her alcoholism by another, more acceptably feminine name, like "nerves" or depression.

But even when it is no longer possible to go on pretending to themselves, others go out of their way to avoid confronting a woman with her alcoholism. A husband will nervously "protect" his wife's illness from friends and neighbors—or leave her in disgust to work out her "problem" alone. An employer will fire a woman or ignore her unexplained absences and uneven work record rather than discuss with her the possibility of a drinking problem. A friend will pretend not to notice a woman's increasingly frequent blackouts at parties, or the incoherent phone calls late at night. A physician will listen somberly to the alcohol-related symptoms of his woman client, then give her a prescription for tranquilizers rather than refer her to an alcoholism treatment program. Any dodge, excuse, or apparent misapprehension will do, as long as it keeps others from having to confront the disquieting truth. Consequently, by the time many problem drinking women finally become visible and get help, their alcoholism has wrought extreme, sometimes irreversible physical and emotional damage. Some women never emerge from hiding, and die of alcoholism.

But the double standard on alcohol abuse does more than keep the problem drinking woman invisible. She is likely to internalize her culture's harsh judgment of her and learn to view herself with hopelessness and hatred. Studies repeatedly show that alcoholic women suffer significantly more guilt, anxiety, and depression than alcoholic men, have lower self-esteem, and attempt suicide more often.[6] "I hated my guts," remembered a forty-three-year-old community organizer from New York who recovered from alcoholism three years ago. "I remember walking to my office in Manhattan from the subway some mornings and noticing that people were looking at me strangely and I'd realize that I was talking to myself out loud, cursing: 'You goddam, horrible, miserable woman, you're a pig, you're full of shit'— whatever I could think of to express how rotten I felt about myself." A young woman from rural Pennsylvania who was addicted to both alcohol and pills recalled her multiple suicide attempts: "I just felt I had no right to live and that it was unbearable to live. My mental image of myself was as a worm or some kind of bug, too low to stand on my own two feet. There was no way out of those feelings."

The crippling sense of self-disgust and generalized "badness" suffered by many problem drinking women pushes them still deeper into alcoholism, for often the most accessible antidote to their misery is yet another drink. It can also seriously impede any eventual treatment, for even with years of therapy, such rock-hard convictions of worthlessness can be difficult to dislodge.

Why do we consider it "worse" for a woman to abuse alcohol than a man, and consequently respond to her illness in ways that prolong and intensify her pain rather than ease it? This double standard, like any sex-based double standard, is rooted in the dichotomous roles of men and women in our culture, which demand a radically different and mutually exclusive set of behaviors for each sex. But because of the specific ways in which excessive drinking affects the performance of these roles, attitudes toward male and female alcohol abuse are more divergent, and more passionately held, than dual standards for many other aspects of behavior.

Although alcohol is actually a central nervous system depressant, it goes to work first on those brain centers which inhibit behavior. So, initially, instead of acting as a sedative, it tends to expand the personality, releasing a flood of usually repressed impulses. After several drinks, a person may become louder, blunter, more boisterous, more aggressive, more violent, more sexually open. Feelings of personal power expand while, simultaneously, judgment fuzzes over. One is readier to risk, to challenge, to act on sudden feelings of invincibility and freedom.

By current cultural standards, this kind of unfettered, unsocialized behavior released by alcohol is fundamentally masculine. One of the archetypal elements of the male role is an allegiance to the instinctual self, to one's primal, animal nature, in defiance of "feminine" civilizing norms. The man who drinks may not actually live out this virile ideal, but at the very least, alcohol and the drinking environment allow him to *feel* more manly. In the cool semidarkness of a bar, with a few like-minded cronies, he can temporarily be the hard-drinkin', hard-livin', hard-lovin' man of the American dream, a born-again Hemingway. Writer and erstwhile drinker Pete Hamill described the masculine fantasies elicited by alcohol in a 1974 *New York Magazine* article entitled "Memoirs of the Drinking Life":

> Drink was the great loosener, the killer of shyness, the maker of dreams and courage. . . . And everyone around you was witty, interesting, full of morning. They told you all the stories of your life, stories that would fill a hundred books, stories of busted marriages, great disasters, lost heroism. War stories and sea stories and sex stories. There was never any way for the stories to be ruined by the truth.

To the extent that men affirm their masculinity through drinking, alcohol is used as a tool, a rite, and a symbol for that purpose. Through the ages it has served—and still serves—as a test of physical stamina, a reward for heroism, proof of independence from authority, an escape hatch from the world of women. Consequently, when a man develops a *problem* with alcohol, he has, in a sense, only become a victim of "too much of a good thing." He may be called weak or irresponsible, but his lapse is the consequence of going too far with a legitimate, even praiseworthy masculine pursuit. And so we may judge him but, finally, we are likely to understand and forgive him.

When a woman goes too far with her drinking, however, our tolerance runs dry. For just as the use of alcohol enhances and celebrates the male role, it poses a potentially serious threat to the female role. Men are the repositories of "animal" values in our culture; women are the vessels of moral and spiritual virtues. And although standards for women's behavior are gradually loosening, the "good" woman is still expected to be sexually monogamous, devoted primarily to husband and children, and to serve as a kind of unofficial moral guardian to her family and community. Moreover, in carrying out these prescribed duties, style is nearly as important as substance. A truly "feminine" woman is gentle, unaggressive, refined, both decorous and decorative in appearance. And alcohol is the deadly enemy of this womanly ideal. Under the influence of too many drinks, a woman "forgets" to be feminine. She may talk more loudly than usual, swear a blue streak, put her arms around somebody else's husband, express anger. She may cease to care if her lipstick is on straight, if her words become a little slurred, if her legs remain primly crossed. The more uncontrolled her behavior, the less she conforms to society's image of the "good" woman. In a book entitled *An American Woman and Alcohol,* written ostensibly to "help" the problem drinking woman, the author sternly rebukes her: "Your appearance, the facade you present to the world outside, will become slovenly, unkempt and finally revolting. You—the pretty, charming, bright American woman—will fall hard and fast. The higher you are, the lower you fall."[7]

But it is not simply the disintegration of a romantic vision of womanhood that accounts for society's virulently negative response to the alcoholic woman. What is really at stake when a woman drinks too much is the threat of a major shift in the sexual balance of power. For the roles of men and women are not simply opposite sides of a coin; they are fundamentally unequal, and further, they are interdependent. Men cannot keep their grip on their dominant place in our culture unless women remain squarely in their subservient, dependent place. And the hoisting of women high upon a pedestal is an extraordinarily effective means of ensuring their continued powerlessness. For by insisting that women are "better" than men—more virtuous, more loving, more self-sacrificing—men in fact consign women to a life of enforced altruism and severely restrict their autonomy. How can a bored housewife demand to launch a career of her own when a "real" woman is dedicated first to husband and children? How can a woman insist on her right to an orgasm when a "good" woman is only concerned about meeting a man's sexual needs?

It is not as though most men consciously maneuver to protect their position of privilege by restricting women's behavior; such restrictions are built into the structure of the culture itself, through socialization processes, institutions, law, custom, the weight of history. The deeply embedded nature of this oppression also makes it appear somehow preordained and "natural," and, consequently, often difficult to recognize for what it is. The moral role of women is generally accepted by society as reasonable and just even though no woman can possibly live up to it. Not only is it based on a rarefied vision of femininity that has little to do with flesh-and-blood women, but, because of the function the role serves, even the slightest deviation from its precepts triggers male anxiety and consequent accusations of failure. Simone de Beauvoir writes in *The Second Sex:*

> Woman is doomed to immorality, because for her to be moral would mean that she must incarnate a being of superhuman qualities: the "virtuous woman" of Proverbs, the "perfect mother," the "honest woman," and so on. Let her but think, dream, sleep, desire, breathe without permission and she betrays the masculine ideal.[8]

But if the average woman has trouble meeting the demands of her sex role, the alcoholic woman is doomed to utter and outrageous failure. For when a woman is chronically drunk, she loses a large measure of the control that is absolutely necessary to the performance of her rigidly defined functions. And because the effects of alcohol are at once so overpowering and so unpredictable, there is no telling what taboo she will break next, what tacit agreement between the sexes she might expose and reject. The possibilities are frightening in precise proportion to the threat they pose to the sexual status quo. The most threatening of her potential acts of defiance—and thus those she is most frequently and bitterly accused of—are first, that she will become indiscriminately sexual, and second, that she will no longer be able to take care of men and children.

Drunkenness in women is not simply associated, but *equated,* with rampant sexuality. This cynical connection has been the single greatest source of anxiety about the alcoholic woman throughout history, and the primary reason for her degraded status. And it remains so today, the so-called sexual revolution of the last decade notwithstanding. Recovered alcoholic Susan B. Anthony summarized the prevailing public attitude toward alcoholic women at the 1976 Senate hearings on women and alcohol problems: "We are suspected of being either prostitutes or not quite nice women, a problem men do not have. Therefore we are looked down on far more than the man alcoholic at any level, no matter whether we are upper class, lower class, bottom; because there is that added sexual note with the woman alcoholic."[9]

A fifty-two-year-old recovered alcoholic woman from Seattle remembered her husband's first words on discovering that she was abusing alcohol: "I guess the lady is a tramp." A San Francisco commercial artist in her mid-thirties recalls the response of her doctor when she finally summoned the courage to tell him she thought she had a problem with drinking. "I hope you're on the pill, and if you're not, you better start thinking about it." Jan DuPlain, former director of the Office on Women for the National Council on Alcoholism and a recovered alcoholic, believes that this knee-jerk assumption of promiscuity is deeply destructive to alcoholic women. "Most of us, to begin with, grow up with this divided image of ourselves as virginal Doris Day on the one side and the wanton Happy Hooker on the other. The whole angel-whore dichotomy is built into the culture's view of women. When we drink and it's assumed that

we've gone over to the camp of the Happy Hooker, the shame
and remorse and guilt is overpowering. Most of us react by just
drinking some more to get rid of those 'bad girl' feelings and
allow ourselves to feel like we're okay again."

The facts do not support the widespread assumption of
rampant sexual activity among alcoholic women. Research has
demonstrated that drinking, drunkenness, and even alcoholism
are not necessarily predictors of increased sexual activity among
most women; in fact, they decrease many women's interest in or
likelihood of having sex. In a recent analytical review of the
literature on female alcoholism, researcher Dr. Edith Gomberg of
the University of Michigan concluded:

There is far more talk about the promiscuity of women with
drinking problems than there is evidence. Lack of sexual
interest is probably far more common than promiscuity. Many
women alcoholics drink at home, alone or with husbands, and
while infidelity and promiscuity undoubtedly occur, they are
not inevitable concomitants of female alcoholism.[10]

Dr. Marc Schuckit, an alcoholism researcher at the
University of Washington, concurred in an article entitled
"Sexual Disturbance in the Woman Alcoholic": "The popular
image of the scarlet woman is a fiction. Promiscuity is
appropriate to only five percent of all women drinkers. Most of
the other 95 percent complain of diminished interest in sex."[11]

However, although most alcoholic women may not be
more sexually active than average, it cannot be denied that *some*
women may be more apt to engage in sex after having too much
to drink, especially if they do much of their drinking in public
places. Alcohol does in fact loosen inhibitions, among them those
repressing sexual impulses. Some women who usually guard
themselves carefully against expressing or even feeling their
sexuality may, under certain circumstances, find themselves

spontaneously acting on sexual feelings after a few drinks, or at least being more receptive to men's advances. But even if these responses do not occur, a woman who has had too much to drink is less able to fend off any sexual initiatives that may happen along the way, particularly if force is applied. She may be too woozy, too unsteady, too sick, or, if she has drunk enough, too uncaring to stop a sexual advance, or even a rape. She may even be unconscious when it happens.

This increased sexual *vulnerability* of alcoholic women is enough to precipitate wholesale accusations of promiscuity, regardless of whether or not actual sexual involvement is extensive. For the restriction of women's sexual freedom is one of the key means by which men traditionally have exerted control over women. A woman who exercises her sexuality at will is asserting her rights over her own body, her freedom to act as she wishes, in short, her independence from any man's ownership. Even if a woman is thought to have submitted to sex by force, as some women do when drunk, she is still seen as available to men at large, no longer the property of any one man. Man's need to control woman's sexuality in order to ensure his exclusive possession of her is so intense that even the *threat* of losing that control often activates male fear and consequent outrage. Thus the problem drinking woman, whose usual clamps on her sexuality may in fact be somewhat loosened by alcohol, is denounced as a "whore" even before the facts of her sex life are known.

Attacks on alcoholic women for their actual or imagined sexual behavior are also blatantly hypocritical. For as noted above, a woman's sexual involvement when "under the influence" doesn't happen just by chance, or even on her own initiative in many cases. Men have always relied on alcohol as one of their foremost seduction tools, pressing it on their female companions to make them more amenable to sex, then crying "slut" at them when their ploy has worked. This double message is communicated to women even more aggressively today than in the past, not only by individual men on the make, but by the media and Madison Avenue as well. On the one hand, movies, television, magazine and newspaper articles, and especially alcohol advertising increasingly link alcohol with sexual sophistication in women, in effect encouraging women to use it to enhance their erotic appeal. But on the other hand, "nice girls" are still taught to be leery of the seductive potential of alcohol, to view it as a dangerous substance which may make them too pliable in the hands of the wrong man. Such conflicting messages may not only undermine a woman's ability to develop a healthy outlook on sex, but also foster a fundamentally ambivalent attitude toward alcohol which is believed to contribute to the development of drinking problems.

Linked to the image of the alcoholic woman as hopelessly promiscuous is the vision of her as shockingly neglectful of her family responsibilities. This theme is a favorite of women's magazines and newspaper feature pages, which almost invariably portray a woman's alcoholism as a tragedy primarily for her children and husband, and only secondarily for the woman herself. These articles are often capped by such incriminating headlines as "Johnny Has a Drinking Problem: His Mother," or "Women's Alcohol Problems Tear Families Apart." The subtitle of a "true-life" story in a contemporary woman's magazine is typical:

> *Once alcoholism was a man's problem, but now a tragic number of women are turning to drink, bringing misery to their families' lives. Our reader has triumphed over this weakness and her story will bring hope to other women who have found drink a temptation.*[12]

Both recovered alcoholic women and treatment specialists attest to the intense guilt and self-hatred borne by alcoholic women because of society's judgment that they have failed as wives and mothers. "I still run tapes through my head about how rotten I was to my family," said a forty-eight-year-old secretary from Houston who stopped drinking five years ago. "I can tell myself I was sick, that I was out of control, but it still eats at me. Sometimes I lie awake whole nights and go over all my crimes and it's almost enough to make me run screaming for the bottle again."

Daryl Kosloske, director of the Palm Beach Institute, a private residential alcoholism facility in Palm Beach, Florida, believes that guilt about family neglect is one of the major issues faced by alcoholic women in treatment. "There is a pervasive sense that 'I've failed them.' In terms of children, in terms of husband. Feeling that they've ruined things for the family, that it is all *their* problem. And in many cases, the husband views it the same way. Whereas when the man is alcoholic, the wife is more likely to say: 'Did *I* do something wrong? Am I not being a good wife?' "

Outrage at the alcoholic woman for her shirking of family responsibilities usually centers on her inability to properly care for her children. Ardelle Schultz, former director of Today, Incorporated, an alcohol-drug treatment program in southeastern Pennsylvania, observed that "the issue for the addicted woman is still learning how to forgive herself for one of society's biggest crimes—failure at motherhood." The problem drinking woman is viewed as the classic "bad mother," neglectful, capricious, inconsistent in her responses, possibly even physically abusive. And in fact, as women are the primary caretakers of children, there is good reason to be concerned about the welfare of children of alcoholic mothers. As alcoholism researcher Joan Curlee-Salisbury noted: "No one likes to think that the hand that rocks the cradle is a shaky one." While there is little hard evidence that many alcoholic women physically abuse their children, neglect and emotional scarring are almost inevitable. A woman who is chronically drunk can barely attend to her own basic needs, much less the myriad, never-ending physical and emotional demands of children.

But concern for the welfare of children of an alcoholic mother and attacks on the woman herself are two very different matters. Upon hearing of harm befalling children as a consequence of their mother's drinking, the typical response is: "How could she do it to *them?* Isn't she just *terrible!*" But in fact, what is a woman's alternative to inflicting her alcohol problem on her children? The average woman is assigned primary responsibility for the care of her young, usually within a nuclear family structure that leaves her totally alone with her children most of the day. Our society considers such a division of labor and family structure ideal. If an alcoholic woman is fortunate, she may have a husband who at least comes home in the evenings to help care for the children. But more likely her alcohol problem has culminated in divorce or desertion, and she is left with sole responsibility for her children's safety and welfare.

Even if she is able to ignore the societal contempt that is almost certain to attend her admission of her drinking problem, treatment is all but impossible for an alcoholic mother, particularly if her children are small. For if she checks herself into an alcoholism facility, who will take care of them? Few alcoholism programs make either internal or outside arrangements for child care, and it is a rare woman who can find a relative or friend to care for her children during an extended period of treatment. It seems grossly unfair to blame a woman for her inadequacy as a mother when she is trapped by a system that forces her to care for her children even when she is physically and emotionally unable to do so. By doing what a "good" mother should—remaining with her children at all times—an alcoholic woman is doomed to be a "bad" mother.

The alcoholic woman is attacked not only for her failure at motherhood, but for her abandonment of more general nurturing and caretaking functions that are at the core of the female role. "Good" women are primarily concerned with the needs and welfare of others, serving as perpetual feeders, replenishers, cleaners, healers, and emotional stabilizers to those around them. These services make it possible for men to carry out their daily lives more comfortably and conveniently; indeed, they give men the freedom necessary to achieve, create, and exercise power in the larger world. But when women become alcoholic, they shed this you-first, me-last role and begin to live, however unhealthily, for themselves. And without their continuous domestic and emotional services, the equilibrium of men's lives collapses. All at once, no one is available to wash socks, salve egos, make dinners, dispense aspirin, admire accomplishments—and take proper care of children. In effect, the help has quit. And when women are no longer willing or able to serve men's daily needs—even for reasons beyond women's control—the response is usually not support or sympathy, but anger.

Studies show that men are significantly more likely to leave their alcoholic spouses than are women, and although the reasons are partly economic, they are also largely attributable to women's nearly total responsibility for the care and nurturing of others. When a man develops a drinking problem, his wife is already somewhat prepared to deal with it, as ministering to those who are sick or in trouble is central to her role. But when a woman becomes alcoholic, a basic role reversal is required within the marriage. Not only has she abdicated her caretaking responsibilities, but now she requires an enormous amount of personal care and emotional support from her husband, functions he has never been socialized to provide and which he may have little taste for learning now. He was formerly the nurtured party;

now, suddenly, she is demanding to trade places with him. It may be easier for a man to leave his marriage than to make the basic life-style and psychological adjustments necessary to meet the needs of a wife who is both physically and emotionally ill. And since the alcoholic wife is seen as having shirked her family duties in the first place, a husband can rationalize his exit by claiming it is "all her fault." She is not likely to dispute that judgment.

But the alcoholic woman's failure to fulfill her nurturing function makes her more than simply a "bad" woman. For the female caretaking role, which serves men's needs so well, has been justified and even sanctified by the label "natural." Male-created philosophical and medical theory holds that women's reproductive organs mysteriously make them "naturally" fit for a home-centered, nurturing existence; to refuse to live out such an existence is, by definition, to be an "unnatural" woman. Despite the entrance of fully half of American women into the labor force and the steadily decreasing numbers of women who choose to marry and have children, this theory is still doggedly advanced. Noted psychiatrist and author Erik Erikson claims that a woman's "somatic design harbors an 'inner space' destined to bear the offspring of chosen men, and with it, a biological, psychological and ethical commitment to take care of human infancy."[13] Bruno Bettelheim, another leading contemporary psychiatrist, argues that "as much as women want to be good scientists and engineers, they want, first and foremost, to be womanly companions of men and to be mothers."[14] Biology is still being sold as woman's destiny.

And because of it, the alcoholic woman is not only considered a failure as a wife and mother, but an unnatural woman as well. This is a devastating label, for besides denying a woman one of her most basic sources of self-esteem, it robs her of her very sexual identity. She is not simply an evil woman but a *non*-woman. This cruelly obliterating judgment is probably the single most destructive aspect of the stigma borne by the alcoholic woman, and it is one that largely lies outside the experience of alcoholic men. For although men with drinking problems may fail their families as completely as their female counterparts, and although they may be denounced consequently as "weak" and even "no-good," men are never *unsexed* by their alcoholism the way women are, for they never violate the precepts of their sex role as profoundly as do women. In her book on the social underpinnings of mental illness in women, *Women and Madness,* psychologist Phyllis Chesler comments on this crucial distinction:

> . . . most women experience the male's physical or emotional abandonment of his family or children as either cruel or cruelly necessary. He is a "louse"—or a "victim" of harsh job realities. His behavior is human. However, the female's similar abandonment of her family—for any purpose—is viewed as "unnatural" and "tragic." The female's social role is still a biological one: as such she is seen as transgressing against nature when she attempts to change her social role.[15]

In recent years there has been a growing awareness among activists in the alcohol field of the particularly harsh stigma attached to female alcoholism, and that unless the stigma is effectively defused, women will continue to fearfully deny their drinking problems and isolate themselves from treatment. The primary response of those concerned has been to initiate ambitious public education campaigns on the issue, in the hope that the presentation of the alcoholic woman as a sympathetic, suffering human being will undermine stereotypes and spur more enlightened, compassionate attitudes. And, in fact, the recent outpouring of information on women and alcoholism—the TV and radio spots, the pamphlets stuffed in supermarket racks, the conferences and seminars—has had some impact. Undeniably, alcoholic women are somewhat less invisible than they were twenty, ten, or even five years ago.

But however intelligently conceived and carried out, the approach of public education is necessarily limited, for it fails to grapple with the real roots of the stigma: the immediate and symbolic threats female alcoholism poses to the sexual balance of power. Society's contempt for the alcoholic woman serves two crucial functions in the maintenance of this balance: It punishes the ill woman herself for daring to overstep the bounds of her feminine role; and, more importantly, it serves as a warning to other women to remain soberly in their places lest they, too, be branded sexual outlaws, bad mothers and wives, and finally, unnatural women.

Once again, there is no conspiracy at work here, nor are most individuals even conscious of the real basis of their anger and disgust. The responses to women necessary to the preservation of the sexual status quo are so deeply embedded in our culture and in the psychic structures of both men and women as to be largely unconscious and automatic. We simply "know" that the alcoholic woman has committed an unforgivable offense, and our consequent condemnation seems only right, natural, and deserved. And as long as women are judged by superhuman standards of behavior that both seal and conceal their subordinate status, our response will not soften.

2

BACCHANTIC MAIDENS AND TEMPERANCE DAUGHTERS

The taboo on female drunkenness is not simply a twentieth century response to growing rates of alcohol use and abuse among women. Throughout Western history, women have been subject to more restrictions on their alcohol use than men, and have been punished more harshly for their defiance of sex-typed drinking codes. And as is the case today, the real issue has never been drunkenness per se, but rather man's fear that the alcohol abusing woman will abandon her role and careen out of his control. Wherever drinking among women has been limited in history, it has been linked to promiscuity and neglect of home and hearth; it has always sparked a terrifying vision of what she might say, do, or be once freed by alcohol from her otherwise predictable state of being. The historical record is testimony to the depth and power of our current belief system about the woman who abuses alcohol.

The historical picture is not a uniformly bleak one. Because women's drinking patterns have been so closely tied to their societal role, their freedom to imbibe has fluctuated somewhat depending on their overall status. Where women were permitted some measure of freedom from traditional feminine standards, they were usually permitted to drink more, and more frequently. Class was also an important factor and remains so today; rich women in some eras were freer to drink and get drunk than women of lower classes. This distinction was not only a product of a more liberal sexual code sometimes allowed the upper-class woman, but also of her ability to rely on servants to care for her children and perform necessary household duties while she was nursing a hangover. Her drinking, in short, usually posed a less serious threat to the status quo.

The level of tolerance for women's drinking—and men's, to a lesser degree—also has been a function of a given society's attitudes toward alcohol itself. Historically, in some Western cultures alcohol has been looked upon as a primarily beneficent beverage, used variously as a symbol of hospitality, a medicine, a social catalyst, a healthful adjunct to the diet, or a simple expression of communal values. In other times, such as Prohibition, alcohol has been condemned as an insidious killer drug threatening every moral value held sacred by society. But we are dealing here with trends, and the prevailing trend in Western history has been to stigmatize and otherwise punish the hard-drinking woman rather than help or even tolerate her.

Disapproval of women's alcohol abuse and even their drinking pervades the earliest of Western cultures. In accounts of social life in classical Greece, animated descriptions of male wine-bibbing parties and symposia (literally, "drinkings together") abound, but comments on female drinking are few and usually critical. Where it is mentioned at all, women's alcohol abuse is usually linked to deleterious effects on unborn children. The ancient Greeks may have been the first to take note of the fetal-alcohol syndrome, a pattern of physical and mental abnormalities found in some babies born to alcoholic mothers. Aristotle charged that "foolish, drunken or harebrain women for the most part bring forth children like unto themselves," while Plutarch more succinctly stated that "one drunkard begets another."

Sparta, which carefully nurtured the health of its young freewomen so that they might breed robust and sturdy Spartan stock, forbade them to drink any wine at all unless it was well diluted with water. While the Greeks displayed impressive powers of observation and deduction in their early notice of the effects of drinking on the fetus, they rarely shifted the focus of their concern from the baby to the woman herself. As is largely true today, the alcohol abusing woman was worthy of attention because she was a mother, not because of any concern about her own health or well-being.

Predictably, when a drinking woman in ancient Greece was not seen as a hurtful mother, she was viewed as a threat to men. Nowhere is male fear of the woman unleashed by drink revealed more sharply than in the Greek myth of the Bacchantes, the wild, forest-dwelling priestesses of the wine god Dionysus. When the Bacchantes drank wine as part of their sacred rites to Dionysus, they whipped themselves into a drink-crazed frenzy and took off through the woods, whooping and singing with ecstatic abandon. Sometimes they ran up to the mountaintops and made collective love to Pan, the half-goat, half-human god. But just as often the wine made the mythical priestesses savage and brutal, and they could be found attacking wild animals in the woods, ripping them to shreds with their bare hands and eating the raw meat. And animals were not their only prey. After one wine-soaked rite, the drunken Bacchantes mistook Pentheus, king of Thebes, for a wild mountain lion and tore him to pieces. But their most shocking crime occurred in the course of an attack on Orpheus, a priest of Apollo, whom Dionysus wanted killed. According to the myth, the Bacchantes stormed the temple where Orpheus was worshiping, only to find their husbands there with him, also in worship. Since they knew their husbands would try to protect Orpheus from their impending attack, the Bacchantes acted quickly. With ferocious shrieks they fell upon their own husbands, murdering them. Then they finished off Orpheus.[1]

The Bacchantes myth embodies a profoundly terrifying image of the drunken woman which still resonates with us today. The drink-crazed Bacchantes are both sexually promiscuous and stripped of their femininity; once corrupted by alcohol they are beyond the control of men and deaf to any appeal for womanly mercy. In their drunken abandon they actualize one of man's greatest fears: that woman will overpower and destroy him. The prominence and emotional power of this myth, created as it was in a society that is a direct predecessor of our own, suggests the depth of our heritage of fear of the woman who abuses alcohol. The myth even partially survives in current custom: The mythical Bacchantes were tattooed by the few men who survived their murderous attack, the tattoo serving as a visual reminder of their heinous crime. To this day, in some small Grecian villages, men tattoo their wives as a symbolic warning of their murderous potential.[2]

The terrorist reputation of the mythical Bacchantes, however, didn't stop some women in ancient Greece from performing actual rites of worship to the god Dionysus. Every other year the Thyiads, as the women in this mystic cult were called, came from Athens and Delphi to Mount Parnassus, where they worshiped their god amid much wine-drinking, dancing, singing, and ecstatic cries. Since men were strictly barred from these celebrations, the Thyiads may have participated in one of the only legitimate all-women's drinking parties in history. Their semiannual gatherings continued through the Hellenistic age.

Roman women also worshiped the wine god, and for many years the Roman rite also remained exclusively female. At some point during the second century B.C., however, one woman admitted her sons to the rites, and from then on, men flooded the festivities. With the addition of men, what had once been a drunken but essentially harmless and joyful celebration among women became an extended sexual orgy which the historian Livy claimed included all manner of violence and perverted practices. The debauchery continued unchecked until 186 B.C. when an extraordinary session of the Roman senate was convened, forbidding men to participate in the Bacchanalia and sentencing thousands of male and female participants to death.[3] Following the senatorial decree, small bands of women resumed their wine-tinged worship, free again from male interference. It is ironic that although women's drinking is typically linked with sexual insatiability, the female worshipers rarely sought out the company of men for their celebrations, and prior to male participation there were few reports of violence or sexual activity of any kind.

Although drinking among Roman women was permitted by the second century B.C., it was considered a serious crime in the early Roman period. During this era Roman society was wholly patriarchal, with the male head of each clan having powers of life and death over his wife and children. Since a man virtually owned his wife, adultery was her most unspeakable crime, and since it was assumed that the drinking woman was only a sip away from another man's bed, she was punished as severely as the adulteress. Dionysius of Halicarnassus, a chronicler of the reign of Emperor Augustus, explained the penalty for female drinking and the tortuous logic that justified it:

. . . Romulus permitted them to punish both these acts (adultery and wine-drinking) with death, as being the gravest offenses women could be guilty of, since he looked upon adultery as the source of reckless folly, and drunkenness as the source of adultery. And both these offenses continued for a long time to be punished by the Romans with merciless severity.[4]

The Roman husband had a virtually foolproof method of determining whether his wife had been drinking behind his back. Each day a woman was forced to kiss all of her male relatives as well as those of her husband on seeing them for the first time, so that the telltale odor of wine could not be missed. If a woman smelled of alcohol, her husband and male relatives would meet to decide whether execution was deserved, and could lawfully carry out her fate on the spot.

This law was no mere scare tactic. Although it is not known how stringently it was enforced, there are documented cases of husbands who executed their wives for drinking wine. Valerius Maximus, a contemporary of Emperor Tiberius in the first century A.D., tells of the fate of one Roman matron whose husband caught her in the wine cellar:

Egnatius Metellus . . . beat his wife to death because she had drunk some wine; and this murder, far from leading to his being denounced, was not even blamed. People considered that her exemplary punishment had properly expiated her offense against the laws of sobriety; for any woman who drinks wine immoderately closes her heart to every virtue and opens it to every vice.[5]

Other women met equally agonizing deaths for their mere intent to drink. One Roman lady was caught simply opening the purse that held the keys to the household wine cellar, and was condemned to death by the male members of her family. She was locked in a room and starved to death.

Historians characterize the Middle Ages as plagued by widespread drunkenness in both Britain and Europe, yet the tracts of the era are all but silent on women's drinking. Women regularly used alcohol at least for medicinal purposes, with many wine-based potions concocted especially for female "needs." Wine laced with ginger and cinnamon bark was thought to "beautify women . . . (and ensure) a white, subtle, and pleasant complexion," while rosemary wine, according to a well-known medieval physician, "rectifies the uterus in the body and helps in childbirth." In an age which idealized virginity to the point of mystification, however, heavy drinking was almost certainly censured, and Chaucer's *Canterbury Tales* indicates that drinking among women was still linked with sexual excesses. In the "Prologue to the Wife of Bath," the lusty, lustful Wife laments:

> But after a drink, Venus gets in my thinking,
> For just as true as cold engenders hail
> A thirsty mouth goes with a thirsty tail.
> Drinking destroys a woman's last defense
> As lechers well know from experience.[6]

Women appeared to drink fairly openly during the Renaissance, particularly the highborn ladies who graced the courts of England, Germany, and Italy. This age of cultural, religious, and intellectual ferment spawned "La Querelle des Femmes" (The Dispute about Women) which challenged traditional views on women and may have loosened restraints on female drinking to some degree. By the sixteenth century, drinking among women of the German court was so commonplace that the Duke of Gotha, tongue only half in cheek, issued a "drinking order for the princely women." Yet Renaissance writer Alexandre Pont-Aymerie noted in 1596 that one could traverse the whole of Germany, "that empire of drunkards," and not find a single inebriated woman—an obvious exaggeration but an indication that some sanctions undoubtedly were still in force.

Historically, public outrage at the drunk woman may have reached its height during the infamous "gin epidemic" of London in the first half of the eighteenth century. The outbreak of alcoholism and alcohol-related deaths occurred after Parliament lifted nearly all restrictions on the making and selling of domestic gin in 1701 in hopes of increasing local revenues. As a result, cheap and often badly adulterated gin flooded the country, doing its worst damage in London's slums. Between 1700 and 1750 the population of London actually declined, and children especially were dying in record numbers. Between 1730 and 1749, three out of four children christened had died before the age of five.[7] Since no serious epidemic had swept through the city during that period and since the standard of living for London slum dwellers was actually rising, if very slowly, gin seemed the most likely cause of the deaths. And if babies were dying of too much gin, whose fault was that? Suddenly, public attention focused sharply on the alcoholic mother of London's slums. Amid cries of "bad mother" and "debauched woman," she became the scapegoat for a national scandal for which she bore little responsibility and from which she suffered as acutely as did her children.

The gin epidemic produced the first observations since classical Greece of the connection between hard-drinking mothers and sickly offspring. But in making this connection, indifference to the mother's alcoholism was only exceeded by the blame heaped on her for her children's afflictions. Apothecary James Sedgewick in 1725 described the babies of gin-drinking mothers as "only the secondary Sighs, and Groanings, the

evidential Marks, and Reproaches, of parentive ill-spent Life.
. . . These consequences, nay without doubt, will be brought
on Infants, by the Debauchery of the Mother. . . ."[8] And a
report of the Middlesex sessions in 1736 stated that "unhappy
mothers habituate themselves . . . children are born weak and
sickly, and often look shrivel'd and old as though they had
numbered many years. Others again daily give it to their
children . . . to taste and approve this certain destroyer."[9]

Henry Fielding, in a persuasive 1751 pamphlet that
helped to influence Parliament to finally stem the gin tide with
legislation, seemed less concerned about the effects of alcohol on
individual babies than on the cumulative effect of the legions of
gin-swilling mothers on the robustness of the English race:

> What must become of the Infant who is conceived in *Gin?*
> with the poisonous Distillations of which it is nourished both
> in the Womb and at the Breast. Are these wretched
> Infants . . . to become our future Sailors and our future
> Grenadiers? . . . Doth not this polluted Source . . . promise
> only to fill Almshouses and Hospitals, and to infect the streets
> with Stench and Disease?[10]

But probably the most effective piece of anti-gin propaganda
produced during this period was a print entitled "Gin Lane"
made by painter and printmaker William Hogarth in 1751,
which was sold by the hundreds on street corners for a shilling
each. The print "Gin Lane" is as powerful an indictment of
gin-drinking women as ever was produced in this period. The
central figure of the print is a drunken, slovenly woman sitting
on some steps as her child falls screaming out of her arms to the
street below. Amid a crowd gathered in front of a distillery, two
unattended little girls are sharing a glass of gin. Elsewhere, a
woman is pressing gin on her child. It is a scene of motherhood
gone mad.

Much of the public comment on the effects of gin-addicted women on children was done in the service of a good cause, namely, to induce Parliament to pass legislation stemming the unrestricted flow of gin into London's slums. And many of the charges were true: Some alcoholic mothers did produce sickly babies, many did neglect their children, and a few probably even did cause their deaths. But to cast the mother in the role of villain was to miss that she was as victimized by the gin epidemic as her children. The slum-dwelling woman of eighteenth century London lived in desperate, hopeless poverty, and the sudden availability of cheap gin in every grocery shop offered temporary escape from a wretched existence. Under such circumstances, addiction was an almost inevitable consequence for many. Moreover, the gin-drinking woman was suffering and dying from alcoholism right along with her children, yet there was an almost total absence of concern for her as a sick individual. Her alcoholism was seen only through the prism of her motherhood.

Across the Atlantic in the young American colonies, alcohol was a largely welcome fact of life, even in Puritan New England. An important part of the local economy, it was considered not only a sociable beverage but also a medicine and a healthful addition to the daily diet of men, women, and children alike. Many a colonial housewife brewed beer and fermented cider in her own home for family use; some worked back yard stills as well, selling their product to supplement the household income. And the early American tavern was the social center of nearly every good-sized town, providing not only strong drink but a hearty meal, the latest gossip, and possibly a bed for the night. Both men and women frequented taverns (although respectable women usually did not drink there), and it was not unusual for a woman to run a tavern of her own.

Female drinking was not confined to the privacy of the colonial home, however. At balls and dances and private parties, women sipped wine, rum punch, and fruit brandies along with the men. Their freedom to publicly enjoy alcohol was part of a generally relaxed social code for women of this period, particularly women of the upper classes. At a fancy dress ball in Boston or Philadelphia or Williamsburg in the mid 1700s, it was not uncommon to see exquisitely dressed and coiffed young women not only drinking, but also playing cards, shooting dice, and trying their hand at backgammon. But as always, there were distinctions drawn in the matter of alcohol. Nice women could drink, but never too much. At private dinner parties, for example, men and women enjoyed food and wine together during dinner. Afterward, the ladies discreetly retired to a separate drawing room for coffee and conversation, while the men brought out reserves of peach brandy and wine and continued to drink far into the evening.

Since alcohol was also considered a medicine, the colonial housewife used it in a wide variety of homemade nostrums, salves, and ointments. Recipes for various alcohol-based remedies were handed down from mother to daughter and exchanged among neighbors and friends. *The British Housewife,* a popular handbook among colonial women, recommended Aqua Mirabilis, a cordial, as "excellent in the Cholick, and against that Sickness and Uneasiness that often follow a full Meal." Another book of home remedies offered a recipe for "Stomachick" which called for a mixture of snails, worms, hartshorn shavings, and wood sorrel stewed in brandy and seasoned to taste with spices and herbs. Alcohol also was a popular cure for "breeding sickness," despite warnings from England of the dangers of drinking during pregnancy. And both beer and rum mixed with milk were regularly prescribed for nursing mothers.

If alcohol use was widely accepted in colonial America, drunkenness was not. Inebriety and its companion evils— gambling, fighting, and consorting with "bad" women—were loudly inveighed against by the churches, and their influence was felt in civil law. The Puritan fathers of the Massachusetts Bay colonies fixed legal consumption of alcohol at half a pint per person per half hour, beyond which a person was considered indisputably drunk. The convicted drunkard could be consigned to any number of unsavory fates, from a public whipping to imprisonment to the wearing of the terrible red "D" as visible testimony to one's guilt.[11]

Although both men and women were discouraged from excessive drinking, drunkenness was commonly viewed as more shocking and shameful in women. In the year 1626, a Virginia court official saw one Goodwife Fisher reel and stagger on the street and finally stumble and fall on top of a cow. He hauled her into court and testified that when he saw this otherwise respectable woman in her drunken condition, his companion at the time remarked that it was a "great shame to see a man drunk but more a shame to see a woman in that case." He also noted that a man would be set in the stocks to "lie neck and heels" for such an offense, implying that in the name of early American chivalry, a woman might escape such a fate.

However, early colonial authorities were far less chivalrous with women who encouraged drinking and its associated vices in others. In 1671 the Widow Alice Thomas, tavernkeeper, was tried before the Suffolk County Court in Boston for, among other things, selling liquor without a license, providing unseemly entertainment for children and servants, and giving "frequent secret and unseasonable Entertainment in her house to Lewd, Lascivious & notorious persons of both Sexes, giving them opportunity to commit carnal wickedness, & that by common fame she is a common Baud." Convicted on all counts, tavernkeeper Thomas received a harsh punishment even for that era: thirty-nine lashes and nine months imprisonment. After serving her sentence, she was literally banned from Boston, and her case led to the enactment of Boston's first law prohibiting prostitution. But the moral indignation of the court was not of lasting stuff. For a year later Mrs. Thomas contributed generously toward the construction of the sea wall in Boston Harbor, and she was soon after mysteriously readmitted as a city resident.

Alice Thomas's occupation as a tavernkeeper was shared by hundreds of women in colonial times, although most businesses were more respectable than that of the notorious Boston widow. Women got into the tavern business in the American colonies at least as early as the 1650s, and by the mid 1700s they were as likely to own taverns as men. Thousands of travelers stayed overnight at places such as Ann Hawkes's At the Sign of the Bacchus in South Carolina; or in Philadelphia, Mrs. Jones's Plume of Feathers, the Widow Withy's Blue Anchor, or Margaret Ingram's Rose and Crown. Tavernkeeping, an important and prestigious occupation in colonial America, usually fell to women more by necessity than by choice. Upon a husband's death, often a woman's sole inheritance was the roof over her head, and only by converting her home into a tavern could she continue to support herself comfortably. Further, since many colonial taverns doubled as inns and town social centers, many of the responsibilities of a good tavern owner—planning meals, maintaining clean lodgings, entertaining guests—were quite in keeping with the home-centered role of the colonial woman.

The generally accepted view of tavernkeeping as "women's work" is underscored by the trouble male tavern owners sometimes encountered in keeping their liquor licenses once their wives died. After innkeeper James Leonard of Taunton, Massachusetts, buried his wife in 1663, the general court of Plymouth County revoked the hapless widower's permission to sell liquor, declaring him "not being soe capable of keeping a publicke house" without the participation of his wife.

There was one problem, however, with female ownership

of taverns—the inevitable presence of liquor. How could a respectable widow pour and serve spirits, surround herself with drunken travelers, and still retain her respectability? Some of the colonies solved this problem by "protecting" women from tending bar by law. Thus when the Widow Clark of Salem requested a liquor license in 1647, the courts approved it only on condition that she "provide a fitt man who is godlie to manage ye business"—in other words, if she hired a good male bartender. This law survives in some states today, still in the name of "shielding" women from the corrupting influence of liquor.

However, some women in colonial America both owned and managed their taverns alone, and proved more than able to take care of themselves without male protection. One such woman was Hannah Brown of Long Island, who turned to tavernkeeping after her husband died in the Revolutionary War, leaving her to support herself and a large family of orphaned grandchildren. She was alone with the children in her house late one night in 1777 when suddenly a small band of armed British troops stormed through her door and demanded all of her liquor on the spot. Mrs. Brown ran toward her liquor storage room, but instead of opening it she wedged her body between the muzzles of the soldiers' rifles and the door, protecting the barrels of beer and jugs of rum that were her livelihood. She then addressed the commanding officer, Barbara Frietchie-style: "You unfeeling wretch, you hired tool of a tyrant, your conduct is worse than a savage . . . I despise your threats, and if you pass the threshhold of this door, you will first pass over my lifeless body." Stunned by her spirited response, the officer glared at her speechlessly, then stalked out empty-handed, his rifle-wielding corps behind him.

Women continued their active participation in American drinking life until the early 1800s, when many began to vigorously *oppose* the use of alcohol. Their vehicle was the temperance movement, which after more than one hundred years of prayer, persuasion, hatchet-wielding, and hard-nosed lobbying, reached its goal of nationwide Prohibition in 1919. Like no other period in Western history, the temperance era expressed and sometimes even caricatured the tortuous double standard associated with women's use of alcohol. The female temperance crusader was the very embodiment of the "good" woman, her abstinence stance identified with the will of God, a Victorian ideal of purity, and the primacy of home and family life. Alcohol, by contrast, was labeled "the unclean thing" during this era, stinking of sin and degradation. But the temperance woman was in fact more radical than her image suggests. Even as she crusaded for an antidrinking cause that embodied the most traditional female virtues, she took important steps to further the liberation of women from their powerless, home-rooted place. And for the first time she was able to transform the age-old double standard on drinking, at least officially, into a nearly single one.

The most compelling reason for women's involvement in temperance was not some abstract notion of alcohol as an evil substance, but rather their own misery and helplessness in the face of men's drunkenness. By the early nineteenth century, westward expansion, the growing industrialization of cities, and the greater availability of liquor had combined to make alcohol abuse a serious social problem in the United States, primarily among men. A woman married to an alcoholic husband had little protection from financial ruin, severe family disruption, and physical harm to herself and her children. Divorce during this period was almost unthinkable, and the rare woman who went to those lengths was usually left without money, property, or realistic hope of supporting herself or her children.

But large numbers of women in mid-nineteenth-century America were also easy marks for any campaign that appealed to their self-images as ladies of sterling virtue. Victorian culture had hoisted the middle-class woman upon a pedestal so towering that she was barely recognizable as a human being. The image she projected from that rarefied plane was an exaggerated version of the traditional feminine role: supremely dutiful, loving, and passive, and almost wholly asexual. Morally above reproach herself, she was designated the guardian of the morals of men, children, and the community at large. For a woman defined by such a role, alcohol was a natural enemy. As portrayed by early temperance preachers, liquor not only ruined the men and children for whom she had moral responsibility, but even more dreadful, it threatened her own virtue.

Temperance manuals repeated the same theme ad nauseam: When a young boy was introduced to alcohol, he deteriorated to a lustful, animallike state and subsequently died; when a girl tasted the evil stuff, she lost her head and was either seduced, raped, or lured into a life of prostitution. Richmond P. Hobson, an antiliquor lecturer infamous for his lurid scare tactics, denounced alcohol as "the primary cause of the condition of feeble-minded, unbalanced female sex-perverts, and of those women and girls who . . . were taken advantage of through the temporary suspension of their higher faculties as the result of drink."[12] In the South, antiliquor leaders hysterically predicted that alcohol would "bring white virtue into the black brute's power" via drunken rapes.

It was no wonder that when the churches began recruiting women to the temperance cause they found a ready volunteer army. Here was an issue that traumatically affected women's lives and played on some of their deepest fears, and was consistent with their self-images as guardians of family and community virtue. It was also a cause which they could pursue within the respectable framework of the church. The churches' leadership role in the dry cause was crucial to women's ability to become involved in it. Since the only approved role for middle-class women outside of wife and mother was that of public protectoress of morals, the only activities sanctioned for women outside the home were church-authorized "good works" involving the edification of the depraved and downtrodden.

Thus when the churches called on women to help save souls drowning in alcohol, they could leave their kitchens for the organizing halls with clear consciences. Many also left with a sense of excitement and relief. For many, the temperance cause also served as an escape route from the daily monotony of their lives, and an opportunity to exert substantial intellectual, organizing, and leadership abilities that had found little outlet within the home. More than any other social movement thus far in American history, the temperance cause was able to nurture and harness these capabilities in women, and finally unleash them with such power that most historians acknowledge that were it not for women, Prohibition could never have been enacted.

Not all women fought the temperance fight, of course. The dry cause was a primarily white, middle-class, rural Protestant movement, and attracted mostly women of similar background to its ranks. A minority of women continued to drink throughout the temperance era, among them wealthy women who considered themselves above "bourgeois" morality, immigrant women from the wine-drinking countries of Europe, and poor women of all ethnic backgrounds. Alcohol abuse in women during this period was not uncommon, particularly among the urban poor. According to one magazine writer commenting on "Women and the Drink Problem" in 1899, no less than eight thousand women were arrested for drunkenness in New York City in the preceding year.[13]

Drunkenness among both sexes was often punished by imprisonment; however, Victorian morality may have imposed an even harsher fate on some chronically drunk or alcoholic women. In an address before the Medico-Legal Society in 1897, a

Brooklyn physician recommended that the alcoholic woman "be desexualized . . . whether maid or matron" if she failed to respond to routine treatment.[14] As "desexualization"—removal of a woman's uterus and ovaries—was a fairly common procedure performed on sexually active or otherwise unruly women in the late 1800s,[15] it is likely that this operation was carried out on at least some alcoholic women during this period.

If the stigma attached to female drunkenness during this era seriously harmed some women, the guardian angel image of the temperance woman also had its limitations. From the beginning, male antiliquor leaders exhorted women to limit their participation in the dry cause to an ethereal brand of "moral influence" appropriate to their sex, while leaving the dirty—and more substantive—work of policymaking to men. This vision culminated in the "Women's Crusade" of 1873–74, in which women throughout the country marched on saloons and taverns, praying and singing hymns to tavern owners to shame them into closing down. The theory behind this strategy was that no man, however brutish and insensitive, could withstand the devastating moral force of the "good" woman, who represented purity, motherhood, and the will of the Creator Himself. After all, "Who is left to (suppress saloons) but God and the Women?" demanded the *Crusade Temperance Almanac* in 1875. But apparently even this impressive duo couldn't do the job. Although Bible-quoting women did manage to shame or embarrass thousands of tavern owners into closing down their businesses, just as often their prayers were answered with buckets of dirty water thrown in their faces, drenching blasts from firehoses, and repeated arrests. And of the thirty thousand some saloons that did sheepishly close under moral pressure, nearly every one reopened within a year.

A few women rejected this passive, prayerful role from the beginning and opted for direct action. As early as 1853, Mrs. Margaret Freeland of Syracuse, New York, marched alone into her alcoholic husband's favorite saloon and smashed it to splinters with a club. Other women, primarily in the Midwest, began to follow her example, banding together in search-and-destroy missions, wielding hatchets, clubs, and rocks. Although most male leaders of both the dry and wet causes denounced this more aggressive brand of activism, a few supported it: When a group of Illinois women were arrested for roughing up a tavern, an eminent lawyer named Abraham Lincoln volunteered to defend them and got them off with only a reprimand.

Hatchet-bearing women usually have been dismissed as comic figures of the temperance era, but their violence in most cases was an expression of intense anger and frustration over the devastating effects of alcoholism on their personal lives. It is no accident that Carry Nation, one of the most vehement temperance fighters of the era, was married to an abusive alcoholic.

But by the mid 1870s, dry women had largely abandoned both their roles as hatchet-bearing shock troops and as moral cajolers. They were weary of public hostility, arrests, and most of all, the reality of shut-down saloons reopening almost as soon as they left the scene. Also they were increasingly frustrated by their systematic exclusion from a policymaking role in the temperance movement, though its male leaders thus far had had little success in stemming the liquor traffic. Women's attempts to gain equal participation with men in temperance conventions through the 1850s and 1860s had been repeatedly thwarted, prompting temperance fighter Susan B. Anthony to write angrily to a friend: "Men like to see women pick up the drunken and fallen!—repair the *damages* of society! . . . But to be master of circumstances— that is man's sphere!"

The abysmal failure of the Woman's Crusade, a male-orchestrated scheme, was the last straw. On November 7, 1874, dry women took matters into their own hands for the first time by gathering at Cleveland's Second Presbyterian Church and voting into existence the National Woman's Christian Temperance Union. The WCTU was to become the largest women's organization in the country to date, and a powerful force for national Prohibition.

The phenomenal growth and power of the WCTU in the last quarter of the nineteenth century was due in large part to Frances Willard, the organization's president from 1879 to 1898 and its most brilliant theoretician, policymaker, and tactician. Willard's broad vision encompassed not only Prohibition but a range of other social causes, including prisoner's rights, the eight-hour working day, and the minimum wage. But next to Prohibition—and some say on a level with—Willard fought hardest for the cause of female suffrage. For though at first glance the prim and ladylike dry women and the militant suffragists seemed ideologically at odds, Willard was quick to see their natural affinity. Not only did she understand the relationship between male alcoholism and the oppression of women, but from a purely practical point of view, she believed that women needed the vote in order to win Prohibition. For their part, many of the foremost proponents of woman suffrage, including Susan B. Anthony, Elizabeth Cady Stanton, and Lucy Stone, sincerely supported the temperance cause, having honed both their organizing skills and their feminist principles on the antiliquor movement. The suffragists needed the support of the WCTU, moreover, because the respectable temperance organization attracted far more women in the late 1800s than did the more radical suffrage movement. At the turn of the century, the WCTU boasted ten times as many members as the still struggling suffrage cause.[16]

The two causes clearly needed each other to succeed, and further, shared many common goals and values. But if this very real alliance of interests between suffragists and dry women had been an open one, it could not have been tolerated by many temperance advocates of either sex. Many feared the social vision of the suffragists, and psychologically needed to maintain an image of temperance women as home-centered Madonnas unsullied by more worldly ambitions. Frances Willard simply outwitted these potential opponents.

Committed feminist though she was, Willard adorned her organization with the trappings of pure and diaphanous womanhood. She nicknamed the WCTU "organized mother love," chose a white ribbon symbolizing purity for its emblem, and made its motto: "For God, Home and Native Land." Meanwhile, she and the WCTU membership worked hard to expand rights and responsibilities for women beyond the home. Along with the organization's Departments of Social Purity and Health and Hygiene was a Department of Suffrage, which produced five million pages of literature per year—more than the suffragists themselves did. In 1884, the WCTU national convention endorsed woman suffrage, a risky step that Willard made safer by calling the ballot "a necessary weapon for home protection."[17]

Willard and her supporters got what they wanted. In 1919 a constitutional amendment instituting national Prohibition was ratified; in 1920, women won the right to vote. That temperance women were instrumental in winning both battles is ironic. Perhaps within no other historical era were nondrinking women so rigidly identified with the traditional virtues of purity and family allegiance. Yet in their efforts to protect those very values through Prohibition, female temperance fighters helped to make possible the expansion of women's home-bound role through the tool of suffrage. Moreover, these reputedly proper temperance ladies were more than willing to get their hands dirty in the process of winning their goal—whether with the saloon dust that greeted the Women's Crusaders, by wielding hatchets in the name of home protection, or by the ultimately successful politicking of the WCTU. So within an era and a cause that idealized woman's traditional role, women temperance crusaders—some consciously, more probably unconsciously—slowly undermined that role. And in so doing they made way for a social environment that brought women new freedoms, including, it will be seen, the freedom to drink alcohol.

A final irony undercuts the sober, straight-laced role of temperance women. Many of them, even as they were vocally and sincerely opposing alcohol, were quietly abusing both alcohol and drugs in the privacy of their homes. "Nice" women didn't drink, but nice women were permitted and even encouraged to use the popular patent medicines of the day, which contained up to fifty percent opiates or alcohol and were available over the counter. Sold under such reassuring names as Ayer's Cherry Pectoral, Mrs. Winslow's Soothing Syrup, and of course, the infamous Lydia Pinkham's Pink Pills for Pale People, these nostrums promised miraculous relief from a dizzying variety of "women's troubles" from menstrual pain to sagging ovaries. Their true ingredients, however, were rarely listed on the bottles. It is difficult to estimate how many women became dependent on alcohol through the use of patent medicines, but it is clear that many regularly and unknowingly imbibed substantial amounts—including many official teetotalers. Edward Bok, editor of the *Ladies' Home Journal* in the late 1800s and a leading opponent of the patent medicine business, surveyed fifty members of the WCTU and found that three out of four used patent medicines with an alcohol content of one-eighth to one-half pure spirits.[18]

But not all women used drugs unknowingly. Many chose to soothe their ills with one of the widely available legal painkillers of the era: opium, heroin, morphine, or cocaine. From the mid nineteenth through the early twentieth century these drugs could be purchased from drugstores, groceries, general stores, and even mail order houses, and because they were sold as medicines, they were eminently respectable. So many women became dependent either on legal opiates or patent medicines that from about 1850 to 1920, twice as many American women as men were addicted to narcotics. Moreover, the typical female drug abuser of the Victorian age was neither a prostitute nor an impoverished slum-dweller, but rather middle-aged, middle-class, and white. An Iowa study of the late 1800s reported that "the majority of them (addicts) are to be found among the educated and most honored and useful members of society; and as to sex, we . . . find females far ahead so far as numbers are concerned."[19] Other surveys confirmed this profile.

The marketing of these drugs as medicines was the key to their widespread use among women. Drugs of all kinds—including alcohol—traditionally have been approved for women as long as they are used, at least officially, for health reasons rather than for pleasure. For when used medicinally, drugs are more likely to be taken when alone and thereby less likely to expose women to sexual activity or other threats to her image as a "good" woman. So just as the modern woman is considered safer popping ten milligrams of Valium than relieving her tensions at the local bar, the Victorian lady was deemed in less danger taking her "medicinal" opium than enjoying an after-dinner brandy with a gentleman. And since her motive was the enhancement of her health, she personally saw nothing inconsistent about returning from a hard day of prayer and crusading against the evils of alcohol to soothe her aches and pains with a powerful narcotic. Of course if she was using a patent medicine, she probably wasn't even aware of the chemical basis of its potency. She only knew she "magically" felt better, just as the label promised.

However, for a woman to use drugs medicinally, she had to be sick—or someone had to convince her she was. Drug manufacturers have long exploited the myth that women are physically and emotionally more prone to illness than men and thus in need of special "help" in order to cope. But middle-class Victorian women were particularly vulnerable to manipulation by patent medicine marketeers, for in no other period of Western history was a class of women so imbued with notions of its inborn ill health. The Victorian lady was encouraged to see herself as a rarefied, delicate creature who was "naturally" weak and subject to constant illnesses of mind and body. The patent medicine industry seized on this cult of invalidism by pitching most of its advertising directly at women, promising swift and total relief from real ills and concocting new ones which their products were guaranteed to cure. Advertising focused primarily on gynecological difficulties, which were encased in euphemisms such as "women's troubles," or "female weaknesses," and on "feminine" emotional problems such as nerves and depression. Products were often cozily nicknamed "the woman's friend."

These marketing ploys were highly successful; by the turn of the century Americans were buying $100 million worth of patent medicines per year, and the majority of consumers were female.[20] In a 1915 article in *Harper's Weekly* entitled "Suffering Women," George Creel attacked the patent medicine industry's blatant exploitation of women:

> Women, not men, are the financial props of the patent medicine swindle . . . "Female weakness" are magic words that rarely fail to tap a golden stream, and it is among those who prey on the terrors of the mother sex that the great fortunes are found . . . Scientific analysis has failed to reveal a single so-called "woman's remedy" that, in its essence, is not a cheat, working inevitably to the hurt of the victim.[21]

The exposé goes on to lambaste two particularly successful and misleading "women's friends:" Wine of Cardui, a mixture of

vegetable extract and twenty percent alcohol which was advertised as a "certain cure for menstrual disturbance," and Viavi,
which promised to "bring women into a closer relationship with
Nature and Nature's God" as well as to ensure a better marriage,
and was comprised entirely of extract of hydrastic and a little
cocoa butter.

By 1920 drug addiction among women had declined
sharply. The downturn stemmed partly from the passage of the
Pure Food and Drug Act of 1906, which outlawed false
advertising and thereby exposed both the misleading claims and
the heavy drug and alcohol content of patent medicines. But
more important to the sudden drop in the female addiction rate
was the passage of the Harrison Narcotics Act of 1914 which
made narcotics illegal. Since the typical female addict was a
middle-class law-abiding woman who bought her "fix" at the
local grocery or drugstore, she was unlikely to follow her addiction into the underground world of the black market and the
pusher. No longer legal and no longer primarily medicines, narcotics ceased to be options for the respectable woman. Today, only
about twenty percent of those addicted to illegal drugs are
women. [22]

By the 1920s, many women had less use for patent
medicines and legal opiates, anyway. For after a century of
viewing alcohol as an agent of their physical and moral
destruction, women had begun drinking again. The Volstead Act
of 1919, which prohibited the sale or use of alcoholic beverages
in the United States, had barely been ratified when millions of
women began drinking openly, sometimes defiantly, at cocktail
parties, in speakeasies, at women's luncheons and bridge parties,
at country club dinners, in cars with their dates. And it was not
only the young and consciously rebellious "new woman" of the
1920s who was drinking. An article published in *Harper's
Monthly* during the Prohibition era reported:

It is no secret that well-protected, charming women, probably chaste, often beautiful, of taste and manners above the average, now drink more or less habitually. So do many good wives and beloved ones. So do women who are excellent and scientific young mothers and skillful housekeepers . . . These facts may seem shocking, but there is no use trying to beat them down with moral maxims.[23]

The revolution in drinking among middle-class women was the result of several interlocking factors operating between 1915 and 1930. First, women's roles and self-concepts were changing. World War I gave thousands of American women their first jobs and, consequently, their first taste of freedom from their husband's or father's authority. The winning of the vote for women in 1920 strengthened this emerging sense of autonomy, and with it came a new resistance to double standards of behavior. Importantly too, in the 1920s sex had begun to come out of the closet. From Vienna, Sigmund Freud had sent Americans the message that sexual expression was neither evil nor distasteful, but rather a necessary component of mental health. It became acceptable and even fashionable in some circles to talk openly about sex—no small achievement in a society that only a decade before had decorously referred to women's legs as "limbs."

The double standard on sexual behavior remained in force, but not quite so rigidly. Young women began attending necking and petting parties, and some even went so far as to buy the newly marketed contraceptives. A woman who engaged in premarital sex was still looked down upon, but she still stood a chance of making a "good" marriage—a state of affairs her mother could not have imagined. This gradual loosening of restraints on female sexuality allowed women to engage in a variety of behaviors that had been taboo in the past: shortening their skirts, cutting their hair, smoking cigarettes, experimenting with cosmetics, learning "wild" dances—and drinking alcohol. Particularly for younger women, these new behaviors were not only pleasurable in themselves, but represented a violent and conscious break from the stifling Victorian past of their mothers and grandmothers. A drink not only became a new way for women to socialize, but also an expression of their emerging sense of equality with men and a dependable way to shock their elders.

And, ironically, Prohibition itself served to encourage women's drinking rather than limit it. No sooner had the Eighteenth Amendment become law than a large segment of the wet population began to defy it, outraged that the federal government should try to legislate the right to drink. Liquor engulfed the nation from a variety of sources, among them organized crime, the independent bootlegger, the front-parlor speakeasy, and household kitchens where whole families concocted their own "home brew." Rebellious drinkers made a point of serving alcohol to both men and women in their homes, even taking the trouble to create a new occasion for drinking—the cocktail party. And the enormously popular speakeasies, unlike the taverns of a generation before, welcomed women of all classes as well as men. Millions of Americans had become preoccupied by alcohol: how to get it; where to serve it; how to avoid getting caught. In this drink-charged atmosphere, the ancient question of whether "good" women should be allowed to drink "evil" booze had been nearly swallowed by the larger confrontation between wets and drys of both sexes. Dorothy Parker spoke for many drinking women when she quipped that the Nineteenth Amendment—which gave women the vote—came just too late to stop the Eighteenth.

There were still some, of course, who took exception to the new generation of drinking women, and for the usual reasons. In a magazine article entitled "Lit Ladies," a female writer anguished:

But this drinking among decent, well-bred women, this touch
of bacchanalia in orderly society must have its reasons . . .
What has happened to the restraints of custom, taste and
habit, what has broken down the age-old female fear of what
lack of control may mean?[24]

In a similar vein, muckraker Ida Tarbell noted darkly that
women "set up bars in their homes, boast of their bootleggers
and their brews, tolerate and practice a looseness of tongue and
manner once familiar only in saloons and brothels.[25] But this
brand of moral hand-wringing, so effective in keeping the
Victorian lady away from the bottle, had little effect on the
1920s woman. Many not only drank liquor, but went a step
further and made money from it. Many a housewife had a favorite
recipe for "home brew" which she mixed, bottled, and sold to her
neighbors after setting aside a good supply for herself and her
husband. Often home-brewing was a family enterprise, as this
popular song of the era describes:

> Mother's in the kitchen
> Washing out the jugs;
> Sister's in the pantry
> Bottling the suds;
> Father's in the cellar
> Mixing up the hops
> Johnny's on the front porch
> Watching for the cops.[26]

Other women profited from Prohibition by going into the
speakeasy business, sometimes with the backing of organized
crime. Two of the most famous female-run speakeasies in New
York were Belle Livingstone's five-story famous Country Club
and Mary Louise "Texas" Guinan's El Fey Club. For a five-dollar
cover charge Belle offered ping pong and miniature golf as well as

access to an enormous bar, while Texas's club, which netted $700,000 its first year, specialized in bizarre entertainment, including a girl who danced nude with an eight-foot python wrapped around her body. Both of these flamboyant and highly successful women were legends of the Prohibition era. But for every Belle or Texas there were hundreds of women who quietly owned and managed speakeasies on a smaller scale in the front parlors of their own homes.

If she was sufficiently cool-headed and daring, a woman could make money from Prohibition in yet another way—by bootlegging. The female bootlegger, or "ladylegger" as she came to be called, was no oddity of the era; in 1920, according to prohibition headquarters in Washington, D.C., more than fifty thousand women in the United States were involved in some aspect of the bootleg business.[27] Many, in the gun moll tradition, were wives or girl friends of male bootleggers and primarily made automobile deliveries or rode "cover cars" behind autos loaded down with liquor. But not all. Prohibition investigator Walton A. Green stated in the *Omaha Bee* magazine in 1926 that "a growing number of women are making their living by bootlegging, not merely as the wives or employees of male bootleggers, but as self-sustaining, freelance criminal operatives." Some were highly successful in their profession, at least partly because they were less likely to arouse the suspicions of Prohibition officials. Some even took children with them to make pickups and deliver their goods, thus establishing the perfect cover. After all, who would suspect that a *mother* would have anything to do with the illegal booze trade?

The large numbers of women who drank and who made money from Prohibition not only reflected changing attitudes toward women's relationship to alcohol, but also the colossal failure of Prohibition itself. The flow of liquor was unstoppable. For every hapless imbiber, maker, or distributor of liquor nabbed by Prohibition officials, hundreds of thousands of dollars were pouring into the pockets of organized crime and independent bootleggers, thousands of Americans were getting sick, or dying, from the rotgut manufactured by illegal stills, and millions more were enjoying cocktails in speakeasies and living rooms and the backs of parked cars. The country was becoming increasingly disenchanted with Prohibition; in 1926, a national newspaper survey reported that eighty-one percent of the U.S. population was in favor of modification or repeal of the Eighteenth Amendment.[28] So when a powerful coalition of business and political interests began working for repeal in the mid 1920s, many Americans supported it. But despite changing social values, few expected that a leading role in repeal would be played by an energetic and highly effective organization of women.

The Women's Organization for National Prohibition Reform (WONPR) was founded in 1929 by the darling of New York City's smart set, Pauline Sabin, and was led by the wives of some of the richest and most powerful men in the country. These women represented the leisured, self-indulgent life of society's upper crust, in stark contrast to the solidly middle-class, home-centered image projected by the WCTU. Predictably, the drys seized on the amoral image of these upper-class women in its counterattack on the women's repeal organization. They labeled WONPR members the "Sabine women," linking them with drunkenness, sexual misconduct, and unfeminine ruthlessness.

The *American Independent,* a dry newspaper in Kentucky, claimed that it was a rare woman who openly advocated repeal "who is not either a drunkard or whose home life is not immoral," and as for the WONPR, "most of them are no more than the scum of the earth, parading around in skirts, and possibly late at night flirting with other women's husbands at drunken and fashionable resorts." The chairman of the National Prohibition Committee, David Leigh Colvin, described them as "Bacchantian maidens, parching for wine—wet women who, like the drunkards whom their program will produce, would take the pennies off the eyes of the dead for the sake of legalizing booze."

The target of the drys' hysteria reflected the real threat to Prohibition posed by the one-million member women's repeal organization. For the power of the wet women stemmed not only from their wealth or even from their right to vote, but from the fact of their femaleness. The drys won Prohibition largely on the strength of their portrayal of women and children as the innocent victims of drink. But no sooner had their goal been reached than their most powerful propaganda began disintegrating before their eyes. It was difficult to continue portraying drinking women as sexually at the mercy of men when increasing numbers of women were using contraceptives and openly asserting their sexual rights. And as for protection of children, it became an unconvincing issue to the millions of mothers who were regularly serving cocktails in their homes under the eyes of their children.

Already weakened by the changing mores of the 1920s, the temperance cause was dealt a deathblow when one million WONPR women publicly stood up for alcohol. With so many women lined up against Prohibition, the drys not only lost some of their most powerful allies, but also the symbols of their entire movement. Yet, ironically, the antiliquor forces had eased the way for the success of the women's repeal organization. For it was the temperance movement that had given women political skills, a proven model of organized womanpower, and enough support to get the vote, even as it seemed to be protecting the most traditional image of womanhood. The WONPR, in turn, used these fruits of the temperance movement to regain the right to drink. And they used them well. With the repeal of Prohibition in 1933, WONPR and other proliquor forces had destroyed in only a few years what the WCTU and its allies had toiled sixty years to achieve.

But by the time Prohibition was repealed, women were less likely to use their newly legalized right to drink. As the

Depression settled over the country, many women, by necessity, left the workplace and returned to the home. In general, there was a renewed national emphasis on traditional, family-centered values, and, consequently, less tolerance of "deviant" behavior in women. Women didn't stop drinking altogether—it was much too late for the imposition of a neo-temperance ethic—but they tended to drink less often and less openly than a decade ago. This shift in attitudes and behavior apparently went unnoticed by Eleanor Roosevelt, who addressed the issue of drinking among young women on national radio in December 1932, shortly before repeal was ratified. The average girl of today, Mrs. Roosevelt told the listening nation, "faces the problem of learning, very young, how much she can drink of such things as whiskey and gin, and sticking to the proper quantity."

The public response was explosive. Although she received warm congratulations from WONPR, fifty representatives of several large women's organizations angrily charged that the address was "an insult to the American girl" and that Mrs. Roosevelt herself had "put a severe strain on the loyalty of countless American women."[29] Apparently, that response was fairly representative of women's attitudes on drinking nationally during the 1930s. In 1938, the *Ladies' Home Journal* conducted a nationwide survey of drinking attitudes among women and found that the majority would not teach their daughters to drink, although most did not object to alcohol use by their sons. More than fifty percent of all the respondents thought it was wrong for women to drink at all, while fully two-thirds believed that women should not be seen imbibing in public.

But that was before a world war once again shook the nation. World War II and the increasing industrialization, urbanization, and affluence that followed in its wake opened up new opportunities and roles for women. Although women continued to face discrimination in nearly every traditionally sex-typed endeavor, after 1945 many began to experience an unprecedented degree of independence. More women than ever before were attending college, driving automobiles, using contraceptives, buying their own homes, divorcing and remarrying, getting involved in politics, working in nontraditional jobs. With this expansion of women's roles, a dramatic increase in female drinking was almost inevitable. According to the Gallup Poll, from 1939 to 1978 the number of women drinkers in the United States jumped from 45 percent to 66 percent, while the number of male drinkers rose more modestly from 70 percent to 77 percent. In other words, in the last forty years nearly three times as many women as men began using alcohol. And, if anything, this trend appears to be accelerating rather than tapering off: Between 1974 and 1977 alone, the number of women drinkers increased five percent, while the male drinking rate inched up only one percent.[30] Among younger people, the gap between male and female drinking is closing even more quickly. Although more men still use alcohol than women, by the year 2000 many experts predict that half of all American drinkers will be women.

Never before in the history of Western culture, as far as we know, have women of all classes, regions, and ethnic groups been as free to drink as they are now in the United States. Not only are more women using alcohol, but women also are beginning to drink at an earlier age, more frequently, and more publicly than in most past eras. This recent widespread acceptance of women's alcohol use represents a real historical shift. For even in past periods that permitted drinking among women, in most cases a significant part of the population believed it was immoral for some or all women to even touch alcohol. Today, women's drinking is all but taken for granted. This new laissez-faire attitude has prompted some social commentators to proclaim a "new equality" in drinking codes for men and women.

But it is equality only up to a point. Beyond the realm of social drinking, we are still very much in the grip of an oppressive history. As in the past, we continue to fear and punish women who drink to the point of drunkenness. Certainly, we no longer execute problem drinking women, nor do we discuss or perform "desexualization" as a form of treatment. But we continue to penalize the alcoholic woman, although more subtly and silently now, because we still equate her drunkenness with a threatening abdication of her social role. The history of women and alcohol demonstrates the depth and power of this equation in Western culture.

3

THE SCOPE OF THE PROBLEM

In the spring of 1978, shortly after Betty Ford announced to the nation that she was battling alcohol and drug problems, a large-circulation national magazine proclaimed that alcoholism among women had reached "epidemic proportions." Several weeks later, the *Washington Post* ran an article by a well-known health writer who reported that alcoholism was still "relatively rare" among women. Neither statement was true.

In any given month of media reportage, one can learn that the majority of alcoholic women are housewives, jobholders, or shadowy barhoppers of indeterminant employment; that most alcoholic women are from the middle and upper classes, or conversely, that the majority are on welfare, driven to the bottle by brutal poverty; that the typical female alcoholic begins hard drinking by the time she is fifteen, or that most women don't begin abusing alcohol until they approach the dangerous middle years.

In view of such consistently contradictory reports, it is little wonder that most people are thoroughly confused about the scope of women's alcoholism: that is, the number of women who have drinking problems and the types of women most likely to develop such problems. But before trying to provide more accurate answers to the questions of "how many" and "who," it is necessary to explore why we have been getting such unreliable information thus far. The fault lies beyond the newspaper or magazine reporter who is weak on checking facts, although that is part of the problem. The truth is the reporter, most often, has had very few facts to go on. Until very recently, no one has been concerned enough about the woman with a drinking problem to bother finding out who she was—or even if she existed.

Since the late nineteenth century, researchers have been assiduously collecting, analyzing, and publishing data on alcoholics, but have largely done so as though alcoholism were a sex-determined illness, contracted almost exclusively by males. Most studies have been conducted entirely with male subjects, with the results assumed to be transferable to the handful of alcoholic women thought to exist. When women have been included in studies, their numbers have usually been too small to have any significance; one study of alcoholism in urban Connecticut, for example, used 1,200 men and 42 women in its sample.[1] Another study, widely cited in support of the theory that alcoholic women are promiscuous, is based on the case histories of three women.[2]

Until very recently, this lack of research contributed to a widespread public impression that problem drinking women barely existed. Since these women weren't being studied, data on them was not filtering down to the major social institutions that shape and channel public information: educational institutions, medical and scientific journals, government information centers, and the mass media. The message that issued from all of those channels was that insofar as alcoholism existed at all, it was a male disease that struck women only rarely and somewhat haphazardly, rather like freak lightning. This general information blackout was further ensured by the rigid taboos shrouding the subject of alcoholic women.

Then, in the early 1970s, it began to look as though women's alcohol problems might finally receive a serious hearing. Several new surveys were published that pointed to a dramatic increase in women's drinking, and some interesting studies appeared which focused on ways in which women's alcohol problems differed from those of men. It was during this time, too, that the women's movement was beginning to make itself felt within the notably male-dominated alcoholism field. Feminists—among them researchers, treatment counselors and recovered alcoholics—were beginning to ask some hard questions about the invisible status of problem drinking women: Why weren't they being researched? Why weren't they coming in for treatment? Why was society generally trying to pretend they didn't exist? Before long, the federal alcoholism agency and several private alcohol organizations began to pay attention to the "woman question," and finally, the media caught on. By the end of 1976, nearly every woman's magazine in the country had published a major feature piece on the subject; Phil Donahue and Merv Griffin had chatted with recovered alcoholic women on national television; newspapers and TV stations across the country had put together local stories. Even the U.S. Congress got involved; in September 1976 the Senate held its first hearings on women and alcoholism, with such well-known recovered alcoholic women as actress Jan Clayton and journalist Susan B. Anthony testifying on societal hostility and indifference toward the woman with an alcohol problem.

But although some of this recent publicity has been beneficial, more of it has succeeded in only further confusing the issue. For in gathering its information, the media, the alcoholism organizations, and the U.S. government have had to rely primarily on the poorly designed and biased studies that still comprise the bulk of existing data on alcoholic women. As a result, the media and other information channels have transmitted a great deal of inaccurate data on both the scope and the nature of women's alcohol problems. Still further distortion has resulted from some writers' inability to resist sensationalizing the issue. Statistics have been magically produced on the "skyrocketing" rate of alcoholism among groups such as housewives or teen-agers or menopausal women, supported by little beyond the author's hunger for hot copy.

Given the mass of poorly researched and contradictory information on women's alcohol problems, it is not surprising that few people—be they friends and family of an alcoholic woman, members of the medical profession, or even those working in the alcohol field—have an accurate view of either the dimensions or the nature of the problem. But the alcoholic woman herself is the real victim of the current confusion. Once totally ignored, she is now so stereotyped and misrepresented that any attempts to give her the support she needs usually miss the mark. Efforts to identify alcohol problems are misdirected, theories on the causes of women's alcoholism are based on inaccurate premises, and treatment programs often overlook some of women's most pressing needs. And many people still aren't sure whether alcoholism in women is widespread enough to deserve serious attention in the first place.

In view of the current state of confusion on the subject,

one may question whether it is even possible to arrive at at a real understanding of the scope or dynamics of alcoholism in women. I believe that it can be done, up to a point. It is very difficult to make definitive statements about any aspect of alcoholism, for it is a singularly complex problem to define, observe, and measure. And certainly until more sensitive studies are conducted on alcoholism as it specifically affects women, little can be said about women's problems with absolute confidence. Yet because of the upsurge of interest in women's alcohol abuse over the last decade, some interesting and useful data have been uncovered in recent years. In addition, research currently underway on related women's concerns, particularly in the fields of sociology and psychology, has suggested new connections between women's drinking problems and other aspects of their life experience. And finally, alcoholic women are beginning to talk about themselves for the first time, insisting that their reality be acknowledged unfiltered by researchers' biases and "expert" opinions. By integrating all of these new sources of information, it is possible to bring the blurred, shifting image of the alcoholic woman into focus and begin to see her as she truly is.

The process of defining the alcoholic woman must begin with an exploration of the basic dimensions of women's alcohol abuse. Specifically, just how many women in the United States have problems with their drinking? And is women's alcoholism really increasing, as the media often insists, or are statistics only rising because the problem is more difficult to hide than it once was? Further, what kinds of women are at highest risk? Is the housewife really most susceptible, as many reports have it? And how do questions of race, class, marital status, age, and even place of residence affect a woman's likelihood of developing a drinking problem?

Any discussion of the scope of alcohol problems among women has to begin with a look at the status of women's drinking per se. After all, a woman cannot develop a drinking problem until she first begins to use alcohol, and there is evidence that as per capita consumption rises, alcohol problems may increase in even greater proportion.[3] Given this association, the sharp increase in women's drinking since the beginning of World War II is highly significant. As the preceding chapter noted, during the last four decades three times as many women as men began using alcohol, so that by 1978, 66 percent of women were drinking with some regularity, as compared to 77 percent of men. Women are also drinking more alcohol on a greater variety of occasions than they were a generation ago.

This swift narrowing of the gap between male and female drinking has been even more dramatic among young people. The percentage of drinkers among male college students rose a bare three points between 1947 and 1971 (from 77 percent to 80 percent), while the number of college women drinkers jumped by twelve percent (from 61 percent to 73 percent).[4] The most recent large-scale college survey, conducted in 1977 at thirty-four New England colleges, discovered that a startling 95 percent of both college men and women drank alcohol, effectively closing the sex gap as well as indicating a sizable increase in college drinking generally, at least in the New England states.[5]

Studies of high school students' drinking indicate a similar movement toward equality in the proportions of boys and girls who use alcohol. A survey of high school students in San Mateo, California, showed that in 1968, 68 percent of high school boys drank, compared with 62 percent of high school girls. In the next few years, however, the rates soared for boys and even more so for girls, so that by 1973, 82 percent of the boys and 80 percent of the girls were drinking.[6] Other high school surveys have reported similarly sharp increases.

The upswing in drinking among both men and women

since World War II is the product of several interlocking factors, including the increasing acceptability of social drug use in our culture, expanding leisure time, increasing urbanization and affluence, and, of course, the wider availability and promotion of alcohol itself. But the much more rapid rise in women's alcohol use, compared to that of men, needs further explanation. Widespread drinking among women is usually seen as a "symbol of liberation," tangible evidence of the social equality of men and women. But in fact, women's increased drinking, along with their greater freedom to smoke cigarettes, drive sports cars, and wear pants to work, is not so much a sign of actual equality as it is a cheap substitute for it. Despite gradual changes in the status of women, widespread sex discrimination still exists in such basic areas as employment, education, health care, and division of labor within the home. Efforts by women to remedy these fundamental inequities have met with entrenched resistance, for such changes profoundly shake the status quo.

But it costs society little to offer women some of the more superficial symbols of entry into a "man's world," such as alcohol, cigarettes, and automobiles. In fact, a variety of industries have profited handsomely by equating these products with the liberation of women; the cigarette slogan "you've come a long way, baby" is only the most notorious example. Such attempts to confuse symbol with substance are not only dishonest but destructive, for they serve to distract many women from the real aims of their difficult struggle for equality. Sixty years ago, many of our grandmothers flaunted their "freedom" with bobbed hair and bathtub gin, even as they were barred from all but the lowest-paying jobs. How many women today are lulled by their double Scotches and two-packs-a-day into thinking they have "made it," even as a guarantee of equality as basic as the Equal Rights Amendment continues to encounter impassioned opposition?

However, although widespread alcohol use among women is hardly proof of female equality, the sharp increase in women's drinking could not have occurred without some real changes in the social status of women. Somewhat liberalized attitudes toward women's sexuality is one important factor. In a culture that historically has equated women's alcohol use with sexual excesses, there could be no generalized acceptance of drinking among women without at least some loosening of the double standard on sex. Since under certain circumstances, it is now at least possible for "nice girls" to engage in sex without marriage, it is also possible now for women to drink without fear of being labeled "that kind of girl." In fact, drinking is almost expected of women nowadays; the woman who refuses a cocktail is now something of an oddity in many circles, marked as old-fashioned and possibly even dull. Yet the drinking woman had better be able to handle her liquor, or she will very quickly lose her "nice girl" status. For as soon as she becomes very drunk or develops a problem with alcohol, the threat of indiscriminate sexuality rears its head. No one is ready yet to deal with *that* in a woman, even if it exists in the realm of possibility only. The stigma attached to women's drinking still lives; it has only become somewhat more selective.

The changing economic role of women has also had its effect on their increased rate of drinking. The proportion of women in the work force has jumped from 32 percent to 42 percent in the last twenty years,[7] and underpaid though most women may be, they now have money of their own to spend—on alcohol if they so choose. The growing participation of women in the working world also means that they are likely to encounter a variety of drinking opportunities—business lunches, after-hours bar gatherings, office celebrations—that they were once "protected" from in the home. Women are encouraged to drink in most of these situations; they may even be pressured to do so in some of them. Moreover, although many bars continue to try to maintain their status as male preserves, some public drinking establishments have taken note of women's growing economic independence and have begun to encourage female patronage. Singles bars, of course, depend on women for their very survival, but other types of bars actively welcome women as well, particularly those in busy business districts. Many woo female customers with half-price "ladies' nights" and a wide range of drinks popular with women. And since the lowering of the legal drinking age, college bars have sprouted up like the coffeehouses of the 1960s, rarely discouraging female clientele. As with most things, money talks.

The multibillion dollar alcohol industry makes no bones about its growing interest in selling to women. A casual glance through any of the major women's magazines leaves no doubt as to the growing importance of the "women's market" to the liquor industry. Publications as various as *Glamour, Ms.,* and *Woman's Day* are stuffed with advertisements for liqueurs, wines, vodka, gin, and of late, even Scotch and bourbon. In 1976, *Cosmopolitan* was among the nation's top fifteen magazines in liquor advertising revenue, and in 1978, *Better Homes and Gardens* was listed by Seagram, the world's largest distiller, as one of its top five magazine targets for "V.O." *The Wine Marketing Handbook,* the wine manufacturers' bible, acknowledged in its 1977 edition that the "women's market is of great importance" to the wine industry.[8] And that same year *The Liquor Handbook,* the marketing manual for the distilled spirits industry, announced that women would continue to be a major sales target.[9]

The current campaign to attract female customers contrasts sharply with the level of industry attention women have received in the past. Until 1958, the liquor industry code forbade even the portrayal of a woman in an advertisement. And even through the 1960s, the only alcohol advertising likely to be found in most women's magazines was an occasional ad for sherry, possibly accompanied by a recipe for chicken a la king. It has only been in the last decade that the alcohol industry has discovered it is good business to persuade women to drink. For one thing, some of its other important markets have been dwindling, particularly the highly lucrative youth market.

In the late 1960s and early 1970s, when the products of the "baby boom" reached maturity, the alcohol industry very successfully zeroed in on them with pop wines, milk-based alcoholic concoctions, and other sweet drinks more reminiscent of soda pop than alcohol. But by the mid 1970s, this huge and consumption-happy group of eighteen- to twenty-four-year-olds had begun to get older, and the "Ripple effect" lost much of its potency. In addition, the dual pressures of inflation and recession had begun to adversely affect alcohol industry profits. From an average 5 percent yearly growth in the late 1960s and early 1970s, liquor consumption slowed to a paltry .6 percent by 1976,[10] while wine inched up only 2.2 percent the same year.[11] If it was to recoup its losses, the alcohol industry would have to find a large group of new drinkers—quickly.

And by the mid 1970s, the women's market had become a hot prospect for several reasons. Since fewer women drank than men, the female market possessed a healthy growth potential. And although alcohol traditionally was a male beverage, women's roles had evolved to the point where alcohol could be successfully marketed to women; in fact, the goals of the women's movement could be used to enhance the attractiveness of alcohol use. But most importantly, women were beginning to wield substantial economic clout. A study conducted by *Liquor Store Magazine* and widely reprinted in liquor trade publications reported happily that in 1974, more than half of liquor store customers were women, up from just twenty-nine percent in 1962.[12] And *The Liquor Handbook* noted in 1976 that 36.3 million women were then in the labor force and that by 1986 there would be 44.9 million female jobholders, adding that "unless they take their husbands to work with them, they make their own brand decisions."[13] The time clearly had arrived to mine the women's market.

⸢⸣ So far, the industry's strategy regarding women has appeared to combine the introduction of new products, the repackaging of established beverages, and an advertising campaign that offers something to both the traditional and the "liberated" woman. In the last few years alcohol manufacturers have deluged the market with new liqueurs, beverages regarded as distinctly "feminine" in appeal since the first ones were marketed centuries ago bearing names such as Old Woman's Milk and Illicit Love. Now alongside the standard coffee, mint, and orange-flavored liqueurs, women are being urged to try new cordials flavored with tea, peanuts, marshmallow, coconut, caramel, and even the loquat fruit. Industry spokesmen acknowledge that many liqueurs introduced in the past few years were initially pushed in women's magazines, then dropped or continued on the basis of female interest. Significantly, in 1976, a year when total distilled spirits consumption increased less than one percent, consumption of liqueurs shot up an impressive eight percent.[14]

Manufacturers have also stepped up their advertising of established liquors with a good female track record. "White goods," liquor industry lingo for colorless spirits such as gin, vodka, and white rum, are being pushed hard in women's magazines, complete with cocktail recipes that stress the no-fuss, "anybody-can-do-it-even-a-woman" concept of home bartending. The alcohol industry has realized that our gradual transformation from a nation of bourbon drinkers to one of vodka drinkers has a lot to do with women, and is spending its advertising dollars accordingly. Squeezed between ads for high-calorie cocktails and liqueurs, women simultaneously are being urged to drink the new "light" beers and white wines in order to stay thin while getting high.

The impact of this recent alcohol sales campaign on increased drinking among women can only be guessed at, but there is reason to believe it has been substantial. Sagging profits notwithstanding, the manufacturers of alcohol comprise an enormous industrial empire with combined sales of more than $24 billion per year.[15] And the amount of money spent each year to persuade consumers to buy booze is intimidating: In 1976 alone, the industry spent a total of $361.5 million on newspaper, magazine, and television pitches for its products.[16]

But the alcohol industry's influence on women's drinking may have less to do with the size of its advertising budget than with the element of "hidden persuasion" that accompanies the selling of most consumer goods. It is no secret that alcohol is advertised less for its taste or even its relaxing effects than for its supposed power to infuse users with a dazzling array of enviable qualities, from sexual potency to financial success to an indefinable something called "gusto." One doesn't just buy a bottle of bourbon, but a new lifestyle, an overhauled self-image. And in devising its advertising appeals to women, the alcohol industry has taken careful note of the nature of women's aspirations and psychic needs, as well as important differences among various groups.

Thus ads aimed at the career-minded woman portray alcohol as a mark of prestige and independence, borrowing heavily from the status-soaked appeals that have been so successful with men. Other advertisements make their pitch to the sexually "liberated" woman, underscoring the seductive potential of a certain brand of liquor. Probably the majority of alcohol ads aimed at women, however, still center around the traditional female need for the undivided love and attention of a man. These almost invariably portray a man and a woman imbibing together in some lushly romantic setting, suggesting that the particular drink they share is some kind of magic elixir of love. All of these ads, regardless of the segment of the female market they are aiming at, are selling much more than alcohol—they are pushing women's fantasies, bottled, corked, and labeled. It is a seller's market.

Unfortunately, this kind of advertising may do more than merely influence women to begin drinking. By playing on some of women's deepest desires and needs, it may also encourage reliance on a beverage that is also a potentially addictive drug. If an advertiser implies that a certain brand of Scotch will enhance a woman's tenuous self-confidence with men, couldn't some women begin to become somewhat dependent on Scotch for a reliable, if temporary "fix" of confidence? If an ad hints that drinking a particular kind of vodka will heighten a woman's sex appeal, mightn't some women conclude—even unconsciously— that drinking a lot of it, and often, will make them more sexually alluring than only an occasional sip? The association of drinking with certain desirable traits is particularly insidious because alcohol sometimes works biochemically in such a way that the drinker temporarily experiences some of the very advertised attributes she covets. Hence she may begin to turn to alcohol whenever she needs to "be" the person promised by the ad: successful, sexually alluring, loved.

Those ads which link drinking with sexuality may be particularly harmful, for they put a woman in a confusing double bind about the kind of behavior permitted her in drinking situations. What is she to listen to, her mother's stern warnings about self-control, or the seductive promises of sexual power and fulfillment offered by the liquor industry? Such mixed messages may promote a deep-seated ambivalence toward alcohol which some researchers believe contributes to the development of drinking problems. This is not to suggest that alcohol advertising *causes* alcohol abuse among women, for obviously many women are exposed to liquor ads and never experience problems with alcohol. But for women already susceptible to alcoholism, the glittering, bewildering, and ultimately false promises that suffuse much alcohol advertising may well push them further in the direction of problem drinking.

∿ With the fast-growing rate of alcohol use among women and with new social and commercial pressures that possibly encourage abusive drinking, how many women who use alcohol are either problem drinkers or alcoholics? Actually, the terms "problem drinker" and "alcoholic," which are often used interchangeably, describe somewhat different conditions.

∿ A problem drinker is usually described as someone who drinks very heavily on a fairly regular basis and has suffered at least one serious drinking-related problem in an important area of her life. She may have had an accident while driving home from a party; her marriage may be in trouble; or she may have lost a job after too many missed Mondays or unexplained midday absences. Although not yet clinically alcoholic, she risks becoming so; research indicates that a significant proportion of problem drinkers eventually do become alcoholic.[17]

∿ The alcoholic woman differs from the problem drinker primarily in that she cannot consistently choose whether or not to drink, and once she has begun, cannot consistently choose when to stop. She probably has been drinking abusively for at least eight to ten years, and has exhibited such serious symptoms as frequent blackouts, morning drinking, and loss of tolerance for alcohol. Some of the most important areas of her life—family, friends, health, career—have probably suffered painful damage.

The question of just how many women are problem drinkers or alcoholics is not only an academic one, for on it turns important decisions about who gets treated for alcoholism, whose problems are studied, and whose alcohol abuse is deemed worthy of preventive efforts. Outside of the hyperbolic figures that recently have been issued by the media, alcoholism among women has consistently been judged to be a relatively insignificant, low-priority problem. Over the last few decades, problem drinking and alcoholism surveys have reported male-female ratios ranging from 8:1 to 4:1; currently, women are said to comprise approximately twenty percent of the nation's estimated ten million alcoholics and problem drinkers.[18] Consequently, when women's advocates demand more treatment programs and related services for women, budget directors of alcoholism agencies point to the survey statistics and shrug their shoulders, asking: "Why should we spend money on women when women aren't having the problems?" And the available money is used for yet another program for skid-row men, or an outreach program for a male-intensive industry, or for a study of male drinking patterns in working-class taverns.

Even if women accounted for only twenty percent of the U.S. alcoholic population, their needs would still be woefully underserved by current programs. But in fact, the magnitude of alcohol problems among women has been seriously underestimated by most surveys to date. The distorted estimates result largely from an overwhelming male bias in the information collection methods used by alcoholism surveys. For example, many surveys have relied primarily on death rates from liver cirrhosis. This method doesn't take into consideration that cirrhosis may be reported less frequently as a cause of death in women because of the harsher stigma attached to female alcoholism. (Also, although alcohol abuse is a primary cause of liver cirrhosis, it is not the only one.) Other survey estimates have been based on admission rates of alcoholics to various institutions, most frequently prisons, state hospitals, and public clinics. But women rarely encounter problems with the law in connection with their drinking, and are likely to seek help in only the most secluded possible settings; therefore, they are unlikely to be found in large numbers in such institutions.

Surveys of problem drinking, as distinct from alcoholism, also reveal an inherent male bias. Nearly all of these surveys measure problem drinking partially on the basis of how much alcohol one consumes, which appears reasonable enough at first glance. However, the same consumption level is used to determine problem drinking in both men and women, even though women weigh forty pounds less than men on the average and thus are likely to become drunk on substantially less alcohol. Problem drinking surveys also tend to ask male-oriented questions in assessing the social consequences of a person's alcohol abuse. Questions such as "Have you ever been arrested in connection with your drinking?" or "Have you ever gone on extended drinking binges?" are irrelevant to most women, regardless of how much they may be drinking. Further, in responding to survey questions, women may be more likely than men to minimize alcohol-related problems because of more intense guilt and shame.

Attempting to remove some of these biases by investigating private facilities and settings where women might be more likely to seek help for a drinking problem has uncovered significantly higher rates of female alcohol abuse. A national survey of more than thirteen thousand private physicians found that close to forty percent of the doctors saw at least as many alcoholic women as men among their patients.[19] Other surveys of physicians' practices report male-female ratios ranging from 3:1 to 1:1.[20] Most researchers believe that the privacy offered by a physician's office accounts for the larger number of women reported. Dr. Marvin Block, past president of the American Medical Association's National Committee on Alcoholism, wrote as early as 1965:

It is my opinion that there are as many female as male problem drinkers and alcoholics. As a private physician engaged in treating alcoholic patients—and 80 percent of my patients suffer from this disease—I have found this to be true. In conferring with other physicians whose practice is largely in the field of alcoholism, I learn that in their *private work* [italics mine] the same statistics obtain.[21]

Other treatment settings which ensure some protection from public exposure also report a relatively high proportion of female alcoholic clients. One survey of alcoholic admissions to a wide range of treatment facilities showed that while women comprised only about one-seventh of the patients at state and county mental hospitals, approximately one-third of alcoholic patients at private mental hospitals were women.[22] And Alcoholics Anonymous, a worldwide organization of recovering alcoholics which carefully protects the anonymity of its members, reported in 1977 that fully thirty-two percent of its new members were women.[23]

But even these higher figures fail to account for the vast number of alcoholic women who are drinking secretly, thereby eluding statistical tables entirely. No one is sure just how many women are hidden drinkers, but the severity of the stigma associated with female alcoholism has undoubtedly kept large numbers from seeking help. Marty Mann, a recovered alcoholic and founder of the National Council on Alcoholism, believes that "if you added up all the problem drinkers in the country, the hidden as well as the revealed, the sex ratio would be just about fifty-fifty."[24] Other alcoholism specialists have offered similar opinions; no one really knows. It may be premature to assert that fully one-half of all alcoholics in this country are women, in part simply because at present, not as many women as men *drink* alcohol. Therefore, fewer women than men are even exposed to the possibility of developing an alcohol problem. And although norms are changing, men are still pressured to drink more often and more heavily than are women. Hard drinking is still associated with manliness in many circles; nowhere, yet, is it associated with womanliness. Thus on the average, men are still somewhat more likely than women to slide into the kinds of abusive drinking patterns that can lead to serious alcohol problems.

But a precise one-to-one ratio is not necessary to establish that alcohol abuse and alcoholism among women is a widespread and seriously underestimated problem. The few surveys that are relevant to women's experiences indicate that at least one-third of the some ten million alcoholics and problem drinkers in the United States are women. Based on those figures—and they are almost certainly conservative—at least 3.3 million American women are today struggling with serious, largely untreated alcohol problems.

Women's alcohol problems are not only more widespread than commonly assumed; they most likely are increasing. Alcoholics Anonymous statistics, for example, show that the percentage of women in A.A. has risen from 22 percent in 1968 to 26 percent in 1971 to 29 percent in 1977, with women comprising 32 percent of new members joining AA between 1974 and 1977 alone.[25] This jump could result from more women seeking help, but it is doubtful that this could account for the entire increase. Once again, it is useful to look at the startling rise in women's *drinking* over the past few decades. Increased consumption is likely to lead to a roughly parallel increase in alcohol problems when unhealthy attitudes and behavior toward drinking are encouraged.

As discussed above, alcohol is no shortcut to self-confidence, career success, or sexual sophistication, yet the alcohol industry as well as our entire cultural orientation toward drinking encourage women to believe that it may be. And at a time when women are engaged in an often confusing and painful search for more satisfying ways of defining themselves, to urge on them a potentially addictive drug as a means of facilitating that process may increase the likelihood of abusing that drug still further. In addition, as the following chapter will deal with more fully, the very nature and intensity of the role conflicts many women are currently struggling with may make alcohol abuse a more likely avenue of escape than ever before.

Not only are alcohol problems among women probably increasing, but they affect a much wider range of women than is commonly thought to be the case. Insofar as alcoholic women have been paid any attention at all, they generally have been lumped together as a single "type" of woman, despite enormous and quite obvious differences among them. For a long while, the "typical" alcoholic woman was painted as a lower-class, promiscuous barfly who existed precariously on the margins of society. This image was rooted in long-standing cultural stereotypes as well as decades of alcoholism research conducted primarily in prisons, state hospitals, skid-row neighborhoods and other places generally inhabited by very poor and isolated persons. Then, in the 1960s, alcoholism research shifted its focus somewhat to middle-class subjects, and the classic alcoholic woman was reincarnated as a respectable, white middle-aged housewife who did her drinking behind the drawn curtains of her living room.

Researchers began issuing reports such as this one:

> I have attempted to describe the typical alcoholic woman . . . We will name her Mrs. A.L. Cohol . . . She is married and has an average of two children, she is in her mid-forties but looks older than her given age. She has had a definite

problem with alcohol for at least eight years prior to her hospitalization. She is in the middle-income group with better than average intelligence.[26]

Currently, our image of the alcoholic woman seems to shift between the lower-class slut and the middle-class housewife, with the housewife somewhat more in vogue due to the recent attentions of the media. In fact, recent research, as well as reports from treatment programs, have established that substantial numbers of problem drinking women are found in every age bracket, socioeconomic class, racial and ethnic group, employment situation, and region of the country. But the old stock figures are still firmly entrenched in the public imagination. The alcohol abusing woman herself latches onto these stereotypes as desperate justification for her own drinking, proving by her very distance from them that she isn't the "type" to have an alcohol problem. She tells herself that she is too young or too rich or too successful to be in trouble with alcohol, and her family and friends often support her in her rationalizations. The health system, for its part, responds to the stereotypes by restricting its outreach and treatment efforts to very limited groups of women. Particularly if a woman happens to be very young, single, nonwhite, or extremely poor, she is likely to be forgotten by the alcoholism treatment system. She doesn't fit the right cubbyholes.

Yet although there is no "typical" alcoholic woman, it does appear that women with certain kinds of sociocultural characteristics may be more likely to develop drinking problems than others. And it also appears that some of the factors which increase a woman's vulnerability to alcoholism differ from those of men. At present, the most useful source of information on sociocultural differences in drinking problems is a 1975 national drinking survey conducted for the federal government by the

National Opinion Research Corporation.[27] This survey is not the definitive word; it limits itself to measuring problem drinking, not alcoholism, and it also excludes from its purview certain groups of women believed to have very high rates of alcohol problems, such as lesbians and American Indian women. However, as the survey utilizes a nationally representative sample and has made a conscious effort to weed out some of the usual male biases found in alcohol surveys, it does offer some valuable information on the kinds of women and men prone to problem drinking.

The NORC survey, which was based on interviews with 1,125 women and 1,028 men, analyzed those classified as problem drinkers within a wide range of categories, including age, employment status, marital status, socioeconomic class, race, religion, and area of residence. Substantial numbers of women appeared in nearly all of the groupings within each category. Surprisingly, among women and men of any age group, the youngest group (eighteen to twenty) showed the highest rate of drinking problems. This finding can be partially explained by the fact that problem drinking usually develops much more quickly than alcoholism and some young people "grow out of it" by their late twenties. It also may be a function of a greater readiness among younger people to admit to alcohol-related problems, since standards of behavior for young people are generally more relaxed than for older adults. Nevertheless, it remains that a significant proportion of problem drinkers are college-age women, a group not usually considered prone to serious trouble with alcohol.

In terms of job status, problem drinking was most often reported by unemployed persons of both sexes. Interestingly, however, employed women were nearly as likely as unemployed women to have drinking problems, while this was not the case for men. Even more significant, *married* women with jobs reported substantially higher rates of problem drinking than either single working women or housewives, while no such relationship occurred for men. This finding suggests that the dual roles of spouse and worker may be particularly stressful for women, possibly because expectations of women who try to manage both roles are quite different from those for men. In view of current stereotypes, perhaps the most surprising finding in this realm of inquiry was that housewives were less than *half* as likely to have alcohol problems as either working women or unemployed women.

Divorced and separated women reported a disturbingly high rate of alcohol problems. Nearly a third of the women in this group who drank at all, indicated problems—approximately the same percentage reported by divorced and separated men. In no other grouping did women approach the level of alcohol abuse found in men. In the marital status category, single women reported the second highest proportion of drinking problems, followed by married women and widows. These findings further undercut the popular notion that the "typical" alcoholic woman is the house-bound married woman.

A breakdown of drinking problems by socioeconomic status showed that among those who drank at all, poor women were more likely to abuse alcohol than more affluent women; the same was true for men. In terms of race, blacks and whites of both sexes were about equally likely to have drinking problems; unfortunately, no other racial or ethnic group was represented in large enough numbers to allow for comparison. Catholic women were more likely to have drinking problems than women of Protestant faiths; this was also true for men, except that the gap between Catholic and Protestant rates was much larger for males. Rural women reported more alcohol abuse than women living in cities or suburbs; the opposite was true for men.

Although these findings represent trends and approximations rather than absolute reality, they are useful in reorienting and expanding our current conception of the "typical" problem drinking woman. It is clear that certain groups of women who are usually overlooked may be particularly susceptible to alcohol problems, including very young women, unemployed women, married jobholders, and those who are divorced and separated. The high risk of alcohol problems in these groups needs to be given serious attention, not only by the health system but by the women themselves and those close to them. Also important, it appears that women and men of similar backgrounds and lifestyles are not always equally vulnerable to problem drinking. Certain social factors and situations may put more stress on women than on men, and thus are more likely to trigger female alcohol abuse. If this is so, the general propensity of alcoholism programs to treat women as though their problems were identical to those of men can only hinder women's recovery efforts.

But most importantly, this national survey makes clear that no group of women is immune to alcohol problems. It is not an affliction that touches only housewives and a small, shadowy group of bar drinkers, but women of virtually every social background and lifestyle. When the real scope of alcohol problems among women is appreciated—both the broad cross section of women and the sheer numbers involved—the extent of ignorance and denial surrounding this issue becomes that much more astonishing. It also forces one to face an extremely uncomfortable question that is explored in the next chapter: Why? Why have so many women from such diverse backgrounds been driven to escape from their lives and their feelings through a powerful, addictive drug? It is possible that in part, acknowledgment of the scope of women's alcohol abuse has been avoided for so long because society cannot afford to deal with this inevitable next question. For to ask why women drink too much—or abuse other drugs or "go crazy" or exhibit any other symptoms of profound psychic pain—is to be forced to confront the depths and source of women's unhappiness.

4
THE MAKING OF AN ALCOHOLIC WOMAN

"I knew all my life that I was a phony," said Joan, a youngish, soft-faced woman dressed in jeans and a red T-shirt. She looked up at the other women sitting around the circle, her face tight with remembered pain. "I knew that I was intellectually inadequate and physically fat and that I had nothing going for me. But when I drank, baby, I was beautiful. I was bright. I was sharp. And as the years went by, booze became the only thing I could count on to keep telling me I was wonderful. Except that I would wake up each morning and find that I had turned from Cinderella back into a char-girl again—so I would have to drink some more to forget." She let out a long breath and stared at the floor.

After a few moments, Tracy reached forward and touched

her hand. She was a short, middle-aged woman with close-cropped hair and a nervous, tentative manner. "The drinking took the edge off everything for me, too," she admitted, speaking quickly and softly. "It kept me in the fog that I wanted to be in—it kept me from having to be the person I really am. I guess that's what I've tried to dodge all my life. I've always wanted to be . . ." She stopped and bit her lip. "I've always wanted to be that symbol of beauty and grace and perfection that I thought would make my mother love me. Damn! I'm forty-nine years old and I'm just beginning to deal with that."

As the other five recovering alcoholic women in the group took their turns, trying as best they could to articulate why they had turned to alcohol, a shared emotional history began to emerge. Each woman talked of living her life as an outsider, of knocking on doors that never seemed to open, of the daily pain of feeling profoundly and hopelessly unlovable. Each spoke of trying to be more like the person she was "supposed" to be or, alternately, of trying to close herself off from the seemingly impossible expectations of others; all talked of trying and trying and trying and nothing ever getting any better. That seemed to be the worst part: the incessant, ever-expanding fear that it would always be this way, that there was no way out of their bitterness and despair—except, perhaps, through a drug as self-annihilating as alcohol.

Yet, honest and enlightening as the stories of these seven women were, they did not entirely explain why any of them became addicted to alcohol. Not everyone who is miserable drinks too much. Many people look for escape or substitute gratification in outlets other than alcohol: pills of various kinds, food, cigarettes, work, television, sex. Others try to solve their problems through a mental health system that has become big business in America, wading through offerings as disparate as psychoanalysis, the mass marathons of *est,* and literally thousands of messianic self-help manuals. Some despair of solutions altogether and sink into mental illness, sometimes punctuated by violence toward others or themselves. Obviously, many unhappy people try several escape routes in combination or in succession—and drinking may well be one of them. But the reality remains that millions of people, deeply dissatisfied with their lives and veterans of multiple methods of attempted relief, simply never develop problems with alcohol.

In fact, no one is entirely sure what causes a person to become alcoholic. As alcoholism is a complex addiction which only recently has come under study as an illness rather than a moral dilemma, researchers are still stymied over its precise causes, and multiple theories are advanced. Some scientists believe that alcoholism is primarily a biochemical phenomenon, set off by a bodily "trigger" which may be anything from a genetically caused nutritional deficiency to a dysfunction of the endocrine system to the presence of alcohol-vulnerable genes. To date, the only hard evidence for a major physiological component is in the area of heredity: a 1973 study of male children of alcoholic parents found an unusually high rate of alcoholism among these children even when they were raised by foster parents.[1] However, these findings applied only to extremely severe cases of alcoholism and, significantly, were not replicated in a later study by the same researcher using female children.

Although by no means ruling out a possible physiological component, most alcoholism researchers believe that alcoholism is more likely caused primarily by the interaction of environmental and psychological factors. Dr. Edith Gomberg of the University of Michigan, a leading alcoholism educator and researcher, summarized what appears to be the mainstream viewpoint in the field:

> Unless we accept moral or hereditary explanations of alcoholism, we have to look for causes in the alcoholic person's history

and development within the society in which he or she lives . . . a person's body chemistry may make him or her more vulnerable because alcoholic beverages have quite special effects on him or her; more significant, we believe, is the role of life experience, character development, patterns of coping, family and other group experiences, and the frustrations and stresses that are part of the human condition.[2]

The theory that alcoholism is caused primarily by the interplay of social and psychological factors is supported by numerous studies, and resonates as well on a purely personal level. Most of us, at one time or another, have reacted to a stressful situation or emotion with the silent admission: "Could I use a drink now!" Alcohol does dull the prickly edges of reality, allowing us temporary respite from whatever feelings we wish to escape: frustration, anxiety, anger, tension, loneliness. And it is hard to dismiss as entirely coincidental that the United States, one of the most hard-driving, individualistic, and fast-paced societies in the world, also has one of the world's highest rates of alcoholism. In an analysis of the causes of alcoholism, sex crimes, prostitution, and other social ills in America, Margaret Mead observed:

Their form and frequency are indices of the maladjustment that exists in the United States, as in every modern society. They are the symptoms of the state of society, just as the phobias and compulsions of the patient are symptoms. They are systematically related to the culture. . . . Society is the patient.[3]

Assuming that the interaction of social and psychological factors is a key contributor to alcoholism, what kinds of specific stresses in what combinations make a person most vulnerable? Researchers have compiled a fairly extensive list of "risk factors," including particular kinds of family backgrounds, patterns of parental alcohol use, personality conflicts, and adult psychic crises. However, most of this research is weakened by a serious flaw: it has been conducted almost entirely on male subjects, with the results automatically applied to women. In recent years, a few researchers have begun to study alcoholic women directly and have uncovered striking differences in the backgrounds and pre-drinking personality conflicts of alcoholic women and men. But this handful of recent studies, floating among literally hundreds of research reports on all-male groups, has had only limited impact on the alcoholism field's dominant assumption that whatever makes men drink, makes women drink, too.

Throughout the 1960s, one of the leading psychological theories on the cause of alcoholism was the "dependency theory," a psychoanalytically-based hypothesis developed by William and Joan McCord which held that alcoholics drank to satisfy hidden dependency needs that were forbidden expression in adult society. By drinking, the authors postulated in a book definitively entitled *The Origins of Alcoholism,* the alcoholic could satisfy the need to be dependent while simultaneously maintaining the facade of adult sophistication and independence associated with the use of alcohol.[4] Since the McCords interviewed 255 men and not a single woman, their results were not altogether surprising, since the male role does in fact demand a show of self-sufficiency that clashes with the purely human need for support from others. However, as dependent behavior is a key element of the female role and is actively encouraged in women, it is highly unlikely that many women would be driven to gratify dependency needs through alcohol. Nevertheless, the authors concluded that their study results applied equally well to alcoholic women.

The dependency theory received no major challenge until 1972, when David McClelland proposed that individuals abused alcohol not to feel dependent, but rather to heighten illusions of power over others. The more the subjects of his research drank, the more they entertained fantasies of influencing others, of aggressiveness, of sexual conquest, of physical size, strength, and impact. McClelland wrote up the findings of his study in a book appropriately entitled *The Drinking Man,* since he, too, studied only men.[5] And the results of his research, like that of the McCords, do reflect expectations for male behavior: Certain men who are unwilling or unable to dominate others might well drink to quell the "unmanly" feelings they find unacceptable in themselves. But as a woman's feminine identity does not depend on exercising power over others, it is unlikely that many women would use alcohol to conjure up such illusions. Yet, although McClelland did not explicitly claim that his results applied to alcoholic women, his findings by and large have been assumed to have validity for both sexes.

The misconceptions about women stemming from these two key studies—and from several other important studies on alcoholism causation as well—have been seriously destructive to alcoholic women. Results of research as prestigious as both the dependency and power theories do not simply moulder in file cabinets; they are published in leading scientific journals, discussed at conferences, taught in alcoholism training institutes, and ultimately find their way into treatment programs across the country, where they are used as therapeutic bases for treating alcoholics of both sexes. Consequently, for lack of other alternatives, many alcoholism specialists for years have been trying to get to the bottom of their female clients' drinking problems by vainly probing their needs for forbidden dependency or male-defined power. One can only speculate on the effects of such therapy on women trying to recover from alcoholism.

The unsupported assumptions of these studies also have lent credence to the damaging myth that relatively few women are susceptible to alcohol problems at all. Supporters of both the dependency and power studies have acknowledged that the results of this research are unlikely to apply to large numbers of women, yet this insight has not suggested to them that perhaps women drink for reasons altogether different from those emerging from the all-male studies. Instead, many alcoholism researchers have concluded that since women do not seem very vulnerable to the risk factors found in the McCord or McClelland research, women simply are not prone to drinking problems in substantial numbers. These conclusions, widely quoted in the alcoholism field, have only perpetuated the cycle of ignorance about alcoholic women that continues to keep them invisible and untreated.

But from the conclusion that women tend to be relatively immune to alcoholism has issued another, still more dangerous and insidious assumption: that the traditional feminine role must act as a kind of natural "protective shield" against alcohol problems. The McCords themselves noted in a three-page section on women at the end of their book:

> A woman who suffers from intensified dependent longings can find satisfactions simply by living the role most approved by her society. Her conflicts can be assuaged through marriage and homemaking; her need for alcohol as a vicarious outlet is consequently reduced.[6]

Georgio Lolli, another leading proponent of the dependency theory, concluded in the same vein:

> Motherhood makes a woman witness to the blended pleasures of body and mind in her infant and may supply her with vicarious pleasures which reduce the attraction of similar, alcohol-induced gratification.[7]

McClelland, too, implied that the imperatives of the female role protected women from high rates of alcohol abuse.[8]

Alcoholic women pay a high price for this assumption, for if the traditional feminine role is believed to protect women from developing alcohol problems, then a logical therapeutic goal for recovering women is a more successful "adjustment" to the demands of that role. It is a highly suspect prescription for female recovery, based as it is on the studied behavior of several hundred men.

Clearly, the time has come to begin listening to women. And when one examines some of the recent, still largely overlooked research focusing specifically on women, a very different kind of picture begins to take shape. Consistently, this recent research shows that the personality conflicts and backgrounds of alcoholic women differ dramatically from those of alcoholic men; my own interviews with fifty recovering alcoholic women, while not a scientifically selected sample, reveal a pattern of stress factors that by and large echo these findings. To a large extent, the differences in causes of male and female alcoholism appear to be rooted in the social roles of men and women, which tend to produce very different kinds of psychological tensions and life problems. And most important, this recent research indicates that the culturally defined set of behaviors demanded of women, rather than serving as a protective barrier against alcohol problems, actually *engenders* much of the pain and conflict that push women toward abusive drinking. It is true that the harsher stigma attached to women's alcohol abuse probably influences some women to try other, more "feminine" avenues of escape, such as depression or mood-changing pills, instead of alcohol. Yet the very fact that more than three million American women suffer alcohol problems despite the grim social consequences is testimony to the intolerable conditions of many women's lives.

It was 1972 before anyone thought to directly pose the question: Why do *women* drink? Dr. Sharon Wilsnack, then a thirty-year-old research psychologist at Harvard University, had been skeptical for some time about the relevance to women of either the power or dependency theories of alcoholism causation. She was also disturbed by frequent references in the scientific literature to "defective femininity" and "deviant sex role adjustment" in the occasional groups of alcoholic women who had been studied up to that time. She wondered whether women might abuse alcohol to resolve conflicts related to neither dependency nor power, but rather to their adequacy as women in a culture that demanded their adherence to rigid and finally unattainable norms. Perhaps, she hypothesized, at least some women abused alcohol in order to submerge those aspects of themselves that did not conform to the female sex role, thereby allowing them to feel more acceptably feminine.

Wilsnack began her research by conducting a small study of female social drinkers, and found that after two drinks, women did indeed feel more traditionally feminine; the adjectives they used most frequently to describe themselves included "warm," "loving," "considerate," "expressive," "open," "pretty," "affec- tionate," and "sexy." She also found that drinking actually *decreased* women's need for power over others, and had no effect whatever on their need for dependency. Moreover, Wilsnack found in her study that prior to drinking, women who subse- quently drank most heavily were more aggressive and dominant than lighter drinking women. This finding suggested to Wilsnack that certain women with strong power drives may have a greater need for alcohol, as drinking appeared to diminish such "masculine" traits forbidden to women, and to enhance more socially acceptable "feminine" feelings and behavior.[9]

To determine whether her research on female social drinkers also applied to women with drinking *problems*, Wilsnack then studied a group of alcoholic women. Did they, too, drink because of an inner need to feel more "feminine"? Significantly, she found that on a conscious level, the alcoholic women in her study valued traditional feminine norms more than did a control group of nonalcoholic women, but that on measures of *unconscious* sex-role identity, the alcoholic women were substantially more "masculine" than the control group. Further, nearly all of the alcoholic women expressed severe doubts about their adequacy as women. These findings suggested to Wilsnack that some alcoholic women may experience a conflict between a conscious identification with the traditional female role and a less conscious identification with "masculine" attitudes and feelings which serve to undermine their self-images as "feminine" women. Since Wilsnack's earlier research suggested that drinking does in fact make some women feel more feminine, she concluded that alcoholic women who struggled with this type of sex-role conflict might well use alcohol for this purpose.[10]

Wilsnack's findings have been replicated by several other studies,[11] virtually all of them conducted with middle-class women over the age of thirty. Interestingly, an opposite pattern of sex-role conflict is often seen among lower-class and younger alcoholic women: a conscious rejection of the female role and an unconscious need to live up to social norms of femininity. Alcohol abuse may also give this type of woman temporary time out from her sex-role conflict, for there is evidence that the more she drinks, the more "masculine" she feels.[12]

Neither of these types of alcoholic women drink for two of the key reasons men appear to drink abusively: to feel safely dependent or, alternately, to feel aggressively powerful. Although alcoholic women who consciously reject feminine norms tend to feel somewhat more "masculine" after several drinks, they do not appear to be concerned about dominance over others, as do many alcoholic men. Instead, it appears that both types of women drink abusively in order to stifle conflicts generated by a social role that is too narrow for either to negotiate successfully.

The feminine role prescribes a set of behaviors—passivity, dependence, submissiveness—that is patently unhealthy by societal standards of adult mental health.[13] And although norms are slowly changing, that set of behaviors is still prescribed for women and, for many, remains a prerequisite for social approval and love. Thus, the consciously "feminine" woman embraces the female role in hopes of garnering such approval, but by doing so, is forced to suppress the "masculine" elements of her personality that are crucial to emotional wholeness. Conversely, the consciously "masculine" woman, who rejects the feminine role and thereby preserves a measure of personal autonomy, is punished by social contempt and a consequent inner sense that she has somehow failed as a woman. Moreover, in her wholesale rejection of the female role, she may also forfeit some positive aspects of the feminine side of her nature: expressiveness, warmth, tenderness. Whether a woman accepts or rejects her sex role, in short, she is set up for intense psychic conflict.

Yet the presence of sex-role conflict still doesn't entirely explain why some women become dependent on alcohol. The demands of the feminine role are such that most women are probably subject to such conflict to one degree or another, yet many, obviously, manage to escape problems with alcohol. As the next several chapters illustrate, a number of other social factors influence the development of a woman's alcohol problem, including social class, race, age, sexual preference, and even job status. But perhaps even more important are several psychological variables, particularly the emotional climate of one's early childhood, the part played by alcohol in family life, adolescent personality development, and, in some cases, responses to crises in adult life. It is not known for certain whether these factors are actually instrumental in *causing* alcoholism, but they occur in the histories of enough alcoholics to suggest that they are important contributing elements. And although there are many exceptions, recent research shows that, as a group, alcoholic women tend to share a pattern of early experiences and adult stresses that differs substantially from the pattern reported by alcoholic men.

Many alcoholic women share in common an emotionally brutal childhood—more disruptive and traumatic than the childhoods of alcoholic men. Problem drinking women are more likely than men to have lost one of their parents through divorce, desertion, or death while they were still children. They are more likely than men to have grown up with alcoholism in the family, and are particularly apt to have had an alcoholic father. In some studies, up to fifty percent of problem drinking women were the daughters of male alcoholics.[14] The mothers of alcoholic women were often unable to effectively counter the negative influence of the fathers, for these mothers frequently suffered severe emotional problems themselves. More often than men, alcoholic women report that their mothers were cold and dominating, while their fathers tended to be more affectionate and easygoing, and often "bossed" by their mothers. When this was so, women usually felt rejected by and hostile toward their mothers, and gravitated toward their fathers for affection and support. They also tended to view themselves as "a lot like my dad," partly because neither father nor daughter was able to please the mother.

The experience of Eileen, a thirty-six-year-old housewife who abused alcohol for twelve years, was typical: "I didn't like my mother and she didn't seem to like me. My dad was the good guy, my buddy. He was very warm and funny—though unreliable as hell. My mother and him were always fighting and carrying on, and it was only much later that I realized how his drinking must have affected her. At the time, I just saw her as the mean mother, the bitch."

That alcoholic women tend to have suffered more childhood trauma than men may well be linked to the more heavily stigmatized status of female alcoholism. As problem drinking is considered more deviant behavior in women than in men, women might well need more severe pressure from their environment to push them toward the more tabooed escape route of alcohol abuse. To take this riskier step, women also might well need more exposure than men to alcoholism in their family, which is a strong predictor of later alcohol abuse.

There is also evidence that daughters are more influenced than sons by the drinking habits of their parents; assuming this is true, women who identified early with their alcoholic fathers were caught in a particularly dangerous bind, for they not only lived under the same roof with, but viewed themselves as very much *like* persons who solved their problems by abusive drinking. Also, as children they put themselves in the psychologically precarious position of seeking affection almost entirely from individuals who were struggling with serious personal problems of their own and able to provide love and security only on a very inconsistent basis—namely, when they weren't drunk.

Many young girls who later develop alcohol problems grow up, then, feeling deeply insecure about their personal worth and very ambivalent about the power and importance of alcohol as well. As they enter adolescence, they tend to be extremely hostile and distrustful of others, even more so than boys who later become alcoholic.[15] Very likely their more intense unhappiness stems not only from a more disturbed childhood, but from the very real difficulties they face as they stand on the brink of young womanhood. For they confront—as do all girls of that age—the dawning realization that the relative freedom of activity and dreams of glory that marked their childhoods are now part of the past; from now on, they are to groom themselves for a life of curtailed ambitions and deference to the needs of others. This realization comes as a severe shock to many young women, whether or not they are destined for later problem drinking. A recent study on teen-agers and mental illness showed that while boys suffer more emotional disturbance prior to puberty than girls, after the onset of puberty the ratio is reversed, and the reasons appear directly related to the "paring down" of girls' aspirations and independence in preparation for assuming their adult roles.[16]

But as they begin their teen-age years, many young women who later become alcoholic are even less prepared than most to make the required compromises of femininity. For since many of them have rejected their mothers and identified with their fathers, their parental role models are likely to be male rather than female; their mothers, in any case, were unlikely to have conformed to traditional feminine norms. Also, few of these young women have ever felt consistently accepted as they are by either parent, and thus are ill-equipped to develop identities on the basis of real self-knowledge and self-respect. It appears that at this point, many girls who later become alcoholic choose one of two paths in trying to resolve the conflict between who they are told they "should" be and their perception of their own needs.

One type of young woman—distinctly in the minority of those studied to date—rejects all pressures to be ladylike and "good" and embarks on an openly rebellious way of life. She revolts from feminine norms, not by shunning the opposite sex, but by exhibiting a broad spectrum of defiant behavior that may include problems at school and possibly with the law, serious conflicts with parents, sexual precociousness—and abusive drinking while still a teen-ager.

Forty-eight-year-old Pat recalled: "Everything went pretty smoothly until my sophomore year of high school and I just whacked out completely. I was on probation for behavior problems—like stealing the school station wagon or taking off for Chicago for a weekend without permission from my family. And I started getting drunk—every time I drank." Leslie, a twenty-five-year-old single mother from Boston, reported a similar history. "I'd say I was drinking heavily on weekends by the time I was fifteen. And by the age of seventeen I had spent a night in jail for being drunk and disorderly. In general, the wilder and drunker and weirder I acted, the more hip I thought I was."

Many young women view their hard drinking as a way of "getting kicks" or demonstrating their defiance of authority, and these may well be among the initial motives. But their often rapid descent into serious problem drinking or even alcoholism reveals far deeper needs. Many have grown up in an intensely insecure, rejecting environment, which, coupled with a family background of alcohol abuse, may be enough to trigger problem drinking for some. But in addition to such pressures, these young women have adopted a life-style that openly flaunts feminine norms; whether a woman is fifteen or fifty, defiance of these norms rarely goes unpunished. Outside of their small peer group, these girls are likely to encounter repeated rejection for their "unfemininity"; they may even be called "deviant" or "sick." These messages are apt to assault them from so many sources—school, parents, the mental health system, the media—that they are likely to begin to define themselves in similar terms.

For some young women, such social rejection and accompanying guilt—particularly when it is layered on a childhood history of deeply felt inadequacy—may cause a level of psychic strain severe enough to precipitate serious problem drinking. In view of the research discussed above indicating that drinking allows some women to feel more "masculine," abusive drinking for these young women may temporarily resolve the conflict between their conscious rejection of feminine standards and both external as well as deeply internalized injunctions to be "nice girls."

Jan, thirty-eight, who began abusing alcohol while still a teen-ager, remembered: "The last thing I wanted was to get married and live in Silver Spring, Maryland, in a little white house with a dog and a husband. But there was always the guilt, the feeling that I was bad and selfish and even crazy for wanting out of that trap. It was only when I drank that I felt I had made the break from my mother's world and escaped into the world of men—men like my father, Fitzgerald, Hemingway, Errol Flynn—who were dashing and daring and lived for the excitement of the moment . . . and who also drank themselves. With a few drinks in me I felt triumphant and free."

The other primary type of alcoholic woman who emerges from recent research literature makes a very different kind of decision as she enters her teen-age years. She, too, has a miserable self-image stemming from a chaotic childhood; she, too, has been likely to identify with her father and feel rejected by her mother, and thus particularly conflicted about the feminine role she is now expected to unconditionally embrace. But rather than repudiating this role, she opts for overidentifying with it; she becomes feminine with a vengeance. Her solution may be an attempt to ensure some measure of acceptance from a world that has thus far rejected her. And perhaps she also wishes to assure herself that she is "normal" despite an early identification with her father.

This type of young woman is well described in a small longitudinal study of the personality traits of young people who later became problem drinkers. The study's authors interviewed a group of middle-class Californians twice: first in the late 1930s, when they were teen-agers, then again thirty years later, when they were in their middle to late forties, in order to determine which of the group had developed drinking problems. As teen-age girls, the female problem drinkers underwent a dramatic personality change in the tenth grade, becoming intensely self-critical, pessimistic, guilt-ridden and withdrawn. Each young woman apparently tried to resolve her feelings of unworthiness by plunging wholeheartedly into the socially approved feminine role. As the study's authors describe her:

> At 15, life is full of adolescent self doubt and confusion. She fears and rejects life, is distrustful of people, follows a religion which accentuates judgment and punishment. She escapes into ultra femininity. This protective coloration will keep her going through the mating season but very likely she will recognize the emptiness and impotence in later years.[17]

The boys in this study who later became problem drinkers demonstrated very different kinds of needs and conflicts, largely stemming from their emerging sense of what was expected of them as young men. While the girls seemed obsessively concerned about their feminine adequacy, the boys who later abused alcohol were more aggressive, rebellious, and entangled in games of sexual conquest than were the non-problem drinking boys. This research suggests that many problem drinkers of both sexes may be excessively concerned about toeing the lines of their respective sex roles; however, since the roles have different requirements, the resulting behaviors and conflicts take very different forms.

The alcoholic woman who immerses herself in the feminine role is more frequently seen in the alcoholism literature, which may mean she is in fact a more common "type," or simply that she tends to be studied more often. It seems likely, however, that the majority of alcoholic women would opt for allegiance to the feminine role, since deviation from that role entails considerable risk for any woman. The specific factors determining the decision to "go feminine" or "go masculine" are unclear. As the "feminine" women are more likely to be from middle-class backgrounds, it may be that middle-class norms put greater pressure on young women to conform to traditional feminine standards. It may also be that the more "masculine" early drinker, whose family background on the average is more traumatic than that of her counterpart, may feel even more alienated from social norms and expectations. She may believe that regardless of how she behaves, she is likely to be rejected.

The "feminine" woman rarely gets into trouble with drinking as a teen-ager or young adult. Among other things, abusive drinking does not jibe with the ladylike self-image she has adopted, although at times she may find herself nursing a couple of drinks to help her get through a particularly tough day, or having a few too many cocktails at weekend parties. And when she does drink, she is likely to notice its almost magical ability to wash away her feelings of inadequacy and "outsidedness" and make her feel at one with herself and others.

Terry, who recovered from alcoholism three years ago at the age of fifty-three, recalled: "When I first started drinking I felt like I had gone into another dimension. My fears and my distance and detachment from other people disappeared and there was this feeling of really belonging, of being unified with them and with myself and with the whole universe. Alcohol made me flow." Forty-year-old Clarissa recalled her first drink at a college party: "I felt like shrieking 'Eureka!' Suddenly I was no longer too heavy and too tall and too smart for my own good. I was petite and sexy and cute and coy and the whole world loved me. My perception of myself and other people changed so drastically it scared me."

For a number of years, this type of woman is likely to concentrate her energies on raising a family and maintaining a home; even if she has an outside job, she is likely to identify herself primarily as a wife and mother. But contrary to her expectations of fulfillment and self-esteem, she remains acutely unhappy. She feels chronically inadequate in her chosen role, and at the same time deeply frustrated by its limitations. In her quest for unassailable femininity, she has had to violently suppress her forbidden "masculine" qualities and feelings, such as adventurousness, anger, independence, and intellectual curiosity. And, as she is likely to have closely identified with her father, these aspects of her personality may have been particularly encouraged as a child. But as she has moored her adult identity so tightly to the female role, such frustrations only intensify her sense of feminine insufficiency, which she then may try to quash with a frantic, self-defeating "superwoman" performance.

"I wanted to be the perfect wife and mother," recalled Elaine, a Washington, D.C., press agent. "I wanted to be Jane Wyatt on 'Father Knows Best,' always ready with words of wisdom for my whole family, perpetually smiling when my husband came home from work, always available to my children. But I was constantly setting myself up for failure because I could never live up to my ideal, and somewhere deep inside me I wanted to chuck the whole game altogether. I forget when that old Phyllis Diller joke first clicked for me: 'What does every woman need to make her laundry look whiter, the dinner dishes brighter? A martini, of course!' "

The "feminine" woman who becomes alcoholic is likely to have married a man who keeps her at an emotional distance, which serves her needs to the extent that she tends to put little trust in the affection of others and thus fears relationships that require real intimacy. But, ironically, her choice of husband only serves to perpetuate her intense, lifelong loneliness and her conviction that no one could truly care for her. She remains, even in marriage, essentially alone. Moreover, her husband is likely to be a problem drinker,[18] just as her father may have been in years past, thus providing her with yet another model of abusive drinking—as well as easy access to alcohol. As the years progress, she may begin drinking with her husband, ostensibly "just to keep him company," and often with his encouragement, or even insistence.

But before drinking actually becomes a problem for this

type of woman, she is likely to weather bouts of depression, sometimes distressing enough to her—or to others—to warrant hospitalization. Periods of depression prior to the onset of problem drinking occur far more frequently in women than in men,[19] which may be attributable to the intense involvement of many alcoholic women in the traditional female role. Twice as many women as men in the United States and most western European countries suffer from depression, and in a 1977 comprehensive review of the scientific literature on the subject, Drs. Myrna Weissman and Gerald Klerman concluded that this lopsided ratio was rooted in neither genetic nor hormonal sex differences, but rather in the self-denying, literally more "depressing" nature of women's roles.[20]

In a subsequent, highly publicized series of studies on women and depression, Dr. Lenore Radloff, of the U.S. Department of Health, Education and Welfare's National Institute of Mental Health, found that the socialization of women amounts to virtual "training in helplessness" that sets women up for failure, powerlessness, and resulting depression.[21] The "feminine" woman who becomes alcoholic would seem particularly vulnerable to depression, for she grew up in a family environment almost guaranteed to engender a sense of worthlessness and helplessness, then has worked overtime to succeed in a role likely only to reinforce those convictions.

But if this type of woman is set up to eventually become alcoholic, why doesn't she begin drinking when depression first strikes—or drink *instead* of becoming depressed? Quite possibly because for women, it is generally safer to be unhappy than to be drunk. Depression is the quintessentially "feminine" expression of misery, not only because it is an almost natural response to the powerlessness of the female experience, but because the symptoms of depression actually parody many elements of the feminine role: passivity, helplessness, dependence on others.

If a woman expresses her unhappiness through

depression—in Phyllis Chesler's words, "keeping a deadly faith with the feminine role"—she may be rewarded with at least short-term sympathy and support from others. Such sympathy is not forthcoming when a woman drinks too much, or chooses other "male"-typed expressions of misery which undermine the sex-role structure. Thus for the "feminine" woman who becomes alcoholic, depression may serve as a kind of way station on the road to a drinking problem, a relatively safe and tolerated stopping off point before she is thrust into more dangerous and stigmatized territory.

When she finally begins to abuse alcohol, it is often in response to a severe, sometimes sudden crisis that seems to destroy the very foundations of her identity. Significantly, women are far more likely than men to begin problem drinking following a specific traumatic event and without any history of alcohol abuse. Men are more likely to "slide" into alcoholism after years of hard drinking that begins without the impetus of any crisis. This difference is again understandable in light of sex-role imperatives: As alcohol abuse is more heavily stigmatized in women than men, women would be more likely to need a major crisis to propel them toward more forbidden behavior.

The crises women cite most often as precipitators of their drinking problems are divorce, desertion, infidelity, the death of a family member, a child leaving home, postpartum depression, gynecological problems, and menopause. Importantly, all of these crises are integrally related to a woman's role as wife and mother, which the "feminine" alcoholic woman has bought into with almost desperate single-mindedness. In a study of two hundred upper-middle-class men and women undergoing alcoholism treatment, psychologist Joan Curlee found that about a third of the women but only eight of the men could point to a specific traumatic event that triggered their alcohol abuse, and nearly all of those mentioned by women revolved around their reduced status as wives or mothers. Curlee was struck by the extent to which these women experienced the crises as frontal attacks on their identities:

> They all apparently were unusually dependent upon their husbands and/or children for their identities and their sense of worth or purpose. Their lives were built around their families even more than was customary for their social group, and a threat to their roles as "John's wife" or "Sally's mother" apparently created a stress which they attempted to meet with alcohol. They frequently expressed feelings of emptiness and pointlessness and of no longer being needed.[22]

Several other studies indicate that women with a large stake in the feminine role often lose control of their drinking following a crisis that undermines their sense of adequacy in that role. Sharon Wilsnack's study of alcoholic women showed that prior to alcohol abuse, not only did a high percentage of women undergo gynecological difficulties or surgery, such as hysterectomy, infertility, or menopausal problems, but they experienced these events as "chronic threats to their sense of feminine adequacy, experiences which lowered their self-esteem and made them wonder what was 'wrong' with them as women."[23]

Ginny, a fifty-nine-year-old Florida woman who began drinking shortly after her husband died, remembered her feelings of utter devastation: "When I lost him it was like the world had come to an end. It wasn't just that I'd lost the person closest to me—it was also that I no longer had anyone to plan my day around, no one to make me feel that I made a difference. At first I tried to pretend that I was still a housewife, shopping and cooking and cleaning all by myself, but I knew I was being foolish. Without him, I had no reason to be. I amounted to nothing."

The vulnerability of traditionally feminine women to role crises has also been demonstrated by research outside the alcohol field, most notably in a study of depressed middle-aged women by sociologist Pauline Bart. Bart found that women most likely to be hospitalized for depression were full-time housewives and mothers who had recently been jolted into the realization that they were no longer needed by their grown children. Bart noted that women undergoing major role shifts have no guidelines or rituals to help them weather these traumatic changes in their status; in her words, "there is no bar mitzvah for menopause."[24] Moreover, women who identify wholly with the female role are almost certain to face such crises, for the role is simply no longer a lifetime job.

Sociologist Alice Rossi noted that while fifty years ago a woman had only a few years to live after her last child was married, today, the average woman spends forty-one percent of her adult life without children at home, and twenty-three percent of her adulthood without either children or a husband living with her.[25] Thus any woman who makes the wife-mother role the core of her existence is both out of a career and an identity while she still has a large part of her life ahead of her.

Not all women, of course, turn to alcohol to cope with a major role crisis. But for the "feminine" woman with the kind of history described above, alcohol abuse is an understandable response. Deprived of love and security as a child, she has felt profoundly inadequate from her earliest years, and has only been able to survive thus far by clutching at a role that she believed would guarantee her some measure of acceptance and self-worth. But she has remained unhappy most of her life, haunted by a childhood conviction of worthlessness and bound by a role that has limited her ability to be truly her own person, even as she has made it the cornerstone of her identity. And now, at a time in her life when she may already sense her female status slipping in a hundred small ways, she is confronted by a traumatic event that seems to confirm what she has suspected all along: Beneath her facade of consummate femininity, she is nothing but a phony, a con artist, a failure in Miss America's clothing.

During this time of intense psychic strain, the soothing, dulling power of alcohol may suddenly become more seductive than ever before. This woman is no stranger to the charm and potency of alcohol. It may well have been the chosen route to oblivion for both her father and her husband, and significantly, the "magical" beverage that has always been able to make her feel so euphorically, effortlessly alive and close to others. And she may find that alcohol does not fail her now. It may well quiet the conflict between her quest for absolute femininity and a deeper, feared part of her that knows her search is a doomed one, for it denies the reality of her human wholeness. When she drinks, that unwanted part of her may go away for a time, ceasing to badger her with its truth. And then, for a little while at least, she can be Cinderella at the ball, the beautiful, dazzling "real" woman that everyone will admire and love.

5

HOUSEWIVES

A NOTE ON THE INTERVIEWS

The question "what is it like to be an alcoholic woman?" cannot be very adequately answered by research reports and statistical tables. First, from a purely practical standpoint, very few studies exist on the day-to-day experience of women with alcohol problems. But more importantly, research reports rarely uncover much about the content and texture of a person's life, anyway. Amid factorial analyses and mean T-scores, the essence of experience—feelings, thoughts, small and large turning points—tend to get lost. The best way to recover that experience is to give people a chance to talk about themselves, freely and at length. Therefore, the next six chapters are almost entirely devoted to extensive interviews with recovering alcoholic women. The interviews are simply told, painfully honest accounts by eleven of the fifty women who shared their stories for this book.

Each woman talks about some of the factors in her life that may have contributed to her drinking, the consequences of her alcohol problem, and the events leading to her eventual, difficult decision to seek help. There is brutality and horror in these accounts; there is also almost unimaginable courage. These women, after all, survived their alcoholism to tell about it, often in the face of enormous odds.

These eleven women were chosen from the total group of fifty because they seemed to represent most clearly both the commonalities and the differences in the experiences of alcoholic women. Although their backgrounds and life situations varied widely, certain kinds of feelings and experiences kept repeating themselves in the stories of nearly all of the women. As discussed in a previous chapter, research indicates that many of these shared attributes are common to alcoholic women as a group, and significantly, are seen discernibly less often in alcoholic men as a group. Probably the most striking of these commonalities is the sheer, almost inpenetrable invisibility of these women's drinking problems.

With the alcoholic woman's image inhabited as it is by ghosts of whores and bad mothers, without exception these eleven women fled from any knowledge of their alcohol problems, keeping the truth at bay with a hundred different excuses and justifications. And the people closest to them, almost equally threatened by the reality of their alcoholism, only aided and abetted their self-deception. By and large, husbands, parents, friends, employers, coworkers, and even professional counselors and doctors, ignored or shrugged off these women's

drinking problems as determinedly as did the women themselves. Consequently, by the time most of these women surfaced
for help, their alcoholism had left deep, sometimes permanent,
physical and emotional scars.

Other experiences shared by many of the interviewed
women—and by many alcoholic women generally—included
divorce or abandonment by a spouse or lover, physical abuse and
rape, forcible separation from children, agonizing guilt about
failure at marriage and parenthood, extreme economic hardship,
depression, and suicide attempts. That alcoholic women of
widely varying backgrounds and lifestyles share so many of these
experiences, and that they affect men to a significantly lesser
extent, indicate the degree to which women's social condition
affects and is affected by their alcoholism. Powerlessness, low
self-esteem, and punishment for unfeminine behavior are the
heritage of all women; these by-products of the female role are
only experienced more intensely through the violence of alcoholism.

Yet even as they underscore commonalities, the stories
shared by these eleven women also indicate sharp differences in
the experience of individual alcoholic women. Factors such as
age, race, class, sexual preference and employment status shape a
woman's situation as surely as do sex roles, making for real
differences among groups of women. The categories of interviews
that comprise the following six chapters were chosen not only
because large numbers of problem drinking women are found in
each group, but also because each group has very distinct issues,
experiences, and needs that require individual attention. Perhaps
it seems obvious that, for example, an urban lesbian would face
certain problems that would be irrelevant to a suburban married
woman, and vice versa. Yet in the research literature as well as
the popular media, there has been a strong tendency to lump all
alcoholic women together into one undifferentiated mass, as

though all shared identical backgrounds, needs, and feelings. Sweeping statements are made about "the" alcoholic woman, with proposed measures for solving "her" problems. But women with drinking problems resist such homogenization. Although they share many issues and problems in common, they remain individuals, even within the groups they identify with most closely. Each woman's pain and strength are ultimately her own.

HOUSEWIVES

In recent years the middle-class housewife has edged out the lower-class bar-drinking woman as the archetypal alcoholic woman. She has been the subject of countless magazine and newspaper articles, often bearing such seductive titles as "The Lace Curtain Alcoholics," "The Housewife's Secret Sickness," and "Lady Lushes, Secret Sorrow of the Suburbs." When local television documentaries, talk shows, and public service spots have dealt with alcoholism in women, the housewife has nearly always been the focus of attention. She has even made it into the comic strips; millions followed her battles with alcohol recently in two nationally syndicated strips, "Mary Worth" and "Apartment 3-G."

This narrow media focus on the housewife, to the exclusion of other groups of alcoholic women, is partially a reflection of recent research, much of which has focused on middle-class women in the home. But she also makes very good copy, for given cultural myths and attitudes about problem drinking women, what could be more titillating than the image of a middle-class, eminently respectable wife and mother destroying herself and her family in a sea of booze? Her tribulations have sold thousands of newspapers and women's magazines, and have upped the ratings of a good number of television shows. And in the bargain, she has become widely known as the "typical" alcoholic woman, more vulnerable to drinking problems than any other single group of women.

But there is evidence that she is no more typical than several other kinds of problem drinking women. In fact, the NORC survey described in Chapter 3 shows that among alcohol users, housewives are substantially *less* likely either to drink heavily or to have alcohol problems than either employed women or those unsuccessfully looking for work. Specifically, the NORC survey found that *among drinkers,* only seven percent of housewives reported problems, compared to sixteen percent of jobholders and nineteen percent of unemployed women.[1] Although this survey limited itself to measuring problem drinking as distinct from alcoholism, it at least suggests that housewives can no longer be uncritically considered the group of women most prone to trouble with alcohol.

However, problem drinking among housewives is significant enough to merit serious attention; moreover, the nature of the housewife's role and lifestyle may make problems among this group particularly dangerous. First, it is easier for the housewife than the employed woman to hide her drinking, and to do so for a longer period of time. She can simply stay home, pull the shades, refuse to answer the doorbell or the phone, and drink all day long. Unlike the working woman, she has no employer to consistently monitor her behavior or evaluate her work performance.

The housewife is also better equipped than the working woman to keep up appearances of normality. Since she is at home most of the day, she can resort to "plateau drinking," nipping on and off all day to ensure a mild high, but never consuming so much at one time that she actually becomes drunk. Thus, for a long time her family may notice nothing amiss. Moreover, in the home she has at her disposal a wide variety of hiding places for her liquor supply, from medicine bottles and kitchen canisters to clothes hampers, vacuum cleaner bags, and even the flush tanks of toilets. With such a variety of factors operating to shield her drinking from notice, her alcoholism may have progressed to an extremely serious stage by the time her problem is recognized and she finally receives help.

Housewives also may be more likely than other groups of women to mix alcohol with other mood-altering drugs. A 1973 review of research on drug use revealed that housewives were more likely than working women to use minor tranquilizers, barbiturates, diet pills (amphetamines), controlled narcotics, and antidepressants.[2] Other studies indicate that anywhere from twenty to thirty percent of housewives use psychoactive drugs on a regular basis.[3] As alcoholic women are prone to dependence on other drugs in addition to alcohol, the housewife may be particularly vulnerable to such dual addiction. The combination is dangerous not only because the body is forced to absorb two or more powerful drugs, but if they should be mixed accidentally—or purposely—the results could be fatal.

The housewife's close identification with the roles of wife and mother also may make alcoholism a particularly devastating experience. Having built her life around these roles, they may well be her only source of self-esteem, the sole basis for her identity. Yet it is all but impossible to be a "good" mother or wife while in the grip of an addictive drug such as alcohol. No longer in control, a once supportive wife may turn indifferent or angry; a formerly caring, dependable mother may become neglectful and confusingly unpredictable in her behavior. Husbands frequently leave their alcoholic wives, sometimes for other women, but more often simply to escape the chaos of their marriages. Children of alcoholic parents often develop behavior problems, begin having serious difficulties with schoolwork, or get into trouble themselves with alcohol or other drugs. In some cases, alcoholic women are declared "unfit mothers" by the courts and are forcibly separated from their children.

For the housewife, who has constructed her entire life and

identity around her ability to keep her husband and children happy, such crises are apt to be experienced as failures of crushing magnitude, proof of her total bankruptcy as a woman and a person. Her sense of obliteration and the wrenching guilt and despair that accompany it are likely to push her even more deeply into drinking. She may isolate herself from others even further, cutting herself off still more completely from the possibility of identification and help.

DOLORES

Dolores does not conform to the media image of the all-American housewife. At forty-two, she looks closer to fifty-five or sixty—the cumulative effects of a fifteen-year drinking problem, a brutal marriage, the loss of three children to foster homes, and survival on welfare checks since 1964. Her thin, gray-brown hair frames a deeply lined, pale face; her expression is tired, almost beaten. Only two months before our interview, she appeared at the door of a women's alcoholism halfway house outside Boston, exhausted, ill, and alone, recognizing finally that "if I didn't get help quick, I would probably drop dead."

When we met, she was still plagued by serious health, family, and financial problems, and had only begun to work through her feelings about her alcoholic past. But despite the very real difficulties ahead of her, Dolores took pride in one unmistakable achievement of the past two months: She had not taken a drink since she walked into the program, and she hadn't been sober for that long a stretch since she was twenty-seven years old.

"As a child growing up, we lived in a cold-water flat in Cambridge, Massachusetts. I remember being cold a lot, and I seemed to be the one who was always getting sick. That's when my father would say to my mother: 'You better get her some whiskey with water and lemon.' And before long I would start making it myself, on the sly, even when I wasn't sick. This was when I was only five or six. I would always feel safe and secure after my little whiskey and lemon cocktail. That was my introduction to alcohol.

I guess I started drinking for real when I was eighteen or nineteen, and I drank heavy from the beginning. Extremely heavy. But I seemed to be able to handle it. My sister worked as a barmaid at a local neighborhood bar and we used to go down there every Friday night. People would be amazed—I would be amazed—at how much I could put down and still function. I'd have maybe fifteen highballs in an evening, and I could still drive all my friends home. It really wasn't a problem then, even with all I drank. It was just on weekends, and I never got into any trouble.

Then I married my husband. He was in the navy and was out to sea a lot, so I spent a lot of time alone right from the beginning of the marriage. There was talk of a prowler in the neighborhood where I lived and lots of nights I'd be scared to death, being all by myself and hearing noises and all. Then one night one of the girls who lived next door came over and brought me a highball. And I said to myself: 'Gee, this is nice.' I went to sleep that night and wasn't nervous for the first time. I felt safe and calm, and I slept all night. The next day I went out and got myself a bottle of whiskey, so I could make myself a highball whenever I'd start to get edgy. So I did that and found that a bottle would last me quite a while, maybe a month or more. But gradually, I found myself having two highballs before I went to bed. Then three, and then more than I could count. It got to the point where I began having gray-outs—where I couldn't remember what I had done when I was drunk, but when someone would remind me of it later, it would come back to me.

At first, the drinking actually helped. Like I said, I was alone a lot, and when my husband would finally come home after maybe a month or more at sea, I'd want to go out, naturally. After being cooped up for weeks with three small kids in a tiny little apartment, I'd be crazy to go out—for bingo, cards, anything. But he never wanted to go anywhere. So when he'd refuse, sometimes I'd get drunk, to keep the anger down and just to show him, too. And then there was always a lot of housework. But if I would have a few highballs, I would just whip through the work. Or if I had some kind of problem with the kids or money or whatever, I'd have a couple of drinks to help me work them out.

Before long my drinking had gotten to where I had to start defending myself from people saying, you know, 'She drinks.' So I kept my house spotless all the time. And I decided the kids had to be perfect too, so nobody would say I was a bad mother. So I would sit them down after school and make them do homework for five or six hours at a time—this is when they were only in grammar school—and after they would finish I would tear it up and make them do it again and again and again, until it was so perfect that nobody would think I was neglecting them. It hurts me now to think about what I did to them. But I was just terrified that someone would find out I was drinking, that they would see me as some kind of lush out of a trashy book or something. So I used the kids to prove I was okay.

Once the drinking started getting bad, my husband started to beat me for it. If he smelled one drink—*pow!* Black eyes and the whole bit. So I thought, well, if I'm going to get it for one drink, I might as well kill a whole bottle. I remember one time when I got very drunk and he started kicking me and knocking me down and every time I tried to get up again he would kick me again. And I remember crying, 'I don't know why I get like this. Why don't you help me?' And I got another kick for saying that. And then he'd call me a rotten whore. That really hurt, because I never cheated on him. A lot of the women in our building had men in during the day and all that kind of thing, but I never went in for that.

The beating went on for about five years. I was afraid to tell anybody because he told me that if I did, he would kill me. I even lost a baby because of him. One day when I was pregnant and was standing at the top of the stairs with some laundry, he came up behind me real quiet and suddenly I felt a boot in my back and I fell all the way down the stairs, him kicking me further every time I stopped falling. I hadn't even been drinking at the time. While he kicked me he screamed about something I had forgotten to do, like make a phone call or mail a package or something. When I rolled down to the bottom of the stairs I couldn't even get up. I just looked up at him from the bottom of the stairs and I said: 'You're crazy.'

The next day I felt awful, and by the middle of the day I had bad cramps and I ran into the bathroom and it all came out of me. I couldn't believe what was happening. I went to the hospital, but before I left the house my husband said, 'If you tell anyone I kicked you down the stairs, you'll never see your other three kids again.' The doctor who checked me over asked about the big bruises on my legs and back, and I said I had slipped in the bathtub. I don't think he believed me, you could tell by the look on his face. But he let it go at that.

Not long after that my husband divorced me—he had been sneaking around with a girl friend for years, it turned out, and he decided he wanted to marry her. I was glad to get rid of him, but after he left I was under even more pressure than before. I had all the family responsibilities myself. At least when he was home he helped out some. And I had to go to work part-time as counter help in a restaurant, then rush home before the kids got back from school. And we never had enough money—supporting three kids on a waitress's salary and a little welfare is a joke. It just got to be too much. After a while I had to quit the job because I was just too exhausted. Finally it was all I could do to get out of bed in the morning to get the kids off to school on time. I'd yell and scream at them; they'd leave, and as soon as they were out the door I'd either go back to bed or go down to the package store for a half pint just to be able to start functioning again. And at the same time I was still doing everything I could to convince people that I wasn't really drinking heavy, that I was just a nice social drinker. It was hairy as hell for me, and I'm sure it was hairy for the kids.

I feel so bad when I think about my kids. They used to try to get me to stop drinking, any way they could. Once on my way home from work, I stopped for a pint of Seagram's and a big bag of chips and some Coke for the kids. I came home, poured myself a highball, and went out into the living room to drink it. Then, when I went back out to the kitchen a few minutes later to make another one, the bottle was gone. I ran into the kids' room and screamed at them, 'What happened?' None of them said anything for a while, and finally the youngest whispered, 'Mama, Cindy threw it down the sink.' Cindy was about twelve at the time, the oldest. My first instinct was to go after her and beat her black and blue. I took after her, and when I caught her I was just about to smack her across the room when I stopped short. I don't know why, something stopped me. I just sat down and started to cry. I sobbed to Cindy: 'Why did you do that to your mama? Don't you think your mother deserves to have a few drinks once in a while, like other people?' And my eight-year-old daughter, who had come in to see what was happening, answered in a real soft voice: 'But Mama, other people don't get sick like you get sick.' They were afraid for me, and for themselves, too. It breaks my heart to think of the worry and responsibility they put on themselves.

Well, at any rate, things just kept getting worse. My ex-husband was determined to get the kids away from me once he married the girl friend and set up another apartment with her. They evaluated the kids over at Mass General and found them physically and mentally sound, and then their school records and found that all three were on the honor roll and hadn't missed a day of school for over a year. But the drinking went against me anyway. The kids were put up for temporary foster care. It turned out my husband didn't want them after all—he just wanted to make sure I didn't have them. The judge said I had a year to straighten out and if I did, I could have the kids back. Nobody said anything about alcoholism or any other kind of help for me. Just 'straighten up and fly right' if I wanted my kids back.

When I heard the judge say 'one year' it was like somebody had stuck a knife in my heart. It seemed like a lifetime. Nobody seemed to understand what I felt, what having my kids snatched out from under me felt like. I just walked out of the courtroom alone and went straight to the package store. Then I went home and got drunk—as drunk as I'd ever been. So drunk that I went downstairs to the apartment of a new family who I knew needed some furniture, and I told them they could come up to my place and take whatever they felt like taking. Well, people came out of the walls from all over the neighborhood. They swarmed into my apartment and took every single stick of furniture I owned. I mean everything. One of the neighbor women down the hall came over and tried to stop me, yelling: 'Dolores, you don't know what you're doing!' but I pushed her out and told her to shut up. So the whole five rooms of furniture were cleaned out.

I passed out finally, and woke up the next morning lying on the kitchen floor. I got up and went into the bedroom so I could lie down on my bed, and I went into shock. It was totally empty—they hadn't even left any blankets or sheets. Everything was gone. When it all sunk in what had happened, I went straight to the liquor store and got another bottle. I slept on the living room floor that night. Then I collected what little savings I had and went to a hotel for two weeks, and stayed drunk the whole time. I couldn't stand to think or feel anything. Before getting drunk every day I would visit my children at the institution where they were staying, and they would say, 'Mama, when are we coming home?' How could I tell them I had given away our home, that there was no home for them anymore? I would cry myself to sleep every night, or drink myself to sleep—sometimes both. I missed them terribly.

When the money ran out after two weeks, I panicked. I thought, my God, I have no children, no money, no home, nothing. I'm all alone with nothing. *I'm* nothing. From then on, I just lived on the welfare checks, from month to month, staying with each of my sisters for periods of time, then in furnished room after furnished room. It was then that I started hitting bars. I'd see kids coming into the bars to plead with their parents to come home, and the kids would be filthy and wearing the same clothes day in and day out. And I'd say to myself, I'm not like those people—my kids were always neat and clean. But then I'd think: 'Yeah, but they still *have* their kids.' I felt so guilty, so terrible. And I thought the world was rotten and cruel.

I never did get the kids back. I've kept in touch with them all, but they never lived with me again. I kept drinking on and on for nine more years, until I was almost dead. And I never have had a home to go to since I gave my furniture away. I feel like I've been living out of suitcases and sleeping on couches my whole life. Some of the places I've lived, I wouldn't want anyone to see. All I want now is to have a decent place to live, have a job I care for, and have my children come and visit me. I would like to take all my children and sit them down with me and talk about what we've all been through together, especially with my drinking. They've been through so many disappointments in their lives, and I would like them to try to understand. I don't know if any of it is possible. Right now it seems like some kind of dream, the feeling that my kids could love me again, that I could have a real home again, a real job. Probably after everything, I don't deserve it. But that's my dream."

JULIE

A quiet, self-possessed woman of thirty-five, Julie feels fairly good about herself and her life at the moment. Having recovered from alcoholism five years ago, she now has a challenging job on an alcohol research project in St. Louis, Missouri, is involved in a variety of feminist activities, and has a network of close friends. She is divorced and her job doesn't pay enough to adequately support her two children and herself, but having recently won a two-year court battle for child support, money isn't quite as tight as it once was. Most importantly, she feels that she has developed a clear sense of her own needs, and is able to live in accordance with them rather than deferring to other people's expectations.

The ability to live her own life is crucial to Julie, because an earlier failure to do so contributed significantly to her alcohol problem. She married at nineteen and was a mother at twenty, long before she had a chance to figure out what she really wanted. Marriage and children just seemed to "happen"—it was what every woman was supposed to want. But Julie was never cut out to be a full-time housewife. She became dependent on pills by the time she was twenty-five, addicted to both pills and alcohol by twenty-seven, and attempted suicide twice before she was thirty. When she tried to talk to people about how she felt, they would respond in surprise: "But Julie, how can you be unhappy? Why, you have *everything!*"

"Growing up, I just assumed that eventually I'd become

a mother and a wife. I didn't know there were any alternatives. When I was younger I wanted to be a veterinarian; in fact, when I was still in junior high, I had already written to several colleges for brochures on their vet programs. I was always very smart in school and interested in a million different things. But somehow, all that changed in the tenth grade. That was the year I joined a sorority in my high school and got interested in boys and the whole veterinary thing went out the window. Have you ever seen that ad for the Powers School of Modeling that says, 'Stop Nagging Your Daughter, Let Us Do It For You'? Well, that was what happened to me. When I got into high school, my parents sent me to Powers to make a lady out of me.

When I was a freshman in college I started dating my future husband, Ricky. I was having a good time and also enjoying my classes, so marriage wasn't on my mind at the beginning. But by my sophomore year, several of my friends from high school were starting to get engaged and I began to feel the pressure. It also seemed to me that if I stayed single, I had only two choices—to be a party girl or a scholar. And although I was enjoying both of those roles in college, they seemed like lonely paths to follow for a lifetime. One night I was sitting alone in bed eating potato chips and thinking about all my friends who were getting married, and I decided that I didn't want to always be alone eating potato chips, so I might as well get married too. And yet I also knew that some part of me resisted getting married, so I set myself up to *have* to go through with it. I didn't take any birth control precautions, and pretty soon I got pregnant. And I got married.

When my son was born, I felt like I had been plunged into another world. Or more like the world stopped. All of a sudden, I was at home all day without a car and this small baby, and believe me, the feelings of motherhood didn't come automatically. I had never even diapered a baby and had no idea how. I felt frustrated and totally inadequate. And since my husband was gone long hours, going to school and working, I was left alone a lot. I felt that aloneness very much. It was during this period that I began to get into diet pills—amphetamines. The doctor had given me some when I was pregnant because I had gained a lot of weight, and after the baby was born he kept prescribing them for me. When I would take them I found I could get an awful lot done very quickly, so I'd have time left over to read. I read whenever I got a spare moment. Even when I was feeding the baby, I'd prop up his bottle and read at the same time.

After awhile, being home alone with a baby all day and sometimes all night, went from frustrating to intolerable. So I started taking a series of jobs. But no sooner would I settle into one than the guilt would get to me. It was like a tape playing in my head, repeating, 'a mother should be at home, a mother should be at home.' So I'd quit, but before long I'd get bored and restless again. So I would do volunteer work or take classes in Judaism or plant rose bushes. But that wouldn't be enough, so I'd go out and get a job again, and the cycle would start all over again.

It was around this time that I first started drinking regularly. I took to buying a bottle of wine at the 7-Eleven every day, then drinking the whole thing all by myself in the evening. It made me feel less empty and less lonely. The loneliness was really beginning to get to me. I had gotten married to escape from loneliness and here I was lonelier than ever. I started to wonder why my husband was gone so much, whether he really loved me anymore. But when I would broach the subject he would always say he still felt the same way about me, which put the problem back on me. If I felt insecure and lonely, something must be wrong with *me*.

Wherever I turned, I seemed to get the same message:

that something was wrong with *me* if I wasn't happy. When I would tell my friends about my boredom and emptiness, the feeling that life was passing me by, they would talk about my pretty apartment with the purple rug and the white sofa and wall-to-wall curtains and tell me I was crazy to be unhappy, with everything I had. When I tried to tell my mother how I felt, she just told me it was time I started thinking about somebody else besides myself. Once I even tried to talk to my father about it, and he just looked at me and said: 'All men live lives of quiet desperation, Julie. Just learn to accept it.'

Then people started telling me that the answer to my unhappiness was to have another baby. My mother, friends, relatives, and neighbors all started pressing me, saying the trouble was that I was unfulfilled with only one child. I needed to keep busier. By then I had very little trust in my own perceptions. Maybe they were right. And so I got pregnant again. They all gave me a party with lots of presents; they all told me they knew I'd be happier now.

After my daughter was born, my drinking really began to get out of control. I switched from a bottle of burgundy a night to vodka or Scotch, and in the morning I'd start out with a strawberry daiquiri made in the blender. From morning to night, I would reward myself for each and every household task with a drink. My husband encouraged my drinking. He would often pick up a bottle on his way home from work and bring it home to me. He was very ambivalent though, because on the one hand he would bring me bottles or suggest we go out drinking together, but when I actually got drunk and made a scene, he would get very upset and demand that I 'take care of my problem.'

My drinking actually served a very practical purpose for my husband, as long as it didn't get too out of hand. It kept me quiet, from questioning too much. For by this time he had been involved with several different women, and I'm sure he figured that if he kept me quietly drunk I would be too out of it to be suspicious. Actually, I had a feeling something was going on, but I couldn't face the truth, even when some woman's husband once called me to say he'd found my husband's wallet in his wife's car. I still believed my husband when he told me he was sitting there *talking* to her after work one night. I had to believe him—the illusion that he loved me was all I had to keep me going. I remember spending a lot of time twisting my wedding ring around and around on my finger, reassuring myself that someone loved me enough to put that ring on my finger. It was all I had.

In the meantime, I kept on drinking, telling myself it was still 'under control' because I didn't get drunk every single night. Mainly the drinking served to drown the two tapes that played over and over again in my brain: 'you're a shit,' and 'you're a bad mother.' When I drank, they didn't play as loud, or they went away altogether for a while. But there was no way to really escape. I developed skin rashes all over my legs and arms. At night I would scratch so hard that the sheets would be streaked with blood in the morning and scabs formed on my body. Then, in 1970, I began to hear about the feminist movement for the first time. I listened, and my reaction was 'Wow!' Finally, somebody was telling me it wasn't all *my* problem. I joined a women's group and because of the support of those women, I finally got up the nerve to go back and finish college, which I had quit to get married. I loved my courses and felt really excited for the first time in years. I felt that this was where I belonged.

Yet instead of solving my problems, taking on school made things even worse. Since I still had total responsibility for the kids and the house, as well as a horrible need to be 'perfect' in general, I was now under intolerable pressure to do *everything*. I had to prove that I was a super student and a super housewife and a super feminist to boot. And at any rate, the drinking and pill-taking had progressed so far by then that I found I couldn't stop, even now that I had found something satisfying in my life. By then I had two different doctors giving me amphetamines and I was also buying 'black beauties' on campus from other students. They gave me the energy to keep the impossible schedule I had set for myself. I would take pills to stay awake at night and I'd study from the time the kids went to bed until the early hours of the morning. I would sleep in my jeans, clenching my teeth, then jump out of bed a couple of hours later to make my morning classes. The drinking by then was so bad that I had to organize my class schedule so that I could take all my classes in the morning and reserve the afternoons for drinking. There were mornings when my hands shook so badly from both the booze and the pills that I couldn't take notes in class.

And there were nights when I would lay down to go to sleep and would hear rats rustling around in the wastebasket beside my bed. I would leap out of bed terrified and turn on the light, but there were never any rats. Other times I would see tiny faces of women, like bodiless Grecian statues, float in and out of my room, silhouetted against the drawn draperies. They were more fascinating than frightening, but it was a very weird experience. At the time I didn't know I was having DTs (delirium tremens) from all the alcohol.

Finally, it got to the point where I couldn't take it anymore. My life was totally out of my control. I hated myself, I was hurting my kids, my husband didn't love me anymore. I just wanted to go away and let the world go on. So I tried to kill myself with a bottle of my mother's tranquilizers. About a year later I tried again, this time with my husband's tranquilizers. It has often struck me that I was on booze and speed and the two people closest to me were on tranquilizers. Anyway, after the second suicide attempt, the doctor who had now pumped my stomach twice sat me down and said 'Julie, I think you're an alcoholic.'

I couldn't handle the word because I just shook when he said it—I went into a panic. Because all this time I had been denying it, no matter how bad things had gotten. At one point a woman who I worked with on a feminist project told me she thought I had an alcohol problem, and I immediately dropped her. She wasn't my friend anymore. But now that I had tried to kill myself twice and felt totally unable to hold my life together, for the first time I forced myself to at least consider that maybe a part of the problem was booze. But I couldn't face it totally, not even then. I let the doctor give me some local Alcoholics Anonymous phone numbers, but I carried them around with me in my purse for two months before I finally made a phone call to A.A. Finally, in May of that year I stopped drinking—and stopped the pills at the same time.

Since then, I have gotten my support from a combination of A.A., counseling, and feminism. Both A.A. and the professional counseling I've had have been really important to me. They've helped me from slipping back into drinking when things have gotten really rough, like when my husband finally divorced me a few years ago. But I also don't think I would have made it without the women's movement. Until I got to know other feminists, I was really convinced that a wife and mother was all that I could be. It was almost like, 'you've made your bed, now lie in it.' But it was only with the encouragement of other women that I got the nerve to go back to school, and it was my women's support group that gave me the courage to finish once I started, even while my life was such a mess. I was meeting other mothers who were going back to school, and becoming friends with feminist professors. I really believe that if the movement hadn't come along, I would have stayed trapped and I would probably be dead by now. Because if I hadn't had any encouragement to change my life along with my drinking, what would have been the point of getting sober?

Yet, even though I feel much better about myself now,

when something goes wrong, it's still really easy to start playing the old negative tapes again. But my friends are real helpful in pointing out to me how I defeat myself, and I've been working on ways to combat all my self-destructive messages. So now, when I make a mistake and I hear myself repeating the old 'You're a bad mother' or 'you're worthless' tapes, I put on another one that says: 'Julie, you're doing the best you can.' "

6
EMPLOYED WOMEN

Compared with the alcoholic housewife, the employed woman with a drinking problem has been a strangely overlooked
figure in both the popular and scientific literature on female
alcoholism. Her absence is difficult to fathom for two reasons.
First, fully half of all adult women in the United States now work
outside the home, so that female jobholders are now as "typical"
as full-time wives and mothers in American society. But secondly,
as noted in chapters 3 and 5, there is evidence that both working
women and unemployed women actually have substantially
higher rates of alcohol problems than do housewives. The 1975
NORC survey of American drinking patterns established that
unemployed women—those who were unsuccessfully looking for
work—had the highest rate of problems, followed closely by

female jobholders. Both of these groups were more than *twice* as likely to develop alcohol problems as housewives.

That unemployment puts women at high risk for alcohol problems may surprise some, but it is actually quite consistent with the realities of women's relationships to work. Most women work outside the home because they have to, not for "pin money" or some abstract notion of self-fulfillment. So when they can't find jobs, real economic deprivation may result. Moreover, as more women begin to define themselves, at least partially, in terms of their job or career, they are increasingly likely to respond to unemployment with feelings of failure and worthlessness. When these tension-producing factors are combined with increased time on one's hands, it is not difficult to imagine how a bottle of liquor might become a welcome diversion—and eventually, a real need.

The high rate of problem drinking among unemployed women is particularly disturbing in light of the serious unemployment situation for women in the United States. Victims of the "last hired, first fired" policy that also hurts blacks and other low-status groups, women had an unemployment rate of 6 percent in 1978, compared to 4.2 percent for men.[1] For the more than eight million women who head families, and therefore must support both themselves and their children, the unemployment rate is 9 percent.[2] For black women, who suffer dual discrimination in hiring and firing decisions, unemployment is an alarming 11.3 percent.[3]

The NORC survey's finding that women *with* jobs are nearly as likely to have alcohol problems as those who can't find them is significant, particularly since a similar trend does not hold for men. In fact, male jobholders are only about half as likely as unemployed men to be problem drinkers. These findings suggest that, as a group, working women may face intense stress, quite possibly greater than that faced by working men. One reason for this apparently higher stress level may be that female jobholders are significantly poorer than their male counterparts. In the year 1977, the median annual earnings for women in full-time jobs was only 59 percent of a man's earnings: Women made $8,618 to men's $14,626.[4] As the divorce rate soars, so does the number of women who have to support not only themselves but their children on their meager incomes; currently, fully one-third of women-headed families in this country live below the official poverty level.[5] Alcohol is a relatively cheap and available escape from the anxiety and hopelessness that often stem from such poverty.

In addition to financial stresses, most working women are slotted into low-status, repetitive "pink-collar" jobs that offer little challenge or opportunity for advancement. Women comprise 97 percent of typists, 93 percent of telephone operators, 99 percent of secretaries, 91 percent of waiters, and 97 percent of private household workers.[6] Many face the boredom of underemployment, the powerlessness inherent in any low-status job, and if they try to advance, the frustration of job discrimination. For some of these women, drinking may blot out the reality of a despised work situation from which they see few avenues of escape.

The relatively few women who are able to break out of the female job ghettos, however, may face as many difficulties and tensions as those further down the work scale. In higher-level jobs, women face the same competitive, aggressive business ethic as their male coworkers, but their feminine training in passivity and dependence makes them far less prepared to handle it. They may also face a work environment subtly or overtly hostile to female participation, and consequently have to work twice as hard as the men in their offices simply to prove their competence. Not only may these kinds of stresses in themselves contribute to alcohol problems, but professional women are particularly likely to find themselves in situations that encourage heavy drinking. There is plenty of opportunity to seek relief from job tensions in the highly liquored lunches and five o'clock pick-me-ups that are part of many business routines. Gradually, some women may find themselves foregoing their coffee break in favor of a morning eye-opener at the bar across the street from the office, or following their after-work drink with five or six more before they are finally ready to go home.

In addition to the sources of stress described above, those working women who are also married face the burden of juggling two full-time roles: paid employee and housewife. The demands of this dual role may explain why married women in the work force are more than *twice* as likely as single working women to have drinking problems, according to the NORC survey.[7] Few married women have the luxury of ending their workdays at five P.M.; upon arriving home from their jobs, most are still expected to get dinner on the table, take care of the housework, and attend to the dozens of miscellaneous needs of their husbands and children. In addition to sheer physical exhaustion, many working women also have to fight societally induced guilt about "abandoning" their children for their jobs, or hostility from husbands who resent their wives' growing independence. Such psychic pressures are likely to promote or exacerbate the very kinds of sex-role conflicts which are believed to contribute to alcoholism among many women.

Since working women appear to be particularly vulnerable to drinking problems and as their jobs hinder secretive drinking, one might expect their rate of treatment for alcoholism to be relatively high. Yet, compared to men, very few working women with alcohol problems are identified and encouraged to get help. Occupational alcoholism counselors note a consistently low rate of female referrals to company programs dealing with alcohol and drug abuse; male-female ratios of anywhere from 5:1 to 15:1 are cited. Of all clients seen in federally funded occupational alcoholism programs in 1976, only fourteen percent were women.[8]

This sex gap in treatment appears to stem largely from the unwillingness of supervisors to confront female employees with a subject as emotionally explosive as alcohol abuse. A 1977 pilot study of branch managers of a large New York corporation showed that when faced with two hypothetical cases of an alcoholic male employee and an alcoholic female employee, the managers felt both more anger and more concern for the woman than for the man, but were quicker to take disciplinary action against the man.[9] Such behavior on the surface may appear chivalrous, but it more likely reflects the managers' inability to deal directly with the reality of alcohol problems in women.

Some employers prefer to dodge confrontation permanently by simply firing the alcoholic woman on an unrelated charge rather than steering her toward an employee assistance program. Karen Zuckerman, labor liaison to the New York State Division of Alcoholism, recently noted that, from her experience, alcoholic women are more frequently discharged than men because they are more likely to hold unskilled or semiskilled jobs and therefore represent less investment to their company.[10] But often, too, women themselves will quit before they are asked to leave, either to protect their increasingly serious problem from public notice, or because they are no longer physically or mentally able to continue working. In fact, given the likelihood of eventually being fired from a job or leaving in desperation, it is probable that large numbers of alcoholic working women finally become as hidden from view as the housewife. For once they leave their jobs, they are likely to simply go home, close the curtains, and continue their drinking in almost total privacy.

ALICIA

Alicia is a tiny, gamin-faced woman of fifty-four, thoughtful, funny, and articulate. One of the most successful career women of her generation, her account of her life, on the surface, sounded like a success story straight out of *Ms.*

Magazine. She was the first woman ever hired to the advertising staffs of several major metropolitan newspapers, and was enormously successful in her work. By the early 1960s, when the median yearly salary for women workers was $3,500, Alicia was pulling in $38,000. And on top of her career, she was married to a brilliant young economist and was the mother of two lively children, all of whom took great pride in her success. She also had dozens of friends, because Alicia was the kind of person whose talent and good fortune were hard to hold against her. She was too likable and too generous for that. Only half in jest, people used to call her Wonder Woman. Except that when no one was looking, Wonder Woman was putting away nearly a fifth of Jack Daniels a day.

"I grew up in a small town in North Carolina and spent part of my childhood in an orphanage. I hated it and I fought the system constantly. I didn't rebel enough to get thrown out because I didn't have anywhere else to go, but I wouldn't let it overwhelm me. I hung onto a small piece of myself no matter what they did to me or what I was made to do.

I also got out of that experience an extraordinary drive to be successful. I'm sure a lot of it was a compensation for some of the negative effects of the orphanage. But there was always a conflict. I wanted to be successful on my own terms, in my own right. I had a very good mind and I wanted to achieve with that mind. But my culture said that to be successful I was to grow up and get married, hopefully to a brilliant and interesting man who was one day going to make a lot of money, and to have children and be a good wife and a good mother. I went to the movies, you know, like everybody else, and saw Roz Russell wearing her big padded shoulders, being the professional woman. But it was never lost on me that she never got the guy. She was a successful career woman, but this little fluff over here who couldn't find her way out the door always got the guy. And I think the conflict in me was especially strong because I grew up in the South, which was a terrible place to be for a woman with my kind of mind and needs. You might say that I was born at a time and in a place where it was totally inappropriate to be who I was.

So from my early years I felt this kind of bifurcation of me, the feeling that I was two people who could never be integrated. For awhile I was able to pull off being both people, the successful professional and the superb wife and mother. I went into the advertising field, which was a masculine profession, but a natural for me. People usually immediately like me and that's the first order of business when you're selling something as intangible as advertising. I was successful. I became the first woman advertising salesperson for the *Washington Post,* the *New York Times* and the New York *Herald Tribune.* The jobs gave me a good salary as well as a lot of ego benefits, and they were fascinating. I loved working.

But while I was climbing the ladder of success, I had a good buddy who was helping me along. His name was Jack Daniels. I had begun to drink in my teen-age years, and I found out a couple of things right away: I liked to drink, and I had an enormous capacity for drinking. Alcohol altered reality for me beautifully. It was an easy way to feel more acceptable and it was an easy way to feel happy. Everything was more fun if booze was involved. I also found that I had no trouble finding drinking companions, because the newspaper business lends itself to that sort of thing. You went to lunch with a lot of people, and most big-city business people drink at lunch, and I had an expense account. I used to take one particular client out to lunch once a month and we would have, invariably, at least three drinks before lunch, wine with lunch, and then an after-lunch drink. Lunch would start about twelve-thirty and end about three-thirty. And then I'd go home at five-thirty and pour myself half a glass of Jack Daniels.

Along the way I also met and married my husband, who

fit my criteria for success nicely. He was an up-and-coming young economist, a witty man, although in some ways one of the stupidest human beings I have ever known. The biggest problem in our relationship was that he had no perception of another person's emotional needs. He just is not an intuitive person on any level. He's tuned into ideas and books and teaching and all that sort of thing. He was very supportive of my work and toward my achieving, but he never saw me as a whole person. In general, he doesn't have much regard for women. He used to have a phrase: 'Women have no minds and ought not have.'

Since he never saw me as a person with real feelings, I couldn't talk to him about the things that frightened me. He never knew that I lacked any real sense of self, because I was very adept by then at playing the roles that I had assigned myself: the confident professional woman, the wife and mother in charge of her family, the super-woman. I couldn't tell him how driven I felt to prove myself, but that nothing I ever did was quite good enough.

It wasn't until we moved from Washington, D.C., to New York that I really began drinking heavily. It wasn't problem drinking yet because I was coping and I was functioning, but I've seen pictures of myself taken during that period and there is this tension in my face, this extraordinary kind of haunted look about me. And yet at this point in my life I had what seemed to be an extraordinary life—a brilliant and interesting husband, two fine children, a highly visible, successful job—all of the things I had thought I wanted.

But something was wrong. My first glimmer of this came at a good-bye luncheon my colleagues at the *Herald Tribune* gave me when we were leaving New York to move to Cleveland where my husband had been offered a new position. It was an extraordinary luncheon because I had been highly visible in this job in New York, and the crème de la crème of my clients came out to this luncheon to bid me farewell. I had two vodka Gibsons to get through the luncheon, and then, as I stood up to thank everyone, I remember clearly two things; a thought and a feeling. The thought was, as I stood there and looked out over this group of distinguished people: 'Boy, Alicia, this is a hell of a long way from the orphanage, isn't it?' and I was really proud. I really felt good because I had made it in one of the most difficult professions in New York. They don't give any prizes for also-rans in the Big Apple.

And then I had a feeling of disorientation almost, a sense of alienation from what was happening. I had a feeling of not being whoever it was they were honoring there that day. I had a feeling that I had somehow come so far that I had lost myself. And I remember thinking, I'll be glad to get out of this town so I won't drink so much. And that was the first time that I tied drinking to something I knew was happening to me, a kind of subtle erosion of whoever it was I was.

But I didn't think I had a *problem* with drinking at that point, even though by then I had missed work because of drinking and had started taking lunches at eleven and eleven-thirty in the morning because otherwise I'd start feeling shaky. And no one else ever mentioned that I might be drinking too much. A number of my friends from those years were astounded when I told them later I was an alcoholic. They exclaimed: 'But you didn't drink any more than I did!' My husband never believed I had a drinking problem either. To the very end, he equated all of my illnesses, attempts to do away with myself, outrageous behavior, with emotional problems. No doctor, friend, or member of my family ever discussed my drinking during my ten years of alcoholism.

Soon after we moved to Cleveland, my marriage started to come apart. My husband had become involved with another woman, and for me that was the coup de grace because there was no way I could accept that there was somebody else in his life more important than me. It destroyed me, because I had depended on him so much for my sense of self, even though it didn't look that way on the surface. I felt that if someone this interesting and fascinating was married to me, loves me, then I exist. I'm real. So when he stopped loving me I didn't exist anymore. And I was just totally wiped out by it. And it was at this point that the drinking went totally out of control. If I hadn't had the oblivion that booze brought me during that time, I don't think I would have survived. I really don't. It was the most brutal kind of rejection imaginable.

After that I went through a period of time when I was hospitalized over and over again. I became a 'her' a number of times. You hear these conferences going on outside your room all the time, and your husband is saying: 'What's the matter with *her?*' And the doctor is saying: 'I don't know what's the matter with *her.*' What happened to me over and over is what happens to a lot of alcoholic women. We get thrown in the hospital. They come at you with that nice little needle. Boing! And you wake up a week later and you read your get well cards and you smell your potted plants and you go home and start getting potted again. But somehow I was functioning and coping well enough that nobody picked it up. Or at least nobody said to me: 'You're an alcoholic,' or 'You drink too much.' They just went: 'Tsk, tsk, poor thing.'

Then I began the suicide route. I'm not the sort of person who wishes to die. I never have been. But somehow, in that period of drinking, with my whole life coming apart, my relationship with my husband absolutely fragmented beyond belief, everything out of control, I thought, I might as well hang it up. After the closest call—I had taken thirty-six Doriden and half a glass of vodka—I wound up in a hospital for fourteen weeks. Alcoholism was never once mentioned.

In 1968, after my husband divorced me, I wound up back in Washington, D.C. with two children, then ages eight and twelve, and I was a hopeless alcoholic. I got a job doing advertising for *Army Times,* a real comedown from what I had been doing. But I didn't have to worry about my reduced status very long because I was there three months and they fired me. They never said anything to me about drinking, but by this time, I was drunk almost all the time. I had to have a drink to go to work. I was drinking heavily at lunch. I was drinking in the afternoon. I didn't care anymore.

Once I was fired I literally began drinking around the clock. It was the kind of drinking in which I had to have something to drink about every hour in order to keep going. I had a little money, so I took an apartment in Southwest Washington. I let in the housekeeper, I let the kids in after school, and I let Harry's Liquor in to deliver the booze, and I drank.

I drank until I was very close to being dead. Finally, when I began to fear for my children's safety, I called my ex-husband for help. He flew in and decided I needed to be hospitalized, and I was perfectly willing to be hospitalized. My life was over. In my view, I was through. I was finished. All I really was looking for was a kind of comfortable place to lie down and die. And he took me off to a hospital and I stood there in the admitting room, thirty pounds overweight in all the wrong places, wearing a pair of Bermuda shorts, a torn shirt, and sneakers. I had been drunk for weeks and the doctor looked at me and he said: 'Do you know what your problem is?' I couldn't see him very well, and I said, 'I'm sick,' and thought to myself, what a dumb doctor. And he said: 'You're an alcoholic, that's your problem.' And I argued with him, drunk and stumbling around in my sneakers and shorts. But he just repeated, 'You're an alcoholic.' And I was ushered up to my room.

In spite of the doctor's diagnosis, it turned out that the hospital did very little for me as an alcoholic. But when I got out of there, I went home and looked in the Yellow Pages under alcohol, because it was the only thing I could think of to do. I called Alcoholics Anonymous and that night I went to my first meeting. Soon after I went to a drying out spot and then to a fancy six-week treatment program, where I like to say that I made an $1,800 moccasin, one. That was in February of 1969 and I have not found it necessary to take a drink since then.

Since I've recovered I have been very open about my alcoholism. Every time I have had a job interview, for example, I have told my interviewer that I am a recovered alcoholic. And although it has lost me some jobs, it hasn't really hurt me in the long run, because today I have a high-level government position, at a very nice salary, I might add. One of the reasons I decided to be open about my drinking is that I had been two people all my life, and I was tired of it. I was tired of not having an identity that was integrated with whoever it was I was. And the other reason is that if people can look at me now and hear the word alcoholic and not flinch, maybe the myths about alcoholic women that have been present so long will finally disappear.

I can honestly say that I have a fantastic life now. I have a sense of my own freedom as a person—a sense of my own freedom which I sought all my life. There is something about surviving alcoholism that is really very liberating. It took away all of the false values and hopes I had, all of my facades, all of my role playing. And it brought me to the level where I could begin to feel a sense of my own humanity. I guess that is the only way I can describe it. No sham and no shame."

HELEN

Helen has been in treatment for only ten days. She is forty-five years old, and in her worn jeans, graying ponytail, and green cat's-eye glasses, she looks like an old woman dressed up as a teen-ager of the 1950s. She is very thin and sits with her shoulders hunched forward, trying not to shake while she talks.

Life has been difficult for Helen. She never married and has supported herself since she was sixteen, primarily through unskilled, low-paying factory jobs. When she came to work drunk or hungover, she risked not only losing her job but serious physical injury as well. Helen drifted through a series of low-level, monotonous jobs until one day, at the age of twenty-five, she found herself pregnant. She had the child, then a second, then a third. No longer able to work, and without child support from any of the three fathers, she was forced to raise her three children on welfare in a tiny apartment in Hell's Kitchen. The worse things got, the more she drank.

"I grew up during the Depression in New York City, and it was hard. My father and brother were both longshoremen, but my father was an alcoholic so the money was on again, off again. And then my sister started drinking, and then my brother. So it was almost natural that I would follow in their footsteps. I went to work at the age of sixteen at different factory jobs and whatnot. But by the time I was eighteen, I was having trouble with work because of the drinking. I wouldn't drink on the job, but I'd have such a hangover some mornings that I could hardly see. And once in a while I'd come to work already drunk. People used to try to cover for me, you know, 'Helen isn't feeling well,' 'Helen has troubles at home,' that kind of thing. I'd usually hang onto a job until I had done something so outrageous that they had to get rid of me.

At one time I had a job in a cosmetic factory—I was a packer. I worked on this big long conveyor belt and I used to fall asleep standing up because lots of time I wouldn't have gotten to bed the night before until three or four in the morning. Almost every night I'd be out drinking and carrying on. So finally they let me sit down at the conveyor, which turned out to be worse, because it's even easier to fall asleep sitting than standing. And one day I fell fast asleep sitting at the belt, which moves very fast, and I had real long hair at the time, almost down to my waist. Well, while I was asleep, my hair got all tangled up in the conveyor. And nobody saw it for awhile, because everybody else was so busy picking up their own work, you know? So the work was coming down on my head faster and faster, and my head was going around and around and around. I woke up and started screaming bloody murder, and they came running over and stopped the belt and took a scissors and whacked off my hair to get me free.

I just went home and got drunk, I hardly even knew what had happened. But when I finally sobered up the next night and looked in the mirror and saw that my hair had all been hacked off—there was maybe four inches left to it—I got crazy. My gorgeous hair! But when I calmed down I had an even more horrible thought, which was that I would get fired for this. I was so ashamed and scared to go in the next day that beforehand I stopped at a little bar on the way to work and had a few drinks. Just a few beers to give me the courage to face what was coming. But it was the weirdest thing. I walked right in and nobody said a thing about it. Not even the forelady. Somebody told me later that all she said was, 'Well, maybe Helen will straighten up after this.' Fat chance. Finally I had had so many missed days and accidents that they got rid of me. But it took a long time.

Another time I had a job loading up trucks for another factory, a perfume factory. Loading is really a man's job, but because it was during the war in Korea they didn't have enough men and let me do it. I was a big girl then, much bigger than I am now. So here it was bright and early on a Monday morning and I was supposed to be loading cartons of perfume onto this big truck. But I was hung over as hell, as usual. Somehow I got my foot stuck between the dolly and the platform where you stack the boxes, and it hurt so bad I dropped the three boxes I was carrying and I went down with them. There was Helen and hundreds of broken bottles of perfume all over the cement. By a miracle I didn't get hurt except for a couple of cuts. But that was the last straw for that company. They let me go on the spot. So I was on the street again, looking for another job.

And it continued that way straight down the line. With every job I'd get, I either wouldn't appear or I'd have an accident at work. The majority of times it was accidents. The people I worked with would cover for me as long as they could, but eventually I would do something nobody could cover up for. It would get to the higher-ups and I'd be booted out. Nobody ever talked to me about the boozing and there wasn't any counseling or anything for somebody with a drinking problem. They'd just show me the door. Well, I did have one job where my boss told me he thought I better see about my problem with drinking, and I turned around to him and said: 'Don't you dare call me that! I'm not an alcoholic.' It was like he was calling me a piece of trash or something, you know, a slut. So I wasn't ready to hear anything about it anyway, even if somebody brought it up.

I got into all kinds of other trouble too, along the way. I was in and out of jail so much it was pathetic. It would be for harassment, abusive language to the police, ripping off their badges from their uniforms, thinking I was King Kong or Tarzan or something. When you're drunk you just think you're—what's her name on TV? The Bionic Woman. I had trouble with men, too, which is finally what made me have to quit working altogether. I would drink in bars and meet men and eventually found myself with three kids all by different fathers. None of them wanted any more to do with me once they had gotten what they wanted. You just didn't see them no more. Fortunately, I had my tubes tied after the last child. God knows how many more children I would have had after that. But at the time you just don't know what you're doing, you just don't care.

But anyway, once I had the kids I had to go on welfare, since I couldn't work no more. We had to move over to Hell's Kitchen on Forty-sixth Street between Ninth and Tenth avenues. The fathers never paid me a dime to help out with the kids, but every once in awhile they would come around drunk and want to see their kids. It was hard, because I was used to having my own money since I was sixteen, and now I had nothing, either for myself or for the kids. Decent meals and enough clothes were even hard to come by. And I just got deeper and deeper into drinking.

Finally the child welfare people took away my kids, about three years ago. I was an unfit mother, they said. That was the final blow. They shipped them off to a foster home and I got to visit every Sunday. Even today, when I pass by that home and look at the windows of the rooms where my kids were, I think of them, and the memories are very sad. Lots of times when I have to pass by that building I just walk on the opposite side of the street and look the other way. When I'd visit them they would say, 'Mommy, we want to come home. When are you going to buy us a new house so we can come back and live with you?' It was hard.

I've only been getting help for drinking for less than two weeks now, so my mind is still pretty fuddled. But the most important thing is having my children back home with me, where they belong. It's probably too late by now. I feel a lot of guilt mostly because I lost my children and because of what I did to them, more than for what I did to me. I can get by, but for the children, it's harder. I don't know what they think of me today. I can't help feeling that 'Helen, if you didn't pick up that first drink, those kids wouldn't be where they are today.' There's no getting around it.

I've also got to have a job, and that's kind of hard to imagine, because I haven't worked for years. I want to get into some kind of training school so I can get a skilled job. No more factories. But I want to make my own money again, because welfare makes me feel like some kind of beggar. And I'm not kidding myself that some guy is going to come along and marry me and support me—hah! If it hasn't happened yet it sure won't now. I'm on my own. But right now I'm not even thinking about a relationship with a man, because first, I've got to think about getting myself together. If I'm not together, I can't even go halfway with anybody else."

7

MINORITY WOMEN

Minority women are among the most disregarded and devalued groups in American society. Commonly viewed as a secondary group both within a race and a sex already considered secondary and inferior, when acknowledged at all, their blurred profiles are usually those of white women crossed with minority men. And when they are occasionally differentiated, it is usually by means of inaccurate stereotypes that only serve to justify further neglect.

The alcoholism field has no shortage of such stereotypes. It is often assumed that black women tend to be either abstainers or hard-drinking, unreachable prostitutes; that cultural sanctions keep most Hispanic women from drinking at all, much less abusing alcohol; that American Indian women are too busy taking care of their alcoholic husbands to fall prey to drinking problems themselves. As a result of such prejudicial assumptions, efforts to identify and treat minority alcoholic women are almost nonexistent, as are attempts to learn more about the nature of their drinking problems. To date, not a single study exists which devotes itself entirely to the alcohol problems of nonwhite women.

The enormity of such neglect is particularly disturbing in face of the magnitude of alcoholism among minority women. Although black women are more likely than white women to abstain from alcohol, the most recent national drinking survey shows that among *drinkers*, black women and white women are equally susceptible to alcohol problems.[1] Several other studies show a significantly smaller gap in the male-female alcoholism ratio for blacks than for whites. But the most alarming evidence of widespread alcohol problems among black women comes from a recent study of approximately seven hundred insurance policyholders conducted by the Metropolitan Life Insurance Company. The study showed that between 1964 and 1974 alcoholism-related deaths rose thirty-six percent among white women and an astounding seventy-one percent among nonwhite women, most of whom were black.[2]

Among American Indian women, alcoholism appears to be still more serious. Although women are rarely mentioned in studies of drinking problems among native Americans, a report from the National Center for Health Statistics showed that in 1975, women accounted for almost half of the total deaths from liver cirrhosis among American Indians, compared to approximately one-third of cirrhosis deaths among both blacks and whites. Indian women were also more likely to die of liver cirrhosis at a younger age than either white or black women. Between the ages of thirty-five and fifty-four American Indian women died of cirrhosis at nine times the rate of white women, and between the ages of fifteen and thirty-four, they died at *thirty-seven times* the rate of white women.[3] Since liver cirrhosis, if anything, tends to be underreported in women, these figures indicate that alcoholism has reached crisis proportions among American Indian women.

To date, not a single statistic exists on the magnitude of alcohol problems among Hispanic women. However, the NORC national drinking survey did poll this group of women on the extent of their alcohol use. The survey found that although Hispanic women were more likely to abstain from alcohol than either black or white women, among those who drank, eight percent used alcohol heavily, compared to four percent of black women and nine percent of white women.[4] If as many as eight percent of Hispanic women who use alcohol are drinking heavily—about one out of every twelve drinkers—there is reason to believe that significant numbers may also be experiencing alcohol problems. Yet until alcoholism researchers begin to study this group of women, there is no way of making a truly reliable estimate. Even less can be deduced about the drinking problems of women of Asian origin, for they have yet to be included even in surveys of alcohol consumption.

Minority women have more than their share of reasons to seek relief in alcohol. Doubly oppressed by their race or ethnic background as well as their sex, nowhere are they accepted as equals. As racial or ethnic minorities, they are deemed inferior to white women; as women, they are considered inferior to minority men. Outsiders among outsiders, their low status is reflected in their standard of living. As a group, nonwhite women have less education, a lower median income, and substantially higher unemployment than either white women or minority men, and are far more likely than white women to head families subsisting below the official poverty level.[5] Health care for minority women is also notoriously poor; compared to whites, they have a higher rate of maternal mortality, less prenatal care, and fewer available preventive services. Among those on welfare, fewer dollars are spent per person on health care for nonwhites than for whites.[6]

The psychic toll of living on the margins of society can also be intolerably high. Minority women not only have to struggle to maintain their self-esteem in a society that judges them inferior on two separate counts, but they also may be caught in a painful double bind between their emerging identities as women and pressures to maintain their traditional feminine role so as not to undermine the solidarity of their racial or ethnic group. It is a classic no-win situation, for if a minority woman chooses the former, she may be repudiated as a traitor to her community; if she chooses the latter, she may have to sacrifice her own growth and autonomy as a woman. As sex-role conflicts appear to contribute significantly to drinking problems among women, minority women who face this kind of psychic squeeze may be at very high risk for alcohol abuse.

The above-mentioned statistics on alcoholism mortality for black and American Indian women suggest that many nonwhite alcoholic women may literally drink themselves to death before help reaches them. Rates of treatment for minority women are appallingly low: In 1976, women represented only twenty-two percent of the clientele of all federally supported native American programs, seventeen percent of patients in black programs, and a minuscule eight percent in Spanish programs.[7]

The poor showing of minority women in treatment programs stems partially from the stigma attached to female alcoholism which affects all women. Although black women are often pictured drinking heavily and publicly with impunity, evidence contradicts this stereotype. In a study of the drinking patterns of black residents in a St. Louis low-income housing project, for example, half of the men and three-fourths of the women thought it was all right for a man to get drunk, whereas only slightly more than a quarter of both sexes would tolerate drunkenness in a woman.[8]

Cultural taboos against female drunkenness are even more deeply ingrained in Hispanic communities, because of the enforcement of a more traditional code of behavior for women. Alcoholism in a Hispanic woman is considered almost intolerably shameful, something that can barely be spoken about, much less openly treated. Rita Saenz, director of the office on alcoholism for the state of California, noted that "other women may be known as closet alcoholics, but the Spanish-speaking woman is in the basement."

In addition, black and American Indian women in particular have been saddled with an image of emotional strength and stoicism so monumental that many find it extremely difficult to admit to the "weakness" of an alcohol problem. "We are supposed to be rocks," observed Mary Bighorse, a recovered alcoholic and director of social services for the American Indian Community House in New York City. "Combine that with all we hear about being women of loose morals, and not very many of us are going to risk the exposure of treatment." She noted that less than ten percent of the people served in the alcoholism program at her community center were women.

Minority women also tend to avoid alcoholism treatment because many recovery programs fail to relate to their experiences or needs. The vast majority of alcoholism programs are directed and staffed primarily by whites, located in white neighborhoods, and used mainly by whites. Based on bitter experience, many nonwhite people tend to distrust white "helpers" of all kinds, and prefer taking care of their own to participating in nonminority social services programs. Nonwhite alcoholic women who enter the typical alcoholism program may not only risk outright racism, but also may face a treatment system almost wholly ignorant of the values, customs, modes of communication, behavior styles, and sometimes even the language that form their reality. In addition, they are likely to be treated by a predominantly male staff who may have little sensitivity to the special needs of women. Faced with the prospect of treatment in such an alien, isolating environment, it is hardly surprising that many minority women avoid seeking help until their alcoholism is well advanced—and that some never get any treatment at all.

MARGARET

Margaret is a tall, vibrant black woman of sixty-three, the kind of person whose presence electrifies a room. Having recovered from alcoholism twenty-five years ago, she is now an executive secretary with a large Chicago corporation and a well-known speaker and activist in the alcoholism field. But Margaret's current success and self-confidence were hard won. Born in a poor, primarily Italian neighborhood in South Philadelphia, she never knew her father, felt rejected by her mother, and spent most of her childhood unsure of where she really belonged. She also grew up well before the civil rights movement emerged to give blacks many strong role models and a sense of pride in their blackness. Early on, Margaret rejected her color, believing that it—and by extension she herself—represented failure and ugliness. Most of the time, she felt desperately inferior and unattractive, and the world in general seemed a bleak, loveless place. Except when she drank.

"When I was a little girl, I read the story of King Midas and how everything he touched turned to gold. I thought it was the most beautiful story. I was so unhappy, and it seemed that I made everybody else so miserable, that I thought it would be wonderful to have a sort of 'golden touch' and be able to make everybody happy. I used to think and dream about it all the time.

Things were lonely and confusing for me, growing up. My mother had me when she was only seventeen and my grandmother raised me until I was old enough to go to school. She loved me and really indulged me, and I called her 'Momma.' But when I was about six they took me out of my grandmother's house and took me to live with my two aunts, my mother's sisters. Nobody ever explained to me why I had to leave my grandmother, and I was real lonely for her. I felt maybe she didn't want me anymore.

I lived with my aunts during the week and with my mother on the weekends. I never did like my mother. She was a great fancy dresser and I always had the idea that she didn't want me. And at the age of seventeen, no, I guess she didn't. I was illegitimate and it was considered a disgrace, something you couldn't talk about out loud. When somebody would say of me: 'Whose girl is that?' everybody would change the subject, you know, and say something like 'Isn't that a beautiful plant in the window?' It was like I was something to be ashamed of, something that made her unacceptable. It's fine to understand how it all happened, yet, not having the love . . .

When I was still little, I started having real mood swings. Like I would be on cloud nine one hour and just terribly depressed the next. It was frightening, because I knew that something wasn't quite right but I didn't know what it was. I just knew I wasn't quite behaving like other children. It got to the point where I was afraid to feel happy at all, because I knew that something bad was going to happen soon after. And what made it even more confusing was that I started getting spankings both for being too sad or too excited. I just didn't know how to be.

When I was six my mother married my stepfather, who was an alcoholic. He always worked—shoeshining, unloading boats and things—but he got robbed a lot, was always in trouble.

You've seen that kind of a drunk. He was always good to me, though. And my mother's younger sister was an alcoholic, too, a really violent alcoholic. I was terribly frightened of her because she just went mad when she got to drinking. But still, most of my associations with drinking were good ones. I noticed that when they served alcohol at home, at parties and celebrations and such, I suddenly became kind of cute and wasn't a nuisance anymore, and I was allowed to stay up late with everybody.

Growing up black in the 1920s and '30s, I'm sure a certain amount of discrimination came down on me, but it's not something you notice much as a child. I grew up in a part of South Philadelphia that was called Little Italy, so I went to school with mostly white children. I remember some things, like none of us ever got elected officers at school. And I lived across the street from a little Jewish girl named Shirley, and even though we were friends, her mother made me come through the back door of their house.

But mostly I got along okay, although I had to learn to speak some Italian to be understood by some of the kids in the neighborhood. I was always pretty tight with the Italians. In fact, we kind of grouped together as kids, the blacks and the Italians. Every weekend we went down to fight the Polish and the Irish. Sometimes they called us nigger and we would go after them, but I don't remember feeling inferior because we couldn't stand them any more than they could stand us.

It wasn't until we got to the dating age that, well, you kind of knew who you were. Then it was the blacks and the whites, a real division. It was at that point that I began to feel that it was important to be white. Even blacks were kind of segregated among ourselves, like they are now in South Africa, and the fair-complected blacks were given more of—well, whatever it is—than darker blacks. And I might add that the Italians were the same way, in that they admired anybody's children who were blond and blue-eyed. That was the ideal.

I began to hate being black, and it was mixed up with a general feeling of being unattractive and inferior, a real ugly duckling. I wanted to bleach my skin and dye my hair red, and I started to surround myself with very pretty, fair-skinned black people. My aunts kind of encouraged those feelings, because they did a lot of domestic work and they tried to dress me like the white children in the houses they worked in, at great sacrifice, I might add. I had this kind of storybook idea that Goldilocks was the beautiful one, and the witch, all dressed up in black, was the ugly one, and I started categorizing everybody like that. And, of course, the darker ones realized what I was doing and they ostracized me. They called me an Oreo—black on the outside but white on the inside. And at the time I would just say to them: 'So what's wrong with that?' Now I realize how totally I was rejecting myself and hating myself because I was black.

I can't say for sure that any of this helped cause my troubles with drinking, but when I did drink, I wouldn't worry anymore about my race or my complexion or whether I was beautiful or not. And I wouldn't get the depressions, either, as long as I kept enough booze in me. I guess I first started drinking pretty regularly when I was fourteen or fifteen. I knew I was no scholar and I was certainly no beauty, so I thought that if I could fit into the crowd that smoked and drank, at least I would be cool. At that age we didn't get drunk. We'd just go around to the drugstore or the luncheonette and buy ourselves a bottle of blackberry wine and a pack of cigarettes, and split them among maybe ten of us. I'd almost choke to death on the cigarettes but I thought it gave me an air of being with it. It was just a way of rebelling—being where the action was, hanging out with the wise crowd.

But as I got a little older, I began to drink to get drunk. I would go to a party or a dance and immediately look for the alcohol, and I would start feeling relaxed and happy and I would forget that I was too tall and too black and wore glasses. But I would drink until I got sick, I mean sick like I was about to die, every time. They told me I was the life of the party, but I was always the one they had to pull out from under the heap of coats or out of the closet. I would always wonder why I got sick and nobody else seemed to, and I'd feel very guilty. But the very next time I went to a party, I'd get drunk and sick all over again. Nobody ever suggested to me that I was drinking too much. I was just the good-time girl who seemed to overdo things a little.

When I got out of high school I decided I wanted to do something with my talent in drawing. When I was a child I used to draw the Sunday funnies, just for a hobby. And when I was in the twelfth grade I designed the covers for the school magazine. I've always had a bent for the arts. So during World War II, I started taking courses in blueprinting and drafting under the National Youth Act. And one day the instructor came up to me and told me that first of all, I should be aware that this was not a field for women, and secondly, that it was certainly not a field for *black* women. My reaction was: The hell with you! and I was even more determined to stick with it.

But after I graduated from those courses, I began to see what was in store for me. A girl friend of mine who looked very white had taken the courses with me, and when we both applied for a draftsman's job, she got it. I saw that all the good jobs were going to whites, or to blacks who could pass. I finally got a job as a riveter, and then I went down to Washington, D.C. to work at the Naval Gun Factory on turret lathes and presses. A couple of years later I found out about a job opening at the telephone company for a young woman with an aptitude for mechanical drawing, and I ran right over to apply. They told me they couldn't take me for 'certain reasons.' I went over to the Fair Employment Practices Board and they were willing to take the case, but I backed down because I was afraid to take time off from my job to fight it in the courts. At one point I had to work as a maid because I couldn't find any other type of work. I was either angry or very depressed a lot of the time. And the drinking was really getting out of hand.

I had a lot of different jobs in those years, yet nobody ever warned me about my drinking or fired me because of it. If they had, they would have done me a favor, but they just backed off from it. Like at one job, I had no leave saved up, yet I wouldn't show up again and again. My supervisor finally called me in and asked me about it, and I told him 'it's because women have illnesses, you know.' And he said, 'But Margaret, you're sick every Monday.' And I told him I was going through early menopause. I wasn't even thirty yet, but I had to think quick. What could he say? At the time, I thought it was hilarious.

Now that I'm sober and somewhat open about my alcoholism, my current boss will sometimes ask me to talk to certain women about their drinking. And I'll say to him, 'Okay, but *you* have to do the final confronting. I'll just ease the way.' And suddenly he'll back off then decide the problem isn't so serious after all. This is why I think the alcoholic woman is really a tragic figure. She's less accepted by society and yet she's more protected by society, if that makes sense.

The idea that I could be an alcoholic was too terrible to even consider at the time. I didn't want anybody to mention it to me, and I denied it to myself. Since I have always had an appreciation for the fine arts, I used to compare myself to great artists who drank. Van Gogh was mad, I said, so he had to drink. Poe, another great artist, was also a drunk. I tried to find all the big ones I knew who were drunks to justify my own drinking. It made it seem less degrading, somehow.

But it was hard not to feel degraded and disgusting, regardless. I went with a lot of different men, and I used to ask them regularly, 'How come I'm good enough to go to bed with, but not good enough to be seen out in the streets with?' And while none of them ever said it was my drinking, I realize now that it was. I was always the good-time girl because, see, the drinking relieved all my inhibitions. I was the more desirable companion for awhile, but not the kind of girl anybody wanted to take to the altar.

But finally I did get married, to a man who was a drug addict and an alcoholic. It was a miserable marriage and didn't last long—mainly it was two addicts fighting each other all the time. When he was on drugs he would be in another world altogether; he wouldn't even know who I was. He used to beat me sometimes, but I have to say that I may have provoked it. I didn't like being beat up, but I knew that he would be real sorry afterward, and that would make me feel cared about. I might say that when I was a child, I often did the same thing. Whenever I got a scolding or when I was sick, I would get preferred attention for a little while, so there was a tendency to be a little sicker more often, and a little more hurt more often, because then I'd be showered with 'Oh, I'm sorry, honey.' That's what I looked forward to, that extra attention.

Finally, my drinking got so out of control that I went to a psychiatrist—you'll notice I was ready to be crazy before I was ready to be an alcoholic. And I knew that this particular doctor was for me because one of the first things he told me was that he didn't think I was an alcoholic. The man talked on twenty more minutes, but I didn't hear another thing he said after that. He was smart, he was learned, and he said I wasn't an alcoholic. I spent the next two years and two thousand dollars on him, hoping he could straighten out my thinking so I could continue drinking, but without having the problems.

But at the end of two years, it was clear to me that nothing had changed and that I was still as miserable and drunk as ever. So I tried to kill myself. I landed in a state hospital, a horrible place, and it was that whole experience that finally made me see that I had to get help for my drinking. But when I applied to an alcoholism clinic, I was told there would be a two-month wait. Unbelievable. It was fortunate that a friend of mine called Alcoholics Anonymous for me at that point, or I don't know what would have happened to me. I started going to meetings as of that night.

It was in A.A., strangely enough, that for the first time in my life I really stood up for my rights as a black. I started going to A.A. in Washington, D.C., in '53 and the meetings were segregated. We could only go to two meetings a week because there was only one black group in the whole town. I don't know what came over me, but I raised so much hell that they finally assured me that if I got sober and got myself together, I could integrate the meetings. As it happened, by the time I got to that point—'55 or '56—the meetings were already integrated. But I was one of the first to publicly call for it. And even today, whenever I get up to speak at A.A. meetings, I never fail to tell people that blacks who got sober before the mid fifties in Washington, D.C., came through the 'cosmopolitan' group and were barred from white meetings.

But shortly after I got sober, something happened that I didn't expect—I went into a deep depression. Now A.A. is against any kind of mood-changers, but I was so desperate that finally I went to a doctor who gave me some Librium. But they didn't help any. I tried to talk to people in A.A. about it, but they just more or less said 'Stop feeling sorry for yourself and get up and do something for somebody else.' Nothing helped. I was beginning to think, if this is sobriety, then I don't want it. And I just kind of went into the closet and stopped seeing anyone. I even lost my speech.

I was very lucky that a woman in my church knew

something about depression, and sent me to a doctor who helped me understand that I actually had two illnesses: alcoholism and depression. I found out that what had happened was that for years, the drinking had been covering up the depression I had felt ever since I was a little girl. So once I stopped drinking, it all flooded out again, the hopelessness, the self-hating. The doctor put me on an antidepressant because he thought a chemical imbalance might have been involved. But he also worked with me to change the kind of thinking that would get me so down.

Even now, twenty-five years later, I still have to fight depression, although it's not as severe as before and I don't lose as much time from work as I once did. But what is important to me is that other women realize that once they stop drinking, depression can still be a very serious problem. A.A. may sincerely try to help, but not many people in A.A. really understand about depression, how a person just feels helpless and unable to move. It's easy to feel guilty about it, like you should just be able to snap out of it and go on your way. But it's not always that simple. So I'd say to any woman who gets sober, if you feel continually depressed—I don't mean just sad but really, terribly down—then get some help for it, along with A.A. or whatever else you're doing. I know that if I hadn't done something about it, sooner or later I would have picked up the bottle again."

DIANE

Diane is an American Indian, half Osage, half Shawnee. Her drinking problem began on the Oklahoma Indian camp where she grew up, and ended, seventeen years and three marriages later, in a Los Angeles halfway house for alcoholic women where she was the only American Indian. Today, at thirty-eight, Diane is studying to become a nurse and is working at an inner city counseling program for minorities. A tall, intense woman with long, thick black hair, she feels it is impossible to separate her experience as an Indian woman from her struggle with alcoholism. She believes eventual recovery turned on her ability to reject damaging stereotypes about American Indians and discover her own individual needs and strengths.

"I grew up in a little town in Oklahoma, an Indian camp. My father is Osage and my mother is Shawnee. I had only one sister, but my parents took in a lot of other children—twelve altogether—while I was growing up. My parents were the type where if you needed help, they would put you up and help you out in any way they could.

I started drinking when I was still a teen-ager, and I drank to get drunk. Oklahoma was still a dry state when I was growing up and people still made moonshine liquor, so for kids, drinking was a real thrill, kind of challenging and sneaky. We'd go to people in the community who kept stills and buy our liquor from them. It was something a lot of kids did, but by the time I was eighteen, I was the one who had an alcohol problem.

For me it was more than just the excitement. Basically, I'm a very bashful person and drinking allowed me to do things easier. In fact, I think the way my parents were—very warm and friendly and helping people all the time—got me started with my shyness because they're a very hard act to follow. My parents are very well thought of; everybody likes them. And my sister is the same way. I probably don't seem shy, but on the inside I was. I never felt I could do the things they did. And early on I got so that if I couldn't do something perfectly, I wouldn't do it at all. I was always comparing myself to the next person.

Once I left my community, a lot of my competitiveness had to do with being Indian. Because I was an Indian, I always wanted to out-best everybody. I have always felt that people made a lot of allowances for me because I was Indian and didn't think I could make the mark on my own, so they were going to boost me. So I've always been very hard on myself, always having to prove that Indians were better—at work, in school, wherever I was. In my first year of nursing school I came out second highest in my class. I would have even felt bad about being second except that I had been beaten out by another Indian girl. There is always that pressure, having to be the best so they won't say you're a failure, just another dumb Indian.

I went through three marriages because of my drinking and each time I married a little higher up the ranks, so when I finally quit drinking I was almost a silk sheet drunk. My first husband was a ranch hand back home and the father of my only child. My second husband was a policeman, and my last husband was a high level official with the Bureau of Indian Affairs. I didn't start drinking really heavy until my second marriage; my second husband was an alcoholic too. We'd take the baby with us out to bars and meet friends and drink. It all seemed very sociable at the time. I had a million ways to rationalize my drinking. You know; I'm just a social drinker; hey, it's the cocktail hour; everybody has a drink after work; everybody has wine with dinner; everybody has a drink *after* dinner. All the old lines. Or I would stick to something like crème de menthe and think I was just enjoying a little liqueur, except that everybody else would have just one drink and I would finish off the rest of the bottle. And I always worked. I never missed work because of drinking, even if I drank all night. I was a great functional alcoholic.

When my second husband got drunk—especially when we both were drunk—he'd get very abusive. Physically abusive. He never broke any bones, but there were times . . . It's very embarrassing for me to tell you that my husband beat me up. People say, well, you deserved it because you didn't leave him and all that. I think it's even easier to talk about alcoholism than about being beat up. I guess I haven't really come to terms with it yet. Mainly I was just incredibly optimistic. Every time he'd beat me he would swear it would never happen again and I would believe him, but it just kept happening and, finally, it got to the point where we just couldn't be around each other. I was the one who initiated the divorce.

One thing drinking let me do was be angry. My husband was physically violent, but when *I* drank I became verbally violent. I could tear you to shreds with my words when I was drunk. There are a lot of expectations on Indians to be stoic—you know, Indians don't complain, don't show anger, don't show fear, don't show sadness—and it's very inhibiting. We're very passive-aggressive. Growing up I can see now that I was very aggressive in an indirect sort of way, but never confronted anger head on. When I drank I would relax and then I could tell you all the things that bothered me about you that I could never say sober. I think a big reason Indians drink is to let out all that pent-up frustration and anger that we're usually afraid to show. How do we say we don't want your 'help' anymore? We've been helped to death.

At any rate, by the time I married my third husband I was so far into drinking that the marriage really never had a chance. I think that's the thing that bothers me most now, that I never gave him a chance. He was drinking too, of course, but somehow I still feel guilty, because if I had only stopped drinking or at least acknowledged my drinking by then, things would have been different. They might not have, either. But it got to the point where I was totally out of control of my actions once I got drunk. I would laugh one minute and shriek and scream at you the next, and I couldn't control it. And I was getting very sick physically. So finally, in desperation, I went into a women's halfway house in Los Angeles for treatment.

It was very difficult for me there. It was very hard for me to go for treatment at all, because it was like I was fulfilling everybody's expectations. Everyone says, 'You know how it is, Indians can't handle their liquor.' I mean, if you and I were on the street drunk together, people wouldn't remember you, but they'd remember me. I would be the drunk Indian.

So immediately I felt like I had to prove that I really had no problems and be the best woman there because I was an Indian. I had to get well quicker, I had to be the least sick to start with. And the women there made it worse, although I'm sure they didn't mean to. But because I was the only Indian woman there, everyone was saying, 'Guess what, we've got an *Indian* at our house,' and everybody was all excited because it's unusual for *any* Indian to get alcoholism treatment, much less a woman. So I was the token Indian at the halfway house. It was very hard to try to get sober when I was worrying about what everybody else wanted me to be.

I've been sober three years now, and it's been difficult. There is a lot of pressure from the Indian community to drink, whether you're a woman or a man. A lot of socializing is done around drinking, and if you don't join in, they tend to think: So, you're too good for your own people? You're not one of us anymore? So I've had to deal with that. But there have been other problems, too. Like as soon as I came home from the halfway house, I was immediately supposed to be superwoman again, taking care of my family, being the perfect wife and mother and nurse and whatever. I think that's one of the differences between alcoholic men and women. When a man stops drinking he goes to A.A. meetings at night and takes it a little easier and everybody understands that it takes a while for him to get back on his feet. But for a woman, there's no time off. You're not allowed to be sick, to be human.

But I am trying to fight those expectations. Indian women are strong, but we have to be allowed to be real people, to have our feelings. I want to stop believing that feelings are a sign of weakness, that I have to put on a good front no matter what is happening inside me. And I want to stop feeling like a failure unless I am perfect, a super-Indian. Because as long as I don't have my emotions and am not allowed to be who I really am, I am sapped and have nothing left to give. I lose and you lose.

One day recently a black woman came into the community center where I work. Her baby had just died, and when she was in with the counselor you could hear her screaming and hollering with the grief she felt. And an Indian woman who was with me at the time said: 'If she was an Indian, we wouldn't have heard a thing. She would have gone home and silently died inside.' She was right. Most of our grief stays inside, and that's much harder on us in the long run. We can't afford to pretend that way anymore."

8

TEEN-AGE GIRLS

It is hard to imagine a girl of fifteen or sixteen in serious trouble with alcohol. We want to believe that we can somehow protect so young and vulnerable a person from the brutal effects of a drinking problem. We also tend to envision alcohol abuse, as distinct from other kinds of drug problems, as an affliction of middle age rather than adolescence. Yet, although relatively few teen-age girls could be termed clinically alcoholic, thousands are drinking to the point where it is interfering with their schoolwork, damaging relationships with family and friends, contributing to unwanted sexual encounters and sometimes pregnancies, causing accidents and arrests, and generally undermining their emotional and physical health. Some of these young women will be able to shake their abusive drinking patterns by their late teens or early twenties, and go on to pursue relatively satisfying, untroubled lives. Others will not. Research indicates that up to a third of youthful problem drinkers will spend a good part of their adult lives addicted to alcohol.

Estimates of the extent of drinking problems among teen-age girls vary, but most reports show disturbingly high rates. The most comprehensive information on youthful drinking problems to date comes from a 1974 national survey conducted for the federal government by J.V. Rachal and his colleagues, which polled the drinking habits of more than thirteen thousand junior and senior high school students of varying ethnic and racial backgrounds. The Rachal survey found that an alarming twenty-three percent of girls in grades seven through twelve were experiencing problems with their drinking.[1] In 1977 another survey of approximately ten thousand students at several New England colleges showed that fully thirty-one percent of the female college students worried about their alcohol use. About a quarter of these young women reported that they sometimes drank alone and nineteen percent admitted drinking at least occasionally before noon, two practices that are considered signs of a possible alcohol problem.[2]

As with adult women, the magnitude of drinking problems among adolescent girls is partially a reflection of their steadily growing use of alcohol. Drinking among young women has increased much more swiftly than among young men since World War II, and current surveys show that more than seventy percent of American high school girls now use alcohol.[3] Not only are more girls drinking, but they are starting younger, drinking more often and more heavily, and are more likely to use hard liquor than in the past. Particularly in large public schools, the drinking habits of girls now approach, and sometimes even parallel, those of boys.

The drinking patterns of young people of both sexes are influenced by a variety of interlocking factors, including parental drinking habits, cultural and regional attitudes toward alcohol, and inevitably, the weight of peer pressure. But the drinking of young women appears to be particularly susceptible to influence by peers of the opposite sex, perhaps dangerously so. In a series of studies of high school and college drinking patterns between 1972 and 1974 in Walla Walla County, Washington, researcher Lee H. Bowker found that among both high school and college students, girls were influenced to use alcohol by the alcohol and drug use of their boyfriends substantially more than were males by their girl friends' drug use. Among college students, young women were most likely to be initially "turned on" to alcohol, marijuana, and other drugs by male friends, while men were most likely to be introduced to recreational drugs by other young men. Further, only eleven percent of college women bought their own alcohol or drugs, compared to seventy percent of the men. Women were likely both to get their drugs from men and to use them in the company of men.

Perhaps not surprisingly, the Bowker study also found that the tendency for young women to receive alcohol and drugs from men was strongly linked to male sexual expectations. Forty-nine percent of college women reported having sex with one or more of their "suppliers." Approximately two-thirds of fraternity members in the college survey admitted using alcohol or other drugs to render a date "more sexually willing or responsive," with alcohol the most commonly used agent of seduction. Less than a quarter of college women reported ever using any drugs for purposes of sexual conquest.[4]

Such findings suggest that many young women may begin drinking in relatively powerless situations, in which their own judgment about when and how much to drink may be subordinated to their boyfriends' control over both the liquor supply and the dating situation. This kind of introduction to alcohol is not only exploitative in the most obvious sense, but also may keep some young women from developing healthy attitudes toward alcohol use, thereby setting the stage for an early drinking problem.

As with adult women, there is no single "type" of problem drinking teen-age girl. They are found in public and private schools, in urban areas, small towns and suburbs, and among all racial and ethnic groups. Yet young women with alcohol problems do tend to share certain background and behavioral characteristics. Specifically, the Rachal survey of national teen-age drinking patterns found that white, black, and Spanish-American girls who reject conventional standards of femininity are somewhat more likely to have problems with drinking. Interestingly, this relationship was not found among either Asian or American Indian girls, possibly because of different cultural attitudes toward female drinking. The survey also discovered that among girls of *any* ethnic groups who drink at all, rejection of traditional femininity is associated with a broad range of "deviant" behavior.[5]

The Rachal survey also found that on the average, problem drinking adolescent girls start drinking around the age of twelve and begin to get into trouble with alcohol by the time they are fifteen. Compared to young women who do not have drinking problems, alcohol abusing girls are more likely to have parents who drink regularly and who do not openly disapprove of drinking among teen-age girls. They are also apt to have friends who put pressure on them to use alcohol. Compared to non-problem drinking girls, those who abuse alcohol also are more likely to drink alone and in unsupervised situations, to drive after drinking heavily, and to get into trouble with authorities in connection with their alcohol abuse. They are also more prone than other young women to use several kinds of psychotropic drugs, including heroin, cocaine, hallucinogens, amphetamines, barbiturates, and marijuana, and to have friends who use such drugs.

And, perhaps most tellingly, young women who abuse alcohol are likely to be deeply dissatisfied with themselves and their lives. Beneath an often tough, don't-give-a-damn veneer, many feel unworthy of love or affection, and unable to achieve anything worthwhile on their own.[6] There is often a desperate feeling of outsidedness, of being somehow, indescribably *different* from everyone around them. Alcohol may at first dull the sharp edges of such feelings, but only temporarily. For abusive drinking almost inevitably contributes to a variety of other serious personal problems that only serve to reinforce the original feelings of worthlessness and despair. These feelings often generate still more drinking, establishing a vicious, self-destructive cycle that can be difficult to break.

Yet, despite the often brutal repercussions of a young woman's alcohol abuse, the problem often passes almost unnoticed by friends, family, and juvenile authorities. A teen-age girl's companions are likely to interpret her abusive drinking as a sign of her sophistication and daring; in any case, their own drinking and drug use may be equally uncontrolled. Parents and other authorities are apt to view a sixteen-year-old girl's alcohol abuse as less serious than other, possibly related problems, such as an unwanted pregnancy or an arrest for marijuana possession. And like the drinking problems of adult women, alcohol abuse among teen-age girls is further obscured by ignorance and denial. Few people can even imagine someone so young in serious trouble with alcohol—particularly a girl. And parents are especially unlikely to be able to admit that their own daughter could be unhappy enough—or "immoral" enough—to have a drinking problem. Such an admission would force them to confront some extremely uncomfortable realities, not only regarding their daughter and her needs, but their own adequacy as parents and, importantly, the role alcohol plays in their own lives.

NEW HOPE MANOR: BETSY, NAN, AND AMY

Even if a young woman's drinking problem is finally recognized, help is often hard to find. Most teen-age alcohol and drug programs are geared to the needs of young men, and girls regularly drop out of such programs or are refused admittance in the first place. Currently, only two centers in the entire country deal specifically with the alcohol and drug problems of teen-age girls. One of them is New Hope Manor in Manchester, Connecticut.

New Hope Manor was founded in 1972 by four Hartford, Connecticut nurses who for years had watched alcohol and drug abusing young women come through the emergency rooms of the city's main hospital only to be told that no treatment programs existed to meet their needs. Increasingly disturbed by the lack of facilities for teen-age girls, the nurses finally pooled their resources, bought a huge, nineteenth century mansion in the nearby city of Manchester, and opened the country's first alcohol and drug program for young women. The sprawling center includes on-premises schooling as well as intensive counseling for its residents, who usually live at New Hope Manor for approximately a year.

Essentially, the New Hope program tries to help alcohol and drug abusing young women establish stronger, more confident self-concepts and learn to deal with day-to-day problems without escaping into alcohol or drugs. The all-women setting allows them the opportunity to explore a number of difficult problems shared by teen-age girls, including conflicts about femininity, guilt over sexual relationships, difficulties in establishing satisfying personal relationships, and generally negative feelings about their worth and potential as women.

Through the process of living and sharing with other young women, residents also have the chance to experience—perhaps for the first time—real caring and respect from others.

Yet even in women so young, the scars are often deep and hard to heal. Joanne Stowell, the twenty-six-year-old administrative director of New Hope Manor, believes that, in general, alcohol and drug abusing girls suffer more psychic damage than boys. "Every girl who has walked into New Hope Manor has felt rotten to the core about herself," she stated flatly. "They feel guilty, they feel worthless, they think they are bad people.

"How else can they feel, when everything associated with their alcohol and drug abuse is contrary to the feminine role they're expected to adopt? Most of them have been arrested, expelled from school, shunned by girl friends, rejected by boyfriends. And, yes, most of them have been sexually abused. For boys, I think it's a bit different. There's no doubt that their drinking and drug abuse cause them serious problems, but at the same time they can prove their manhood—by sexual prowess, by flaunting authority. But girls feel they have failed totally."

Betsy, Nan, and Amy are three young women now in the New Hope Manor program. Betsy, eighteen, has already run away from the program twice, but she says that now she is committed to sticking it out until she works out her problems. Nan, fifteen, has been drinking abusively since she was ten years old, and thinks she may start again once she leaves New Hope. Amy, seventeen, was so hooked on alcohol that she had to be hospitalized for detoxification a year ago. But she is determined to "make it" once she finishes the program, although she is well aware of the difficulties of staying sober outside the protective walls of New Hope Manor. All three young women feel they have made some progress since joining the program, yet their struggle against self-defeating feelings and impulses is a constant one.

They volunteered to talk about their experiences because

they thought it might persuade other girls in trouble with alcohol to get help before, as Amy put it, "they end up as messed up as me."

MARIAN: When did you first start drinking?

BETSY: I started drinking a lot when I was about twelve, but I can remember even earlier my father giving me beers, and I'd like the taste and the little buzz I'd get. So when I got into the seventh grade I started hanging around with a group of kids who were older than me, and they got their booze from their older brothers and sisters, or I'd steal it from my mother. She's an alcoholic and would never notice if a bottle was gone because there was always so much booze laying around the house.

AMY: The first time I got drunk I was three years old, believe it or not. My whole family went to bars a lot, all together—it was like a social thing. And one time when I was only three, some of the kids who were seven or eight started sneaking up to the bar and drinking their parents' drinks, and they brought some over to me. I don't remember what or how much I drank, but it's been a family joke ever since: My folks thought it was really funny to have this three-year-old staggering all over the place. They crack up every time they tell the story.

NAN: I started drinking when I was about ten. Mostly I'd steal it from my parents' liquor cabinet, whiskey and stuff, and I'd take it outside and hide and drink it. I was feeling really lonely at the time because we had just moved to a new town and I didn't have any friends, and I had two younger sisters that seemed to get all the attention from my parents. So I just felt lousy most of the time. For about two years I drank all by myself, and then I started drinking at school and found out I could make friends that way. It got around that I was drinking, so I was considered cool.

MARIAN: What did drinking do for you?

NAN: When I drank, it was mostly to escape, because I was always feeling really hurt inside. And I didn't want to feel like that—it scared me. So mostly I'd drink until I got so tired out that I could just forget about my problems. From the beginning, even when I was only ten, I'd always drink to get drunk.

BETSY: I was pretty much like Nan, in that I mostly drank to escape. Right around the time I started drinking my parents were getting a divorce, and there were lots of pressures on me at home. And I wasn't doing well at school and I was having a hard time with kids my own age. I always felt different from everybody else, I guess because I thought I was the only one who had parents who were splitting up and because my mother drank. So I started hanging around with a group of older kids who drank a lot, and when I drank I just felt a lot looser and I didn't care what I did or said.

AMY: For me there were a lot of family troubles, too. My mother was sick all the time and had to take a lot of medicines. And when she would take her pills and drink at the same time, it would make her crazy; she wouldn't know what was going on at all. And my father was drinking real heavy too, and he would get really mean. It got so I didn't even want to be there. And at school I never felt accepted, I was always real shy and awkward. But if I drank or took any kind of drug, I would always be happy. I would laugh, everything was funny, and I could have a good time. I'd feel real cool, like I could handle anything.

MARIAN: Where did you do most of your drinking?

BETSY: Well, I'd always have some beer stashed in my bedroom so I could have some as soon as I got up in the morning. I drank in school a lot, too—sometimes in the girls' room, but sometimes we'd just take off in the middle of the day in cars and drink. Most of the time it was beer, some whiskey. A couple of times I finished off a case of beer in one day. It got to the point where it didn't matter when I did it, where I did it, or who I drank with. Sometimes I'd just drink by myself.

AMY: I used to get on the school bus in the morning about seven o'clock and somebody would have something in the back of the bus, and we'd all share it. Then we'd get to school around eight, and instead of going inside, we'd go straight into the parking lot and get into somebody's car and leave to go to the park and drink all day. But every morning I'd get on the bus so it would look like I was going to school, like a good girl.

NAN: I'd get together with some of my friends, mostly seniors, and we'd leave school in the middle of the day and walk down to the package store, and when one of the older kids would buy something, the rest of us would go up and down the shelves and stick pints in our pockets and purses, even down our pants. Anything to get it. I never went in for beer, it was always the hard stuff. Whiskey, mostly. Lots of times I'd drink in my room after school, too, because my parents both worked and didn't get home until around dinner time. If they were around, I'd just go outside.

MARIAN: How did your parents react when they found out about your drinking?

NAN: After awhile, my parents would get calls from school almost every day saying I had missed classes or just not shown up at all, or that I had started fights or was drunk in class or whatever. They would never say much about it. But when I would come home from school I would find that they had smashed my albums or given my stereo away, or let my dog or cat loose outside, or given away all my plants. I never knew what would be wrecked or gone when I came home.

AMY: My mother never knew anything was going on for a long time because I would be failing in school and I'd just take the warning notices out of the mailbox before she got to them. But finally I failed everything one marking period and I think she hit me or something. But I never got grounded and she never really sat down and talked to me about what was going on.

BETSY: I think my mother just gave up on me after awhile. She just took the attitude of 'do what you want, you're hopeless, anyway.' But for a long time, we had a lot of run-ins, pretty violent. She would slap me around some and we would threaten each other with knives and whatnot when we were both drunk. Mostly it would start when my mother would dig up a lot of garbage about me from the past and start throwing it in my face—you know, you're this and you're that—and pretty soon we'd start breaking windows, throwing dishes, whatever was around.

In some ways my mother and I are a lot alike, which is probably part of the reason we can't get along. She's a con artist and a phony and a liar, and so am I—or at least, I was. I got along much better with my father, except that he wanted me to be a boy. I was a real disappointment to him because I was a girl.

MARIAN: What about boys? Did you do a lot of your drinking with them?

NAN: I drank mostly with guys, because they had the booze and the dope. There was a kind of deal where if you had sex with one of the guys, they'd turn you on—booze, drugs, whatever. I thought it was okay at the time because I was so messed up. There was this one guy who had a thing going where if he owed somebody money, instead of paying it back he'd call up the guy he owed it to and say: I've got some girls here—come on over and take 'em. And the guy would get us instead of the money.

AMY: It was mainly a money thing. If you didn't have any, which was often in my case because I was living at home, you'd have to do whatever they wanted to get your booze.

BETSY: I'd go to a party with a bunch of guys and afterward I guess I felt like I owed it to them. You know, they turned me on so now I had to turn them on. Sometimes it was in exchange for pills, sometimes liquor, sometimes grass.

MARIAN: Were you ever sexually attacked when you were drunk?

AMY: It happened to me the first time I ever had sex. I had just met the guy—he was supposed to be real cool—and we got drunk together during the day and he just—well, it was out and out rape. But the dumb thing was, I went back to him after that. He supplied everything—booze, grass, whatever I wanted—and he was cool. That was the big thing for me, to be with a guy who everybody thought was super cool, because then I felt cool when I was with him. By myself I just felt like nothing. I stayed with this guy even though he treated me like dirt. Like he used to love to pull out a knife or a gun on me when we'd have an argument, just to scare me. He thought it was real funny.

BETSY: I felt really taken advantage of by guys. Sometimes they would con me into getting drunk when I didn't really feel like it, so they could get something. One night I went out with this guy and we drank until I passed out. But I only passed out for a few minutes, because when I woke up we were on a bed—he must have carried me there—and he was crawling all over me. I wasn't in any condition to do anything except sleep, I was so drunk. I remember thinking while he was all over me: I can't move. God, I can't even *move*. That's how drunk I was. So I laid there while he raped me.

Afterward I didn't really feel much of anything about it,

but I guess I feel guilty now. I feel cheap. I feel I was used. Abused. I don't know how I'll face a guy now. I mean if I start seeing a guy after I leave here and have to tell him I'm not a virgin, I think I'll just cringe.

AMY: I don't think a guy expects you to be a virgin anymore, but if you get into a close relationship with a guy and you tell him everything you've been into—drinking, drugs, sex, all kinds of trouble—he might just say, see you around. It's not just the virgin thing. It's the whole thing. I think I was trying to prove stuff to a lot of people. I felt so weak and picked on as a kid, and so all the stuff I did seemed like a way of saying, 'Ha, Ha, I'm really cool because I'm doing whatever I want.' But I felt really cheap and like people were looking down on me at the same time. You know, like drinking and sex is okay for a guy, but it's different for a girl.

NAN: All my friends were really sleazy, and so even when I was a virgin, everybody just assumed that I was a sleaze too. So I figured since I had the label, I might as well go through with it. In a way, I didn't feel too bad at the time, because I kind of got sex and love mixed up, and I thought I was getting something out of it. At least I was getting some attention.

MARIAN: Did any of you get any help for your drinking before you came to New Hope Manor?

BETSY: Not help. But at one point I was getting into so much trouble in school that they didn't know what to do with me anymore, so they recommended to my mother that I be put in a mental institution. So my mother committed me. I was there for two months, and it just made me worse, because you didn't have to do anything, it was just real secure. So when the two months were up I was actually afraid to leave. I went home for a month and then I committed myself to the mental ward of another hospital because I couldn't stand being at home with my mother anymore.

MARIAN: What was the experience like?

BETSY: At the first hospital they had something going that they called therapy, but not many people walked out of there any better. Then at the second place I was really drugged up, which didn't help me at all. I would spend all day just sitting around in my bathrobe, smoking cigarettes and drinking coffee and sleeping a lot. And my psychiatrist was a real trip. He would walk in and spend about three minutes asking how I was doing, how my medication was going, and then write a bunch of things down on his note pad and say, 'Okay, I'll see you tomorrow.' He never said a word to me about *me*, never sat and talked to me. He made me feel like I didn't even exist.

NAN: I was at the same place as Betsy for seven months. You could pretty much do whatever you wanted, and there were drugs everywhere. Friends and relatives could bring them in, and nobody ever got checked. I think the whole place was just in it for the money. Nobody ever said a word to me about my drinking. I was real quiet all the time, so they diagnosed me as depressed.

BETSY: That's what I was diagnosed as, too. Depressed. Withdrawn. Nothing about booze.

NAN: The worst thing about that place was the body bags. They were gross. They're these canvas bags with wooden slats in them, and they zip up all the way to your neck, so that when you're stuffed into one of them you can't move an inch. You're just totally helpless. When people made trouble in group therapy, we were told to jump on them and pin them down to the ground and force them into the body bag. And usually they'd try to escape and do things like spit and bite, and we were told to spit at them and bite them back. Then after we had stuffed them in, they'd have to lay in the body bag anywhere from three to eleven hours, depending on what they had done. It was really sick.

AMY: These hospitals don't really do much. I was in one for a week in detox, and then got moved over to the psychiatric ward. But they let you go down to the store on the corner with another patient. So what I'd do is find another patient who was into drugs or booze, and we'd stop in the bathroom of the gas station that was next to the store and get high. Or sometimes we'd go down to the park and hang around and get drunk. And nobody seemed to notice, or if they did, they sure didn't seem to care.

MARIAN: What do you want for yourselves once you leave New Hope?

AMY: I just want to be happy and feel good about myself. Right now I feel pretty rotten. I want to have real friends. I want to be able to be honest with people and be myself and stand up for myself, and they can all go shove it if they don't like it. I think it's going to be rough, though, being out there in the real world again after being here where there's so much support. Out there, people will still treat you like shit, push you around, guys will still try to take advantage of you, you still have to deal with your parents. For sure there's going to be pressure to drink again. I don't think I will, though.

BETSY: I want a better relationship with my family. But I guess I've really given up on them. That's really hard to accept, that I don't really have a family to go to. I want my parents. As far as drinking, I think it's going to be real tempting. You know, it's been such a big part of my life. And with my mother drinking and the bottles everywhere—yeah, I could get back into it, I guess.

NAN: I don't plan to stop drinking. I won't get in trouble anymore. I'll just have a beer or two now and then.

AMY: If I ever really get myself together, I'd maybe like to help other kids who have problems like me—you know, like a counselor or something. I think I could help because I've been through it all. I mean, what could anybody say that would shock me? What I think would be cool is if there was some kind of therapy for everybody that you could use throughout your whole lifetime. Starting when you're a little kid. Then you could get yourself straightened out before it's too late and you end up a mess like me.

BETSY: Yeah. Because when I was little, there was nobody for me to talk to, and I just thought I was different and had terrible problems that nobody else had. I felt like there must be something wrong with me or I wouldn't have so many problems. I wish that at the time I had known somebody I could have gone to, somebody who would have just sat down with me and listened to what was going on inside me. But there was nobody.

NAN: You just felt like you were all alone.

9

LESBIANS

If she drinks at all, the lesbian stands a good chance of developing an alcohol problem. She is more likely to abuse alcohol than either a heterosexual woman or man, and may be even more vulnerable to a drinking problem than a homosexual man. The statistics are mind-boggling. In 1970, psychiatrist Marcel T. Saghir compared the psychological adjustment of lesbians with both female heterosexuals and male homosexuals; the subjects were primarily white, middle class, and under thirty-five. Saghir discovered that an astounding thirty-five percent of lesbians had had problems with alcohol at some point in their lives, compared to twenty-eight percent of the homosexual men and only five percent of the heterosexual women. The study also found that lesbians were significantly more likely than the other two groups to use nonprescription drugs and to have attempted suicide.[1]

Other recent studies report comparable levels of alcohol abuse among gay women and men. A 1972 study of drinking habits among blacks in a St. Louis housing project showed that thirty-six percent of the lesbians living in the project were either heavy or problem drinkers.[2] In 1975 a needs assessment of Los Angeles area alcoholism services for homosexuals conducted by Lillene H. Fifield concluded that approximately thirty-two percent of gays in that city had drinking problems.[3] A subsequent study of drinking among homosexuals in four midwestern urban settings found that twenty-nine percent of the gay population had actual or potential problems with their drinking.[4]

How can this staggering rate of drinking problems among gay women and men be explained? Many clinicians and alcoholism specialists simply chalk it up to the inherent "sickness" of homosexuals. According to traditional psychodynamic theory, the homosexual is infantile and maladaptive: at best, a case of arrested development, at worst, a hopeless and possibly dangerous emotional cripple. But in the face of recent research on homosexuality, these labels have become increasingly untenable. Several national associations in the mental health field, including the prestigious and conservative American Psychiatric Association, have officially erased homosexuality from their list of mental illnesses. A recent major study of approximately one thousand homosexuals in the San Francisco area found that the majority of gay women and men led stable lives;[5] other recent studies have revealed similar findings.

The Saghir study concluded that despite the prevalence of unhealthy behaviors among lesbians, "only a minority of the homosexual women showed significant functional and personal disability. The majority of them, like the majority of (homosexual) males, were able to achieve, adapt and be productive citizens."[6] Increasingly, it appears that the "sick" label attached to homosexuality derives more from society's discomfort with the sexual orientation of gays than from the actual presence of deep-seated emotional difficulties.

The high rate of abusive drinking among homosexuals is more likely a product of an environment that openly hates, fears, and isolates them. One does not have to be inherently unbalanced psychologically to respond to societal hostility and discrimination with unhealthy behavior. Most people, at bottom, are profoundly threatened by lesbians, to the point of being unable to tolerate the presence of gay women in their midst. Consequently, homosexual women are forced to "go underground" in order to make contact with other lesbians and find the freedom to express their whole selves. Unfortunately, one of the only available havens for lesbians is the gay bar.

Brenda Weathers, cofounder and former director of the Alcoholism Center for Women in Los Angeles, the only alcoholism program for gay women in the country, believes that the gay bar is central to the social lives of many lesbians. A recovered alcoholic lesbian who regularly frequented gay bars for more than a decade, Weathers described their critical function in a 1976 report entitled "Alcoholism and the Lesbian Community":

> Bars for lesbians have taken on the characteristics and significance of the community center, the coffee break, family gatherings, clubs, societies, and the church picnic. In a society which has openly oppressed the gay minority . . . lesbian women usually are forced to socialize in very limited environments . . . Traditionally, these environments are bars, and lesbian women look to them as places for meeting friends, finding partners, relating with peers, and performing most other human social functions. Bars provide the atmosphere where "it is o.k. to be me", even if only for a few hours a week.[7]

That gay bars form the nucleus of social life for large numbers of lesbians is borne out by Fifield's Los Angeles needs assessment survey, which found that homosexual bar users spent an average of nineteen nights per month in gay bars and fully eighty percent of their social lives either in bars or at parties where alcohol was served. Two-thirds of bar users went to bars alone in hopes of meeting new people, and four out of five first met some of their current friends in bars.[8] This heavy reliance on bars as a social outlet almost certainly contributes to the prevalence of alcohol problems among lesbians. If meeting new people is often a tension-filled situation to begin with, and if one's primary social setting is a place whose purpose is to sell liquor, and if the bar setting is one's *only* opportunity to meet new friends and potential lovers, both internal and external pressures to drink are likely to be intense. The Los Angeles survey showed that gay bar users consumed an average of six drinks per evening.[9]

But the gay bar scene isn't the only contributing factor to widespread alcohol abuse among lesbians. The very societal oppression that drives lesbians into bars for temporary freedom contaminates every aspect of their lives, fostering often overwhelming alienation and despair. Lesbians suffer the economic, legal, and psychological oppression of all women, and then some. Because of their sexual preference, they are fired from their jobs, expelled from their schools, kicked out of their apartments, ostracized in their own neighborhoods, and forcibly separated from their own children. Alcohol doesn't solve these problems, but it can dilute the spirit-crushing bitterness and hopelessness that accompany them. It can also provide short-term escape from the internalized guilt, self-hate, and pervasive sense of "badness" that torment many lesbians, regardless of their attempts to close their minds to society's taunts and threats.

The lesbian in trouble with alcohol may never get the help she needs, for she is faced with an alcoholism treatment system which is not only largely oblivious to the needs of women but is insensitive and sometimes even hostile to homosexual clients. In Fifield's survey, only four out of forty-six alcoholism treatment agencies made any outreach efforts to gay alcoholics, and only two offered therapy groups or other special services for homosexual clients. Only 2.2 percent of staff members were known to be gay; reasons given for the poor staff representation included "most gays aren't good workers," "not a concern of mine," and "they like to be with their own kind."[10]

Alcoholism workers are also likely to bring traditional psychiatric theories as well as their own prejudices about lesbians—and about women—to the treatment situation. The Fifield survey reported a strong link between traditional attitudes toward women's sex roles among staff members and judgmental attitudes toward lesbians.[11] Brenda Weathers reported that lesbians are barred outright from many treatment programs if their sexual orientation is known or suspected, and that those who are admitted often meet with hostility from counselors. She noted that many of her gay clients were "refugees" from other treatment programs which demanded that they "work on" their lesbianism as well as—or even instead of—their alcoholism.[12]

RACHEL

Rachel has both the air and the credentials of a winner. Energetic and athletic looking, at forty-two she appears much younger. In the last five years, Rachel has helped organize a women's alcoholism treatment program, started her own successful business, and become an outspoken leader in both the women's and gay rights movements. Her range of talents is impressive, her personality riveting, almost charismatic. She is the kind of person people describe as a "born leader."

Yet for fifteen years Rachel submerged all her vitality and power in alcohol. From an early age, she had been tormented by a vague, nagging sense of being different, of being an outsider even among friends and family. When she discovered just how she was different and "came out" as a lesbian at fifteen, there was a brief period of joy, a feeling of finally belonging somewhere. But her happiness was short-lived, for she found that when she was open about her sexuality, she was punished and sneered at; when she wasn't, she felt painfully divided, alienated, and constantly fearful of being discovered. As soon as she turned twenty-one, Rachel began spending most of her free time in the only places where she could relax and feel accepted—gay bars. Within a year of frequenting gay bars three, four, and five nights a week, she found herself with a serious alcohol problem.

"I didn't know anything about alcohol as a child growing up except what I heard from my father's pulpit. He was a Baptist minister. We lived in a dry county in Texas so I never saw bars, and I never saw liquor stores. The main thing I knew about booze was that you went to hell for it. Neither of my parents drank and we didn't know anyone who drank, so I never even thought about drinking.

In some ways, my childhood was pretty happy. On the one hand, I felt very loved and supported by my family and also by the congregation of my father's church. We were the preacher's kids and that made us sort of special. But even as a kid, I was conscious of feeling different. I always felt out of sync with the rest of the world—a square peg in a round hole. As a child, I didn't have any idea what it was all about. But when I got into junior high school, it became a little clearer. Everybody around me was all atwitter about boys and it just bored the hell out of me and I thought there must be something very strange about me. I felt isolated and lonely. Very lonely.

And then when I was fifteen I came out with another young woman of fifteen. We were in school together. And at that point, everything fit together. I wasn't a square peg in a round hole anymore. Everything was in sync. The birds sang and the bells rang, and I knew what it was all about. But even after that, I still tried to get into the whole heterosexual scene. By the time I was a senior in high school, I was in the 'in crowd' and it was a lot of fun and I dated a lot, but I really couldn't get into the whole thing with boys. And I was really trying.

As for the drinking, I still had not touched a sip of alcohol when I went away to college. And it was a fundamentalist university in Texas, so there was no drinking there, either. I was miserable there because it was a very straight-laced school, and from my experience at fifteen, I knew what it was all about for me. So I had the presence of mind to know that I had to get out of there, and I conned my parents into letting me transfer to Texas Women's University because I had heard there were a lot of others like me there. It was at Texas Women's where I first started to drink. And at first it was the college kid type of thing where you bring out your contraband cigarettes that you've hidden in the air-conditioning unit and you stuff towels under the door so the smoke can't leak out and you pass the bottle around. We were playing. But as I look back, I remember that the bottle of peach wine or whatever cheap junk we drank stayed in front of me a little longer than it did the rest of the group who were sitting in the circle. And within a couple of years I started having blackouts. I was getting drunk maybe a couple of times a week, laid out, falling down, passed out, blacked out drunk. There was only a very brief period when I drank socially.

Well, at Texas Women's I met my second lover and, again, it was the bells ringing and the birds singing and the whole thing was terrific. And then one summer I went to visit her at her home in Houston. Now this was Texas in the fifties and if you were a lesbian, you chose up sides. You were either a butch or you were a femme and there was no in-between. Well, I picked to be a butch because I was more aggressive and I took charge of things. So when I went to visit her one weekend, I was the cat's pajamas. I had the DA haircut and the Levi jacket and the boots—heavy drag. So her parents guessed the scene right away, and while we were out swimming that first day they rummaged through her drawers and found some letters I had sent her. Her father, who was an oil driller, was standing in the front door waiting for us when we got back. He had a piece of rubber hose in his hands. When we walked through the front door he started beating the shit out of both of us with it. He just beat on us over and over again and we screamed and he just kept beating us. It was incredible. The upshot was that he informed my parents and the university of the fact that I was a dyke and so I was immediately expelled from the university.

My parents were very, very hurt and very, very dismayed, but I think they held onto some kind of fantasy that it was only a phase, and they tried to be supportive. But they were afraid that now that I was out of college I would just drop out altogether, so they kept encouraging me to go to IBM keypunch schools and stewardess schools and all these amazing places. It was just a horror show. So finally I moved to Dallas, and that's where I really started into serious drinking.

When I got to Dallas, I still had that old feeling of being very isolated and very lonely, even when a lot of people were around. Always on the outside looking in. And I remember one night when I first got to Dallas, I passed a gay bar, at that time one of the only ones in the city. I remember standing there one night on the sidewalk, looking into this place. It was jam-packed with people and there was loud music coming out of it and everybody looked like they were having fun. They had booze and they were dancing and smiling and the men were with the men and the women were with women and I thought, ah, so this is how it can be. I remember standing there and peering in and thinking that when I got to be old enough to go into that bar, I would truly have arrived.

And the minute I could get into bars, I went to bars, and that's where I stayed for many a year. I drank enormous amounts of booze in those bars, but everybody else around me was drinking enormous amounts of booze too; it was a whole life-style. At least three or four nights out of seven you'd be in the bar. Certainly you were in there Friday, Saturday, and Sunday—no one is not in the bar on those days. It's where you met everybody. There was just no opportunity to meet other lesbians outside bars. Maybe you would meet somebody at work, but it would be a long process of little signs back and forth and it sometimes would take years to have the courage to come up and approach the other person. What if you were wrong? You would lose your job and you would be rejected and there was always this fear that somebody would say something like, 'Oh, God, isn't that horrible. Why don't you go to a hospital and get cured?' or something like that.

The bars were also a place where I could finally let down my guard. I was forced to be two different people—one person when I went to work or visited my mom, and an entirely different person when I was home with my lover. The tension was terrible. It's making all those quick little changes in your life, and not making any slips. For God's sake, don't make a slip. I can remember living in fear and breaking out into cold sweats when I would almost forget and say something to someone at work, like, 'my lover, she . . .' Just one slip and it's over. And the only place where I could let go and be myself was in the bar, and the best way to get really easy and loose and relaxed and so forth was to drink. I'd been saving up all my meeting of new people until I got to the bar, so I had to get a lot of booze in me so I could get moving. The bar was my only chance.

The drinking also made me feel less split within myself. My attitude toward life in general was: well, fuck you. But you know, you can say that, but inside you hear so many messages about how you're sick, about how you need to be cured, about how you need to be dead; you hear that a lot too, no matter how strong you are and no matter how often you say 'fuck you, I'm going to be me.' You just keep hearing it and you just keep pushing it down and that's something booze helps to do. It helps to calm that part, kind of make it all go away for a time.

The way we are forced to be separated from ourselves makes me want to kill, it makes me so goddam angry. I can't tell you how many parties and banquets I've been to, all dressed to the nines, with some faggot as my escort, trying to make some kind of a show, saying, in effect: 'Hey, I'm okay. I'm just like you—normal. So you can accept me, okay?' That's a game we've all played. Unfortunately, it's a game a lot of us are still playing, not so much in New York and Boston and Los Angeles, but certainly in Kansas and Louisiana and Texas and places like that. And the price we pay for it in alcoholism and drug abuse and God knows how many other problems is high. Very high. Because there's got to be some way to get relief from living in those little compartments.

At any rate, while I was in Texas I was drinking to the point of getting drunk and passing out about every other night. Sometimes I would only drink a couple of six packs and I'd be there. Other nights it would take a case. But it didn't hit me that I had a problem with alcohol. Even when it got to the point where I had to have a piece of my stomach removed because of the booze, I couldn't face it. After the surgery the doctor asked me 'Do you drink?' And I said, 'Like socially.' Denial was just incredible. I really did still think I was a social drinker. Amazing, absolutely amazing. For a long time after surgery I could only eat Jell-O and very bland stuff. But somehow I knew, instinctively, when my stomach would be able to handle beer again, and as soon as it could I was out drinking again, getting drunk and staying out till all hours.

Then I moved to Los Angeles and became involved in the gay liberation movement and the women's movement. I began to realize then that a lot of my anger and feelings of outsideness also had to do with being a woman. I can still remember my anger when I was about six or seven and I went to my mother and said to her: 'I want to be a veterinarian when I grow up, Mama.' And she patted my hand and said: 'That's nice, dear. But your place in life is to be a wife to a good man.' And I remember that I was just livid and I thought: 'Why? Why does that have to be?' I also remember as a child being very puzzled about why I would have to give up my last name when I married, and so I became very adamant that I would never marry so I could keep my name. I can remember thinking, 'But it's *mine.*'

So I was angry about a lot of things that were forced on women even when I was very young. As I grew up, more and more things made me angry, but there was no women's movement, no place to share my anger. And the few times I did try to share it, I would be laughed at or scoffed at or called some awful name. So I stopped talking about it. And I think that booze helped me cover up the rage I felt about that, too. I kept myself very anesthetized from the whole lot of things that troubled me deeply.

When I came to Los Angeles I also started taking a lot of psychedelics along with the booze, and after awhile I decided that what I wanted to do was be a hippie and drop out, be on the streets. I had a job as a social worker at the time, and what really happened was that I couldn't work anymore. So I quit my job and opened a little junk store, and that was kind of the beginning of the end. I lived in this little hole in the wall behind the store, and all it had was a mattress on the floor, a peg on the wall for me to hang up the few clothes I owned, and a hot plate to cook on. There was also a sink, an old industrial sink that had layers and layers of old grime and paint on it. And the walls were covered with grease, because the place had been used as some kind of a shop at one time. That was it.

And by this time people that were around me were

gradually leaving me, including my lover. I was drinking wine now, cheap. I would go to the liquor store every single night and buy two bottles of Annie Greensprings, because I knew that's how much it would take. Two bottles in one evening. One bottle wouldn't do it. I would drink the two bottles and pass out and get up the next morning and stumble around trying to open up my store. Dust was everywhere, cobwebs were all over, everything was just thrown around. I didn't give a shit anymore.

It was at this point that I started doing strange, crazy things to hurt myself. Sometimes in the evening—I can remember this so goddam vividly—I'd be so lonely and so depressed and in such a panic that I didn't know what to do with myself. And I'd start at one side of the room and run toward the other side as fast as I could and throw myself against the wall and I would scream something like 'help me,' but I didn't know why I needed help or what I needed help for. I couldn't put it together. And then I would run and throw myself against the opposite wall. Another thing I used to do, when I was about one bottle down and halfway through the second one, was to pick up the empty bottle and bang myself in the head with it. I was so full of rotten feelings and I didn't know where to pin them, so I hated myself—I wanted to hurt myself somehow. A couple of times I got blood poisoning from beating myself over the head and had to go to the hospital.

But incredibly, it still didn't occur to me that alcohol was a problem. I only knew my life had fallen apart somehow. Some mysterious thing had happened to this wonderful person with all this intelligence and zeal and spark for life—but it wasn't alcohol. I just kept telling myself that I was unlucky, I just happened to be unlucky.

But things kept getting worse and I kept getting sicker, and finally it was beginning to dawn on me that maybe alcohol had something to do with it. So I started trying a variety of techniques. First I tried alternating a glass of wine with a glass of orange juice. That didn't work. Then I tried mixing wine with water, and that didn't work. Then I tried saying, 'I'm not going to do that again tonight'—and that didn't work. Then I decided I would only drink as much wine as I could hold in the biggest glass I owned and, of course, that didn't work. I usually started out with the glass but I always ended up drinking right out of the bottle. I can remember pouring the glass full of wine and beginning to drink it and feeling 'I can't get this into my body fast enough. I can't merge with this fast enough.' So I would tip the glass up as far as I could and the wine would pour in faster than I could swallow it so it would go down the sides of my mouth and down my shirt and I didn't care. I just had to have it.

Then one night I went on one of my drunks and I woke up the next morning and I could not move. I crawled onto the floor and for fourteen hours I couldn't get off the floor. Funny things were happening with my vision and when I tried to stand up my legs would buckle out from under me and I would fall to the floor in a heap. And it was at this point that it dawned on me for the very first time that there was a word that applied to me and that word was 'alcoholic.'

I experienced a heaviness and a darkness around my head and my shoulders when I first connected that word with myself. All I knew about alcoholics was that they were doomed. That's just the way it was and the next step was skid row and the next step after that was hell. I can't really describe the way I felt, just kind of crumbly and lost, absolutely lost. Hopeless. It wasn't that I was going to die, it was that my life was going to just keep on like this forever. I was convinced there was no way out, no way an alcoholic could be helped.

So the only thing I could do was prove to myself that I wasn't really an alcoholic. A few more days went by and I valiantly tried not to drink anymore, which, of course, didn't work. And one morning I woke up with a worse hangover than usual and I realized there was no way I could pretend any longer that I wasn't an alcoholic. I just lay there and started to cry and it was a big release, a big surrender. I sat there for a long time and I just cried and cried and cried. I felt that my life was over and I started fantasizing suicide for the first time in my life. I really wanted to die.

But there was this other part of me that was sort of detached and was watching me cry and think about suicide and which didn't want me to die. A part of me that maybe didn't like me too much, but still cared about me and was sorry this was happening. When I talk about the next thing that happened some people say, 'Aw, go on.' But it's true. I wasn't conscious of what I was doing; it was as though some presence picked me up off the bed and got me by the hand and walked me into the kitchen where the telephone was and put the Yellow Pages in my lap. I swear my mind was totally blank while all of this was going on. I opened the Yellow Pages to 'A' for alcoholism and down the page I went, until I found an address close to where I lived. And I called them and they said, 'Sure, come on in. We'd really like to talk to you.'

And I drove my beat-up old van over to this place and I walked in the front door and I looked down this hall. It was real long—it probably wasn't, really, but at the time it seemed real long and dark. And then, at the other end of the corridor, a woman began to walk toward me—and by this time I couldn't stand any longer. I leaned up against the doorjamb and she walked up and said, 'You must be Rachel.' I said 'Yeah.' And she said, 'Well, you're the saddest, loneliest looking thing I've seen in a long time. I'm glad you're here.' And I remember thinking that that was the first time in a long while that anyone had expressed anything remotely like pleasure at seeing me. It felt so good I wanted to cry."

10

WOMEN ON SKID ROW

You may see her as you run to catch the subway at Lafayette and Houston Streets on the edge of New York's Bowery district, or through the window of a taxi heading west from Washington, D.C.'s, Union Station, or as you drive through the outskirts of San Francisco's Mission district. It is unlikely that she will be mingling with one of the "bottle gangs" of skid row neighborhoods, which provide the homeless alcoholic with some measure of companionship and security. Membership in a bottle gang is almost always a male prerogative. Instead, she will probably be alone, on a curb staring at traffic, sleeping over a steam duct to keep warm, or simply wandering the streets, a solitary, rootless figure.

If you linger in the area, she may mark you as a "live one," and approach you for money. As she comes toward you, wrapped in layers of frayed, dirty clothing, her skin mottled and pinched and her eyes empty of hope, it is difficult not to look away. If you give her some money, she will shuffle away to buy herself a bottle, already wondering where she will be able to drink it in peace, without being mugged by one of the men in the neighborhood. Afterward, she'll have to start hustling a place to sleep that night, especially if she spent the previous night out in the cold.

She is a skid row woman, the most desperate and marginal of all alcoholic women. As the embodiment of our most nightmarish image of the "woman drunk"—unwashed, amoral, utterly disassociated from hearth and home—it is no accident that she has been even more blatantly ignored than other groups of problem drinking women. Society's unconcern stems partially from the skid row woman's sheer poverty; the powerlessness of all poor and disaffiliated people renders them invisible to one degree or another. Yet in the alcoholism field, ironically, few groups have been studied more diligently or thoroughly than skid row *men,* even though homeless alcoholics comprise only three to five percent of the total United States alcoholic population.

Skid row men have been observed in flophouses, bars, hobo jungles, bottle gangs, drunk tanks, courtrooms, and clinics, their drinking patterns and social problems the subject of endless research interest. By contrast, the existence of skid row women has been barely acknowledged. And predictably, when they have been noticed at all, their experience and problems have been presumed to be identical to those of men, an assumption which has only served to justify continued neglect.

The one study conducted to date on the experience of homeless alcoholic women, however, reveals that the backgrounds and drinking patterns of skid row women are strikingly different from those of men, and further, that the lives of these women may be lonelier, more alienated, and more poverty-stricken than those of homeless alcoholic men. The study, conducted in 1973 in New York's Bowery district, also discovered that treatment services for skid row women are vastly inferior to those available to men.

The study's authors, sociologists Gerald Garrett and Howard Bahr, conducted their research primarily through extensive interviews with residents of the Women's Emergency Shelter in the Bowery, and with men at Camp LaGuardia, a rehabilitation center for homeless Bowery men. The researchers found that the women were more likely to have been married, to have had children, and to have received more education than the male Bowery residents, suggesting that the women came from more stable backgrounds than the men. Homeless alcoholic women also began abusive drinking later in life than men, apparently, but found themselves on skid row at an earlier age. These findings suggest that for women, the route to skid row was both longer and faster than for men, possibly because women, regardless of their socioeconomic status, have fewer economic resources to keep them from slipping to the very bottom once their lives begin to veer out of control. The crises that began the downward slide to skid row differed strikingly: for women, it was most often a marital crisis; for men, the loss of a job.[1]

Once on skid row, the women were likely to be poorer than the men; only eleven percent of the homeless women but forty-three percent of the men had average monthly incomes of more than one hundred dollars.[2] Drinking patterns also differed dramatically. Among the heavy drinkers and alcoholics on skid row, two-thirds of the women drank alone, compared to only about a quarter of the men. Women were also far more likely to avoid bars and other public places and instead did their drinking in secluded settings, such as deserted parks and alleys and inside abandoned buildings. These findings suggest that homeless alcoholic women, their marginal social status notwithstanding, still may be sensitive to the stigma attached to female alcoholism and therefore hide their drinking to the degree they are able. The research also paints a picture of a very lonely and vulnerable woman, who not only may have little daily companionship, but also few people to turn to for help when she is sick or in trouble—or even to notice if she is missing. In the researchers' words, ". . . homeless alcoholic women may very well be the most isolated and disaffiliated residents of Skid Row."[3]

The study's comparison of treatment services at the Women's Emergency Shelter and Camp LaGuardia revealed sharp differences both in services available to skid row women and men and staff attitudes toward male and female clients. Garrett and Bahr rated the men's program as "very successful" at providing adequate recreational facilities, medical services, and personal security, noting that the residents were generally satisfied with the program and the staff. The men were paid for the work they did at the program and felt that their chances of getting a job upon leaving were fairly good.

In contrast, both the staff and clients at the Women's Shelter rated their rehabilitation and recreational programs as ineffective. There was no work program of any kind and "recreation therapy" consisted largely of bingo, card games, and television. Staff members were openly patronizing and indifferent toward their women clients, repeatedly predicting their failure upon leaving the program. As one caseworker told the researchers: "Anything we do here is useless. . . . I guess they just want to be lost souls and that's it. . . . They are hopeless cases, at best."[4]

The residents of the Women's Shelter, however, were probably fortunate to be there at all. Generally, skid row neighborhoods offer little or nothing in the way of treatment services or even basic shelter for their female residents. Most flophouses and emergency shelters are open only to men, as are many longer term rehabilitation centers for homeless alcoholics. Rita Zimmer, project director of the Lower Manhattan Sobering-Up Station, a Bowery detoxification unit, described the typical "support, system" available to the homeless alcoholic woman in most cities:

"Any woman who's been on the street for any length of time knows that most of the shelters won't take her, so the first place she'll probably try to get help is a detox unit. But if the three or four beds alloted for women are already filled, then she'll probably try the nearest hospital. That's fine if she has Medicaid, but if she doesn't they'll throw her out, unless it's a real emergency. But even if that's the case, they'll release her in five days and she'll be back on the street again.

"If it's not an emergency, the hospital won't take her but they may refer her to a long-term treatment unit in the area. So she goes over there and it's very likely they'll have a waiting list and tell her to come back in two weeks. But let's say they have room. They'll give her a screening interview, but they're very likely to decide that she's 'not appropriate' for the program because she's probably in very poor physical and mental condition. So she walks out the door and she's on the street again. She's run out of options.

"You can also bet she's never going to try again."

MARIE

For the past eleven years, forty-five-year-old Marie has survived on a combination of wits and sheer willpower. When her family fell apart more than a decade ago, she drifted, penniless and drunk, to New York City's Bowery area. By necessity, she quickly became an expert on which alcoholism detox centers had the best food, which subway stations were safest to sleep in at what hours, and most importantly, how to ensure a daily supply of a half gallon of wine. But being streetwise hasn't been enough to protect Marie from the brutality of homelessness. She is also a veteran of repeated muggings, rapes, near starvation, bitter winter nights on the street, and intermittent hostility from male Bowery residents who resent the presence of women on their "territory." Mere physical survival has been a daily struggle for Marie for longer than she wants to remember. And for most of that time, she has been totally alone.

When we talked, Marie had just made a tentative move to escape her skid row existence. She had been sober only five weeks, and was working and living at The Mary House, a Catholic-run center for homeless women. Although she appeared exhausted and pale, her mind, incredibly, did not seem dimmed by eleven alcohol-soaked years on the streets. She had a lot to say not only about the kind of people who lived on the Bowery, but also about the apathetic social system that served to keep them languishing there. She was also touchingly concerned about my personal safety, to the point of escorting me to the "friendliest" subway station in the area. Yet, despite her initial success at getting off the street, Marie seemed to have little hope of really turning her life around. She was still tortured by her past, and had trouble envisioning herself as anything but "just a drunk."

"You name it, I've probably slept there. On the street, in hallways, in abandoned buildings. When I'm lucky, someone might put me up for two weeks here, two weeks there. I've spent a lot of nights in incinerators. You know, those little two-by-three rooms in the hallways of apartment buildings? I'd have to wait until around twelve o'clock at night when nobody would be coming around with their garbage anymore, then I would lock myself into one of them and just sit there all night until it was daytime. Then I'd go out on the street again.

That's the loneliest part, not having a place to go to sleep at night. All the guys would be going off to the flophouses, but they don't let women in, you know. I could have went to the Women's Shelter but they wouldn't take me in when I was drinking. Sometimes I'd just pass out right on the street, especially when it was cold out. When that happened, sometimes one of the guys would find me and try to find me someplace to get warm. There's a place that I call 'The Green Door,' an abandoned building with a big green door, and inside a big room with a fire going, and it's warm. Better than the street, let me put it that way. And when I would pass out, if they could wake me up, sometimes they would try to get me down there. Otherwise, they would try to make sure I had some kind of cover. Enough cardboard over me.

How I got into this state is quite a story. If I had my way, I would have had a home and all my children staying with me. I had fourteen children, nine boys and five girls. The doctor said I was a breeder. But I couldn't take care of everybody alone. To tell you the truth, I didn't even want to get married to begin with. I had a good job selling magazine subscriptions, traveling all around and having a good time. Then when I was nineteen, bingo, I got pregnant. So I married the guy and we got a little apartment in the Bronx. I figured, well, we'll have a few kids and maybe it won't be a bad life.

But I was only married to him for two months when they came and got him for forgery. I was shocked because I didn't know anything about any forging. Well, that was just the beginning. He was in jail when the first one was born. He'd get out of jail just about long enough to get me pregnant again, then they'd come after him again. Forgery, robbery, burglary. And when he was home he would goof off, never working steady, and go to the racetrack with what he had. Meantime, I was having a baby about every year and working in a factory trying to bring in money. I was just about a nervous wreck. We never had enough money. I had to go on welfare I can't tell you how many times.

Well, things started to get really bad when I had to start placing my kids, you know, in foster care. I just couldn't take care of them anymore, all by myself and no money. So I had to place five of 'em one year, in 1957 I think it was. Then in 1963 I had to place five more. I held it against welfare for a long time that they were paying about three hundred dollars a month to foster parents for each one of my kids, when if they had just given it to me I could have kept them with me. I was a good mother, I don't care what they say. I wasn't drinking then.

When they took the kids away I just felt rotten. I was going to take a couple of them back and let them hit me for kidnapping my own kids, but then I figured it would just mix the kids up more. I just figured you can't beat the system. But I was very bitter. It makes you lonely; your arms are empty.

It was in 1964 that I started drinking heavy. That was when my husband went to jail for the fifth time and two of my babies died within two weeks of each other. Do you remember the flu that went around, that they call bronchitis? I think it was around fifty thousand babies that died that year. My daughter was two and my son was four months. They died two weeks apart. She went first, and while I went to her funeral, I left my son with a baby-sitter. They buried her at Calvary—that's a welfare burial place—and I watched them put her in the ground. But when I came home, the guy I had been living with while my husband was in jail had come to my house, knocked the baby-sitter out cold, and kidnapped my baby. He took him out under his coat with just his diaper on and this was the coldest night of the winter. So he got pneumonia and died the twenty-seventh of December. My girl went on the ninth of December.

After that I didn't care anymore. Before that I didn't

drink much—I didn't even like it all that well. Maybe I'd break out a bottle every few Friday nights. While I still had the kids, my husband's father used to come over sometimes with some wine—he was an alcoholic—and we'd drink it together. But now I started hitting the bottle heavy. By '67 I was going through a half gallon of wine a day, and I could only work two days a week doing housework, at fifty dollars a week. That's all I could work, to tell you the truth, because I had to drink the rest of the time. So I had to give up my apartment, and it was then that I came down here, to the Bowery.

I started shacking up with this and that. Sometimes I'd go to bed with 'em, because it was the only way I could stick around. You'd start out and they'd promise no strings attached and they wouldn't get smart, right? They'd say, 'You can just straighten up the place and hang around.' But after three days they'd start chasing you around the room, you know, so you'd either end up in bed or have to find another place.

I could be on welfare but I'm not. I hate welfare. I just do. The last time I was on it they sent me to a hotel on West Ninety-fourth Street to a room that was freezing. No heat in the middle of winter. A crummy little beat-up room and they charged forty-two dollars. You figure it. It was so cold that I had to leave and stay with friends, and when I came back my door was locked and my clothes had been moved out. I found out that they were using my room for tricks. They had prostitutes going in and out while I was away, and the proprietor of the hotel was making a bundle off it. And they did it each time I went away. The third time it happened I went to the proprietor to complain and he threatened me with a knife. That's welfare.

So I just went from place to place, from this guy to that guy, and a lot of the time, I'd just be on my own. Actually, I'm pretty much of a loner. But when you're on your own for awhile, it's hard to keep going. I've been so sick that I couldn't even walk and my legs were like rubber from drinking—and from no food. Lots of times I didn't have nothing to eat. And you know, if I did have a dollar I'd buy a bottle, because I was so shaky I needed that bottle. Sometimes I'd have nothing to eat for as long as five days. I used to steal food, like I'd hide out and watch the milkman put milk outside doors in apartment buildings, then I'd sneak in and drink the milk. I wouldn't even want it, I would be that sick, but I was the kind of drunk that knew I had to eat if I was going to keep going. Lots of drunks don't eat hardly at all, because you really can't stand the sight of food.

It's hard when you're a woman by yourself on the street. I've been mugged, I've been raped, I've been almost thrown out of windows of abandoned buildings. I sound worse than the Perils of Pauline. I ain't kidding you, I went through it all. And I didn't even have to be drunk for it to happen. Once you're drunk and on the streets, the reputation sticks with you—they figure you're drunk whether you are or not. People pull knives on you or hit you over the head with bottles. You've got to expect it. You learn who to stay away from. The number of times I've been raped in my lifetime, I can't even count. And there isn't any kind of guy you can trust for sure. One night there were these characters bothering me and I asked the security guard at the building where we were to walk me home. He said 'Sure, but walk me upstairs first so I can get my dog.' So he got me upstairs and he raped me. And afterward he said: 'Okay, you can get dressed now and I'll walk you home.'

You figure it, that type of thing makes you feel pretty low. All the time I've been on the street I've been scheming how the hell to get away from here. Because it's awful for anybody here, but for a woman it's even worse. A lot of them out there are very proud bums, they don't want any women around. This is a man's world, you know. Most of these guys left decent homes to begin with and they always picture their wives as people who don't drink, and then they look at you. They'll call you any name in the book—I can't even say 'em right here—but you'll sometimes have one guy in the group who'll say, 'Hey, watch your mouth, that's a lady.' And maybe that'll calm 'em down and maybe it won't. If it don't they might start pulling knives or throwing bottles at you, just for the hell of it. Some of the guys have been okay, you can even drink with some of 'em. But there's a lot of 'em that don't want women around.

And like I said, there's no place for a woman to go. There used to be a place called The Haven for Girls, where I lived for awhile. The city ran it. But they closed it in 1975 because a lot of girls got beat up. They were found mugged and drugged, beat-up, raped. There wasn't enough supervision, they didn't care enough to make sure we didn't get hurt. So it was a free-for-all for guys who wanted something. And anyway, the whole place only held fifty girls. When that closed, that was it. The guys have the flophouses, shelters, Salvation Army and whatnot. But if you're a woman you're much more on your own.

Finally, in '73, I was so bad off I ended up in detox for the first time. I was so weak from no food and from the booze that I passed out before I even got in the door. They had to carry me in. But when I came out of there, I had nowhere to live, so they tried to get me into a halfway house. But there was a week's wait, so in the meantime I was out in the street again. And naturally I started drinking again. You can't put a drunk out on the street and expect him to stay sober. And another thing, you need a job. A paying job. Most drunks are really proud people, you know. But they usually only train you for a trade if you've already finished high school. Mainly I think the city and the state don't want to be bothered footing the bill. They don't care where you go once you get dried out—just get out and make room for the new ones, is their attitude.

Since then I've been in and out of detox. But when I dried

out again last October, I got lucky and got a job here at The Mary House. I pay my room and board here by working, so I feel like I'm not on the dole. Most of the women here are what you'd call shopping bag ladies. They go around everywhere with two or three bags, even when they come down to breakfast here. It's ridiculous. I do laundry and make the breakfasts and make the soup for the soup line over at St. Joe's for three hundred men. But after I worked here for awhile I started drinking again, so now I have to go for counseling every day and stay sober or I'm out on my ear. I haven't had anything to drink since the third of last month. I have hopes of staying sober, but you never know. Something could happen and there's no way to tell.

I'd like to see my kids again. I don't even know where they are and they don't know where I am because I haven't stayed anywhere more than three months for the last eleven years. The youngest ones, they wouldn't even know I'm their mother. And my babies that died—of course you think of them all the time. Even now, I know how old they are up in heaven. It's hard for me to talk about my kids at all. I usually don't even mention to people that I have 'em because I get this feeling that I don't have the right to say I had kids, since I didn't raise them myself all the way.

To tell you the truth, if I were to go tomorrow, I would figure I had lived my life. Because the past, it not only haunts you, it's still there. It can't be denied. The past is also the present. It's not supposed to be, right? But it is. Like with the kids, in the past they were with me. The present, they're on my mind. And of course in the future, they'll still be there. And it's that way with everything. I feel like I'm ready to die, because to me, there is no way of straightening out this mess I got myself into. Even if I stayed on this earth thirty more years, nobody would count those thirty years. They'd still say: 'Yeah, but I remember her when she was a drunk.' "

Two months after our interview, I wrote Marie at The Mary House to find out how she was. I never received a reply, and shortly afterward I found out from a Bowery worker that she had left the center and was back on the streets. The last the counselor saw of her, she was standing idly near the corner of Fourth and Houston, watching traffic and occasionally hustling passersby for change. She was alone.

11

THE HAZARDS OF TREATMENT

Nearly all of the eleven women who shared their stories in the six preceding chapters successfully recovered from alcoholism. Likewise, most of the other thirty-nine women interviewed for this book were able to stop drinking and slowly, steadily rebuild their lives. I find their successes astonishing. For even under the best of circumstances, the ability to turn away from a drug to which one is physically and psychologically addicted requires uncommon courage and determination. But most of these women recovered from alcoholism in the face of an appalling lack of support from the doctors, therapists, alcoholism personnel, and others charged with diagnosing and treating their illness. With a few notable exceptions, these women were discouraged by the health system from embarking on alcoholism treatment to begin with, and once involved in treatment, were denied supports and services important to their recovery. They discovered what most alcoholic women who seek help are forced to recognize: that contemptuous attitudes and sheer ignorance about women with alcohol problems pervade the health system as thoroughly and destructively as any other segment of society. There, as anywhere, the real needs and the very humanity of alcoholic women remain invisible.

Within the health system, the first person an alcoholic woman is likely to encounter is her own doctor. And at first glance, he* would seem to be in an excellent position to identify her alcohol problem and steer her toward appropriate treatment. First, as a trained medical professional, a physician would be expected to have the expertise to recognize the symptoms of alcoholism and to lack the layperson's squeamishness about confronting a woman with a drinking problem. Second, a doctor is likely to come into contact with an alcoholic woman fairly frequently. Although it may be unacceptable for a woman to abuse alcohol in our society, it is highly acceptable for her to be ill in more mundane, less threatening ways. An alcoholic woman is unlikely to come into her doctor's office announcing her drinking problem, but she is apt to seek medical attention for a wide range of problems commonly associated with alcohol abuse, including depression, anxiety, stomach trouble, and injuries from alcohol-related accidents or physical abuse. On some of these visits, she may be drunk; at the very least, her behavior is likely to be somewhat erratic. Over time, her pattern of complaints and behavior is likely to suggest the presence of a problem with alcohol.

---

*I use the pronoun "he" deliberately because the medical profession is still overwhelmingly masculine; at present only twelve percent of physicians are women.

Yet physicians appear highly unlikely to diagnose alcoholism in their female patients. In a 1975 survey of eighty-nine women in Alcoholics Anonymous, fully half of the surveyed women said they had tried to discuss their drinking problem with someone who told them they couldn't possibly be alcoholic; twelve received such advice from physicians, five of these psychiatrists.[1] Of the fifty women interviewed for this book, forty-five had been seen by doctors while they were drinking alcoholically, but only seven were ever confronted by their physicians about their alcohol abuse.

A fifty-four-year-old Boston woman recalled: "In all of the times I landed in the hospital during my drinking years, no doctor ever said anything to me about alcoholism. I always either had colitis or a kidney problem or pneumonia, and when they couldn't think of anything else, I would have nerves. Twice I attempted suicide and once wound up in a hospital afterward for three months. And in those three months, I saw a psychiatrist every day and not once did he say a word to me about being alcoholic. And at that point I had been drinking almost around the clock."

Some physicians fail to respond to even clear-cut evidence of alcohol problems in their women patients. "I used to carry a big purse full of beer into my psychiatrist's office and drink right through the sessions," recalled a young Virginia social scientist. "He never said a word to me about it. As I look back, I think I was probably challenging him to say something, to do something, to help me. But he never dealt with it." A Detroit housewife who had a drinking problem while still in college encountered the same kind of reaction from her therapist at a university health service. "There were times when my husband called my psychiatrist in the middle of the night because I'd be so out of control and drunk and hysterical. I remember my husband shrieking over the phone: 'How can I get her to stop drinking?'

But when I would come in for my next session, my psychiatrist would just start talking about my hysteria, my hostility toward my husband, my problems with self-control. The drinking would never get mentioned as a problem in itself."

Probably the primary reason for many doctors' failure to confront alcohol problems in their patients is, perhaps surprisingly, sheer ignorance. Although alcohol abuse affects at least ten million persons in the United States and is considered the third largest health problem in the country, it is one of the most neglected areas of study in medical schools. Although this situation is slowly being corrected, few medical schools even today offer more than one course on the subject, and many limit their coverage to a single lecture. This gap in education is largely due to alcoholism's heritage as a moral problem rather than a medical one, despite its obvious physical and emotional consequences. Further, both because alcoholism still carries connotations of immorality and because its complexity stymies many doctors, it is a notoriously unpopular illness to treat.

It is no accident, for example, that the California Medical Association's Committee on Alcoholism and Other Drug Dependencies is nicknamed "The Committee on Loathsome Diseases." And in a 1972 nationwide survey of thirteen thousand physicians who treat alcoholism, seventy percent declared alcoholics to be difficult and uncooperative patients, while a sizable minority believed alcoholism indicated a "lack of will or morality."[2] Alcoholism also may be a touchy subject among some doctors because it comes too close to home: Recent studies report that physicians may abuse alcohol at a somewhat higher rate than the general population.[3] For doctors who feel uncomfortable about their own drinking habits, alcoholism is undoubtedly a threatening issue to discuss with a patient.

These factors in combination are likely to inhibit many physicians from confronting any patient—female or male—with an alcohol problem. But it is probable that doctors are generally even slower to diagnose alcoholism in a woman than a man. Their professional training notwithstanding, the research noted above indicates that physicians as a group hold many of the same demeaning misconceptions about alcoholics as the average layperson. Further, as the research of Phyllis Chesler and others has demonstrated, doctors, as a group, hold notably stereotypical attitudes about appropriate behavior for women.[4] Consequently, many physicians who believe that alcoholism is a sign of moral laxity may well also subscribe to the double standard rendering alcoholism—i.e. immorality—more shameful in a woman than a man, and thus more discomfiting to discuss with a female patient. Indeed, a study of the attitudes of 161 physicians toward their alcoholic clients revealed that a substantial minority of the doctors believed that compared to the problem drinking man, the alcoholic woman "had loose sexual morals, had more psychosexual conflict such as homosexuality, and was more likely to get into social difficulties."[5]

But if a doctor is unable or unwilling to diagnose a woman as alcoholic, he may give her condition another label instead. All too often a physician notes the distraught state of his alcoholic female client, makes a primary diagnosis of "depression" or "anxiety," and proceeds to prescribe a pill to alter her mood, most commonly a tranquilizer, sedative, or antidepressant. Consequently, many alcoholic women walk out of their doctors' offices not only with their alcoholism undiagnosed, but with a second powerful, potentially addictive psychoactive drug in hand.

A fifty-year-old Maryland woman who abused both alcohol and a variety of pills described her introduction to mood-altering drugs: "I was incredibly jumpy from all the booze I was drinking, so my doctor put me on both Librium and Nembutal—one to calm me during the day and the other to get me to sleep at night. Then about a year later, he put me on

Dexadrine to get me going in the morning, to counteract the effects of the pills—and the alcohol. He actually knew I was drinking, but he never seemed to see it as a major problem."

A young black woman from Washington, D.C., recalled her first visit with a psychiatrist during one of her worst periods of drinking: "I told this man I was depressed and exhausted all the time, but I also told him I thought my drinking might be getting a little out of hand. He told me to be cool about it and handed me a prescription for an antidepressant. In three months I was going through a month's worth of that prescription every ten days."

Psychoactive drug use is not risk-free for anyone, but it is especially dangerous for problem drinkers for several reasons. Perhaps the most obvious danger is that of mixing a mood-altering drug with alcohol. The combination of alcohol and certain psychoactive drugs produces a supra-additive effect substantially more powerful than the effects of any of the drugs taken alone, and consequently increases the possibility of accidental death by overdose.

Access to both alcohol and psychoactive drugs also makes suicide attempts a relatively easy matter, a serious concern in view of the high rate of such attempts—many of them successful—among alcoholic women. "All those pills came in handy when I decided to do myself in," remembered a thirty-six-year-old St. Louis statistician who at one point abused not only alcohol but three kinds of prescription psychoactive drugs. "I put on my best nightgown, took twenty-five Seconal and a glass of bourbon, and lay down to die. I had a massive seizure in the back of my brain and they were sure I would either die or be a vegetable for the rest of my life. But what amazes me most is that when I came to in the hospital, nobody ever suggested that I stop taking pills or stop drinking. All the doctors did was switch me from Seconal to another kind of sleeping pill."

The other major danger of prescribing mood-altering

drugs to an alcoholic is the possibility of cross addiction, that is, dependence on both alcohol and one or more other drugs. Anyone who habitually uses psychoactive drugs may become addicted to them, but the alcoholic is at particularly high risk as she has already established an addictive drug use pattern with alcohol. Cross addiction sometimes keeps a woman drinking for a longer period of time, because she may be able to switch to Valium or another pill temporarily when the effects of alcohol become too staggering for her body to bear. And a woman addicted to both alcohol and pills is likely to face more difficulties in treatment, because she must withdraw and recover from the effects of two or more powerful drugs instead of alcohol alone.

Yet despite these multiple dangers, many physicians distribute these drugs to alcoholic women with an alarmingly free hand. According to LeClair Bissell, M.D., president and chief executive officer of Edgehill/Newport, Inc., a Newport, Rhode Island, alcoholism facility, it is so easy for alcoholic women to get prescriptions for these drugs that, once addicted, many obtain their maintenance supply from several physicians simultaneously. "If a doctor is giving an alcoholic woman pills, don't imagine he is her only source. He is probably part of a long succession of people who are prescribing for her. For instance, the gynecologist is quite capable of writing prescriptions for Librium and Valium. The general practitioner, if there is one, will hear some of her problems and prescribe pills too. If there's a psychiatrist in the act, he'll hear some of it as well. If there's been an emergency of some sort and she has touched base with her hospital emergency room afterward, that may result in yet another prescription for tranquilizers. Even the ophthalmologist taking care of the glasses can prescribe pills. The possibilities are endless."

Since physicians prescribe psychoactive drugs to women in the general population at almost twice the rate for men,[6] it is perhaps not surprising that alcoholic women are far more likely to be cross-addicted than men. A 1977 nationwide survey of more than fifteen thousand Alcoholics Anonymous members showed that twenty-nine percent of the women but only fifteen percent of the men were addicted to other drugs besides alcohol. Of new A.A. members thirty years old or younger, a startling fifty-five percent of women were cross-addicted, compared to thirty-six percent of men.[7] Smaller surveys report similar findings: A study of residents in thirty-six alcoholism halfway houses in Minnesota, for example, found that nearly twice as many women as men were addicted to both alcohol and drugs.[8] Studies of individual treatment programs report similar female-male ratios for cross addiction.

Why are doctors so ready with the prescription tablet when women walk into their offices, thereby contributing to the alarming rate of cross addiction among alcoholic women? Probably one of the most critical factors is the image of women held by the medical profession. Both professional training and prevailing societal attitudes influence doctors and therapists to view women as inherently less stable emotionally than men by virtue of their female biology, and therefore more prone to psychological disturbances. Consequently, many doctors may be likely to misread a number of serious medical problems in women—including alcoholism—as merely "nerves," depression, or another emotional ailment. This image of women as "naturally" given to mental disorders is encouraged by the powerful American drug industry, which spends one billion dollars per year—approximately five thousand dollars per physician—trying to persuade doctors to prescribe mood-altering drugs to their patients.[9] Advertisements for psychoactive drugs in medical magazines not only feature women more often than men, but often suggest that women's unhappiness stems from vague, irrational sources that can be successfully attacked only by chemical means.

That doctors are affected by drug advertising is clear: One

study showed that seventy-three percent of physicians rate advertisements in medical journals as either somewhat or very important to them as sources of information about drugs.[10] In another recent study of twenty-three psychiatrists' reactions to women's portrayal in drug advertisements, approximately half of the respondents said they believed that all physicians are influenced by the image of women in ads for psychoactive drugs. Typical comments about the effects of these advertisements included: "Tends to perpetuate general trend of thinking of women as weaker, more sick"; "subliminally might indicate women are crazier"; "might imprint male M.D.'s with impression mental illness and femaleness go together."[11]

Another, less-often considered factor in doctors' more frequent prescribing of psychoactive drugs to women than to men is that it is more acceptable in our culture for women to take medicine than it is for men. To use medicine implies that one is sick or weak, characteristics that are consistent with the traditional feminine role, and conversely, are anathema to the masculine role. Thus, in a medical context, women are more likely than men to accept even quite powerful drugs, be they the opium and cocaine of the Victorian era or the barbiturates of twentieth century society. Further, as long as they are legal and are taken for "health" purposes rather than for recreation, psychoactive drugs retain an aura of respectability and can be taken by women even in fairly large quantities without fear of stigma. They are quintessentially "feminine" drugs, as surely as alcohol and most other recreational drugs are "masculine."

Given the social dynamics of psychoactive pill prescribing and use, it becomes clear why alcoholic women are so often the recipients of these drugs. In the first place, as many physicians are unknowledgeable about alcoholism and also tend to expect emotional problems in women, the alcohol abusing woman is highly likely to receive a primary diagnosis that indicates an emotional disturbance rather than alcoholism. This is particularly true if she chooses to talk only about her psychic difficulties and remains silent about her level of alcohol consumption. And if emotional problems are diagnosed, not only is a mood-changing drug apt to be judged the appropriate treatment by her physician, but it also may be welcomed or even requested by the alcoholic woman herself. For a tranquilizer or antidepressant not only provides her with another chemical escape valve, but, as a respectable "woman's drug," it can be taken openly and without guilt. And perhaps most importantly, the prescription of a psychoactive drug may serve as a welcome reinforcement of a woman's denial of her alcohol problem. For if her own *doctor*—a trusted expert—is giving her pills for depression or anxiety, she may easily conclude that her emotional difficulties are her primary or even her only problem—not alcohol abuse. Her drinking will almost certainly continue unabated, only somewhat complicated now by the addition of a second addictive drug.

Not every physician, of course, acts as an obstacle to treatment. Some doctors are not only impressively knowledgeable about alcoholism, but will forthrightly confront any patient, regardless of sex, who shows symptoms of the illness. But even if an alcoholic woman is fortunate enough to come into contact with such a physician—and the odds are not good—he can provide no guarantee that she will ultimately receive caring and effective treatment. For once a woman acknowledges her alcohol problem and is ready to seek help, she is then faced with an alcoholism treatment system that, by and large, neither welcomes nor understands her.

The first challenge a woman may confront is simply finding an alcoholism program that has room for her. A 1976 study conducted by the Association of Halfway House Alcoholism Programs of North America reported that of a representative nationwide sample of 161 alcoholism halfway houses, fifty-six percent served men only, thirty-five percent were coed, and only nine percent were open to women only. Further, and perhaps more important, women occupied only nineteen percent of all available beds in the 161 houses, because the "coed" units reserved only ten to thirty percent of their beds for women.[12] Another survey, conducted by the New York State Commission on Women and Alcoholism, found that in forty-five inpatient alcoholism facilities in the state, only seventeen percent of all beds were allocated for women. Some surveyed centers refused to treat women at all, citing inadequate budgets and in one case, the lack of space for a second bathroom.[13]

The scarcity of treatment space for women stems largely from the long-standing assumption by the health system that alcoholism is essentially a male illness. Prior to 1970, the year Congress passed legislation requiring alcoholism programs to offer services to women as a criterion for receiving federal funding, relatively few alcoholism programs admitted women on any basis. And even after the legislation was enacted, many programs added only a few token beds for women rather than providing space on a par with the actual numbers of alcoholic women in the population. It is not uncommon, even today, for a thirty-bed treatment center to reserve only four or five beds for women clients.

Consequently, some women seeking help for alcoholism become names on waiting lists, or are forced to travel far out of their communities to find programs with room for them. Others go the way of many women in our society who are considered troublesome and who lack other options—mental institutions. Although resorted to less often now than in the past, psychiatric hospitals are still used as dumping grounds for some women with drinking problems.

Dr. LeClair Bissell described the typical experience of an alcoholic woman consigned to a psychiatric ward: "First of all, it's usually not hard to get her in there because women have always been willing to self-define as mentally ill more readily than men, especially if the alternative is to be called an alcoholic. And as for her drinking, it plays right into the psychiatric approach that says, 'Find the underlying cause, get a lot of insight, pull up your socks, honey, and guess what? You won't be drinking like that anymore and you'll be having two drinks before dinner just like everybody else.' Never mind that she is physically addicted to alcohol."

The "treatment" of alcoholic women in mental wards is sometimes marked not only by ignorance, but outright brutality. A Washington, D.C., businesswoman remembered: "My husband told me he was taking me to a hospital and I went willingly, no questions asked. I was diagnosed as alcoholic. My husband left and I was told to follow the man who was carrying my bags. And as we walked along I noticed that he was locking doors behind him and I said: 'What are you doing that for?' And he said, 'Don't you know where you are?' And I said 'no,' and he said, 'You're at a federal facility for the insane.'

"It turned out that the hospital had an alcoholism program for men but none for women, so if you were unfortunate enough to be taken there as an alcoholic woman you got thrown in with the violently insane. I will never forget it. I was put in a ward where people were defecating in the corner and ladies were walking around nude. And the people working there were just brutal. Really brutal. Full of contempt. I was treated like an animal just like everyone else there. There were no doors on the johns. You had to take a shower with somebody there watching you. The blanket on my bed smelled like urine. For the first three days I just shook—I was having junior grade DTs. I was withdrawing from alcohol for the first time in my life and they didn't give me any drugs or any other kind of help. I just lay on my cot and shook."

But even if a woman is able to avoid the route of the psychiatric ward and finds an alcoholism program that has room for her, adequate treatment is by no means guaranteed. For by and large, the alcoholism treatment system is still very much a man's world, with most recovery programs primarily used, staffed, and directed by men and designed to meet male needs. As Rita Zimmer, director of a New York Bowery area alcoholism program, summarized the situation: "Just because most facilities now admit some women doesn't mean that most of them make any attempt to develop programs that relate to women. It doesn't mean they really try to reach out to find alcoholic women in the community. It doesn't even mean that they hire staff who have an interest in working with women or who have any knowledge of *how* to work with women." Consequently, many women find themselves in treatment programs which are neither prepared nor committed to meeting many of their fundamental psychological and practical needs.

Perhaps more than anything else, a woman beginning treatment for alcoholism needs to feel cared about and believed in. In most cases, she has weathered years—sometimes decades—of a brutalizing addiction that has left her over-whelmed with feelings of failure and hopelessness about the possibility of acceptance by others. Dr. Edith Gomberg, professor of psychology at the University of Michigan and a pioneering researcher on women and alcoholism, noted from her experience: ". . . in a deviance disorder like alcoholism, the attitude (conscious and unconscious) of the therapist toward women and toward alcoholism and the enthusiasm and interest of the therapist seem far more related to outcome than the technique used."[14] Given the importance of these factors, the attitudes of many treatment professionals toward alcoholic women are deeply disturbing.

A survey of 161 physicians involved in alcoholism

treatment revealed that they generally believed that "women have more basic personality disorders; they are more hostile, angry, unhappy, self-centered, withdrawn, depressed and more subject to mood swings; they are more emotional, lonely, nervous, they have less insight, and are not as likable as men alcoholics."[15] Similarly, a survey of staff attitudes toward women clients at a Newark, New Jersey, drug-alcohol program showed that addicted women were generally viewed as "more emotional, more sensitive, limited by their biology, needing to please men and implicitly 'sicker' than men."[16]

Other surveys note similar negative views of women among treatment personnel, in particular, the notions that alcoholic women are more emotionally unbalanced than alcoholic men, and by implication, more difficult to treat. Such attitudes are deeply destructive to recovering women because they are likely to become self-fulfilling prophecies. Therapists want to succeed at their work as much as anyone else, and if they believe that a certain type of patient is "sicker" and thus less likely to recover than another type of patient, they may well invest less time and energy on the more "difficult" patient, although this selection process may not always be a conscious one. And the patient herself is likely to experience this lack of interest and possibly even hostility from those in authority as a validation of her already deeply felt conviction of worthlessness. Consequently, she may indeed recover more slowly than the more nurtured male patient; in fact, she may even become more emotionally disturbed while in treatment.

As the theory that women are more psychologically maladjusted than men appears to be widespread among alcoholism treatment personnel and can seriously undermine a woman's recovery, its origins need to be examined more closely. It is possible that on average, an alcoholic woman may actually enter rehabilitation more emotionally impaired than an alcoholic man, due to the psychic strain of the particularly harsh stigma attached to female alcoholism. But it is also likely that the "sicker" label springs from deeply sexist notions about the psychology of women held by mental health professionals.

In the study most clearly illustrating these attitudes, conducted in 1970 by Dr. Inge Broverman, a group of psychotherapists was asked to define, respectively, a mature healthy man, a mature healthy woman, and a mature healthy adult. The clinicians, who displayed a high level of consensus in their conclusions, described a healthy male and a healthy female in very different terms. Specifically, they characterized a healthy, mature woman as more submissive, less independent, less adventurous, less competitive, more excitable in minor crises, more easily hurt, and more emotional than a mature, healthy man. Equally significant was their description of a healthy *adult*, which closely paralleled their description of a healthy man, and thereby differed radically from their assessment of a healthy woman.[17] This landmark study, along with others which have replicated its findings, indicates that the standard of mental health in our culture is a clearly masculine one, and, conversely, that feminine behavior is basically inconsistent with society's concept of adult mental health. This dual standard creates an excruciating Catch-22 situation for a woman, for if she behaves like a healthy adult she is considered neurotic and even deviant as a woman, but if she conforms to prescribed female behavior, she is deemed an unhealthy and immature adult. In short, whether she behaves "just like a man" or "just like a woman," she is judged emotionally unbalanced.

This double standard of mental health certainly is not held by all those working in alcoholism treatment, but it probably is the norm. For narrowly stereotypical views of "healthy" and "appropriate" behavior for women are subscribed to not only by mental health professionals but by the larger society as well, and alcoholism personnel are as susceptible as any other group to the prevailing values of their culture. Further, as the majority of alcoholism counselors and program directors are male, their motivation to examine and change their attitudes toward women may be limited. Any serious questioning of the passive, essentially subservient female role would necessitate a corollary—and almost certainly threatening—questioning of the value and functions of the dominant male role. To date, very few alcoholism programs have instituted any kind of in-service training that would encourage staff members to explore sexist assumptions and feelings about women and to develop more positive, egalitarian attitudes.

Stereotypical views of women among alcoholism professionals not only earn many women the damaging labels of "sick" and "hard to treat," but almost inevitably shape the criteria used for women's recovery. If a "healthy" woman is considered relatively submissive, dependent, and unadventurous, such behaviors are likely to be urged on alcoholic women as evidence of emotional maturity, while behaviors that fail to conform to conventional feminine norms are apt to be punished. Moreover, as male-oriented research on alcoholism causation has spawned the theory that the feminine role explicitly "protects" women from alcohol problems, a more thorough adjustment to that role may be seen as particularly important to the recovery of alcoholic women.

When Ardelle Schultz first joined the staff of a drug-alcohol program near Philadelphia in the early 1970s, she found that the staff—until her arrival, entirely male—was bent on such a resocialization process for women clients:

Women were being taught a new set of behaviors to please males. They were told to give up their sleazy bitch ways. . . . If a woman happened to be naturally sexy and sensuous, she was accused of seducing the men and chastized. If she was unfemininely aggressive and angry, she was told she was treacherous and that she was losing her sensitivity and humanity. If she was Lesbian, she was accused of being a man-hater and "sick." In other words, she was learning, again, to repress a part of herself that belonged to her and to become an "honest paper doll" cut out in man's image.[18]

Pressure to conform to such narrowly sexist standards of behavior is seriously damaging to any woman, but it is apt to be particularly destructive to a woman who is alcoholic. The heavy load of guilt, self-hatred, and worthlessness that an alcoholic woman drags with her into treatment is inextricably linked to her failure to live up to a self-denying and impossible ideal of womanhood—the sexual innocent, the nurturing mother, the dutiful wife, and the consummate "lady." To be assaulted in treatment with further accusations of her sins against femininity—whether blatantly or subtly conveyed—can only reinforce her already profound conviction of failure as a woman.

Jan DuPlain, a recovered alcoholic and former director of the National Council on Alcoholism's Office on Women, described the humiliating and guilt-inducing process by which many alcoholic women are "rehabilitated": "When we first get into treatment, a lot of us still feel the conflict between the nice girl we're supposed to be and the wild woman some of us were when we drank. But we never get a chance to resolve this conflict because we get pigeonholed from the start. We get up, in group therapy, in front of a therapist who is male and a bunch of alcoholics who are mostly male and we talk about our bad days, how wild and irresponsible we were, and we repent and put our Virgin Mary suits on again.

"And they don't challenge it—they encourage it. They say, 'we know, you were drunk at the time, but you've made a good confession and bless you, child, you're whole again. Now go back to your husband and children, Susie, and if you're living alone, Henrietta, watch your step with the men this time around.' The message is don't disrupt, don't do anything that would make us men have to confront our feelings about who women really are. Just cross yourself and do your penance, that's a good girl. And we leave the session and wonder why we feel worse about ourselves than ever."

Therapy that imposes a stereotyped vision of femininity on recovering women can intensify the very kinds of conflicts that triggered their abusive drinking in the first place. As discussed in Chapter 4, recent research by Dr. `Sharon Wilsnack and others indicates that many women who become alcoholic suffer painful sex-role conflicts, often between a consciously desired "feminine" self-image and unconscious "masculine" strivings which they experience as unacceptable and acutely threatening to their identities. Any therapy that pushes conventionally feminine behavior on a woman and disparages conventionally masculine behavior is likely only to heighten this sex-role struggle. It can only reinforce a woman's sense that aspects of her personality that are inconsistent with the female sex role are "unnatural" and "bad." Consequently, when she leaves her treatment program, she may well respond to the first crisis that threatens her still unintegrated identity with an old source of relief—a drink.

Insensitivity to the psychological needs of alcoholic women is often coupled with apparent indifference to some of their most urgent practical concerns. For example, the typical woman entering an alcoholism treatment program is in serious financial difficulty and badly needs job training. More often than not, she is divorced, has custody of her children, and is receiving little or no support money from her ex-husband. Her job skills are likely to be minimal and she probably has been unable to work steadily for some time. A 1977 survey by the National Institute on Alcohol Abuse and Alcoholism revealed that of the some sixty thousand women in federally funded treatment programs, approximately thirty percent were unemployed at the time of entering treatment, and only about seven percent held professional-level jobs. The mean household income of all the women surveyed was about seven thousand dollars.[19]

Yet, regardless of these stark financial realities, few alcoholism programs offer serious job training to recovering alcoholic women, either within the facilities themselves or through arrangements with outside agencies. The myth appears to linger among program staff that women don't really need jobs, that a woman's own survival along with that of her children's is never wholly, or even primarily, dependent on her own wage-earning abilities.

This obliviousness to the economic realities of women's lives was underscored in a recent study of staff attitudes toward clients at a Newark, New Jersey, drug-alcohol program, in which researchers asked the twenty-five male and nine female staff members their perceptions of the major problems faced by their clients. Less than a quarter of the staff believed that lack of job training was a significant problem for women, although it was seen as a major concern of male clients. But when the clients themselves were asked what they perceived as their most serious problems, an overwhelming ninety-six percent of the women named lack of job training. No other single problem was named by as many women.[20]

When job training is offered to women at all, it is usually for low-paying "women's work" such as typing and other clerical functions, while men in the same program are often trained for more lucrative, highly skilled occupations. Many alcoholism programs provide no job training opportunities whatever for women, instead assigning them the "occupational therapy" of household chores within the program residence, or brush-up courses on cooking, sewing, and home management. Although these skills may be useful and even necessary to some women, to offer them in lieu of hard-nosed job training almost ensures continuing financial hardship for many women once they leave a treatment program. Unable to find a job that pays enough to support them and possibly children as well, many find themselves on welfare shortly after completing treatment, or are forced to work two jobs simply in order to pay the bills. Clearly, it is not a way of life conducive to staying sober.

Child care is another service crucially needed by recovering women and almost never provided by alcoholism programs. As most recovery facilities are designed for and by men, this gap is not altogether surprising, since men who enter rehabilitation programs ordinarily leave their children in the care of their wives. But women who begin alcoholism treatment have no such convenient caretakers. Even if a woman's husband is still living with her, which is unlikely, he is rarely able or willing to undertake primary care of the children while she gets help for her alcoholism.

Foster care is generally a risky choice, since poor women, in particular, may be declared "unfit mothers" on the basis of their alcoholism and lose custody of their children, sometimes permanently. As for private day care and other kinds of child care services, New York City family alcoholism counselor Sheila Salcedo observed: "Day care centers are prohibitively expensive and have incredible waiting lists, and the homemaker services charge so much money that your average woman could never afford it. So if you have a lady in need of immediate detoxification and other treatment and she happens to have children, you're really in trouble."

Despite this pressing need for child care services, to date only two alcoholism programs in the entire country offer in-house

child care, and few others offer even minimal outside arrangements. Consequently, many women are literally prevented from
getting any kind of alcoholism treatment because they can't find
anyone to take care of their children. And if a woman tries to
begin treatment without having made workable child care
arrangements, her recovery is undermined from the start. Salcedo
noted, "It is very difficult for most women to get the rest they
need in treatment if the kids aren't in good hands. It's easy
enough to say, 'Okay, let's send the woman into rehab,' but if
she's got five kids at home, one of whom is on drugs and
another who is failing at school, and a husband who never really
wanted her to go into treatment in the first place, nothing that
happens in that treatment program is going to make any kind
of impression on her. She gets phone calls from home, she
worries, she feels guilty. What kind of treatment does that
amount to?"

The realities of women's lives are such that they also may
need more intensive follow-up than men after completing a
formal program of treatment. In general, women are likely to
both face greater pressures than men and receive less support
from others once they return from a rehabilitation program to the
"real world." Dr. Bissell observed: "There is usually much less
support from the family of the alcoholic woman than the man. As
soon as she returns from treatment she is expected to begin
taking care of the children and cooking dinner for the husband
and whatnot. And A.A. sometimes rather blandly advocates
'ninety meetings in ninety days' at the beginning, which is fine
in theory, but what about the woman who has a job and whose
baby-sitter leaves every day at five o'clock? or whose husband
refuses to take care of the kids every night? How is she going to
work the mechanics of that?"

Such difficulties assume that an alcoholic woman even has
a family to return to. Since husbands frequently divorce or

abandon their problem drinking wives, many women embark on their newly sober lives with little or no emotional support. Some women have lost not only their spouses or lovers but also their children because of their drinking, and emerge from treatment utterly alone, the family that had been the core of their lives no longer in existence. Many are truly displaced women, without moorings or direction. And regardless of what they may try to become, few women are ever allowed to entirely forget that they were once in trouble with drinking. The stigma attached to female alcoholism dogs many women even after recovery, threatening their relationships, their jobs, and their image of themselves.

A fifty-year-old divorced woman who recently lost both her job and potential remarriage because of her alcoholic past, said bitterly: "I consider myself a victim. I'm a woman, I'm over forty, and I'm an alcoholic. That doesn't mean I can't do anything to help myself. But I am a victim. Society is through with me."

The acute stress and isolation faced by many women following treatment can seriously threaten their sobriety. "You can't just treat a woman, show her how to stop drinking and then tell her to go out and do her own thing," said Clara Synigal, founder and former director of Interim House, a halfway house for alcoholic women in Philadelphia. "You have to go step by step, follow through, and keep in touch with her so she knows she has a home where she can get support at all times." Yet few alcoholism facilities provide any sustained follow-up services to clients once they complete treatment, in terms of either counseling or practical help in rebuilding their lives. Without such support, many women quickly become overwhelmed by the multiple pressures of their new situations, and, sometimes within a few months or even weeks of completing treatment, turn back to the bottle for relief.

The disregard for women's concerns which marks many rehabilitation programs has sparked a small but vigorous movement within the alcoholism field to develop treatment programs specifically designed for women. These programs, which are often staffed and used entirely by women, are committed to providing alcoholic women with a strongly supportive, caring environment and to approaching their recovery needs in the context of women's total experience in society. Many of these programs have initiated services rarely offered in more traditional facilities, including special outreach efforts to alcoholic women still hidden in the community; child care arrangements; health and sexuality seminars; training and placement for skilled jobs; support groups for women with special issues, such as single mothers, lesbians, and minority women; and long-term follow-up services. Generally, those women's programs that have been evaluated have demonstrated better than average rates of client recovery.[21]

Yet, within the alcoholism field, support for women's programs has been grudging at best. Organizers of such programs have found funding hard to come by in a field that has yet to fully recognize the extent of female alcoholism, much less the inability of many traditional programs to meet women's needs. The National Institute on Alcohol Abuse and Alcoholism has funded only twenty-nine women's programs of a total of some five hundred treatment facilities, and although some of these federally supported programs are excellent, they clearly do not begin to meet the extent of women's needs.

At present, many major metropolitan areas and even entire states are without a single women's program or even a coed program that has instituted special services for female clients. Even in New York City, where a highly organized group of alcoholism workers and feminists has been lobbying hard for the establishment of the city's first women's program, New York

City's Department of Mental Health and Mental Retardation has listed it as a "low priority" in its 1976–1980 plan for mental health and alcoholism services.[22] "As it is now, a number of agencies are sending women out of New York to get decent treatment," said Maxine Womble, acting commissioner of the city's Division of Alcoholism and a leader in the effort to establish a New York City women's program. "Women are being sent all the way to Philadelphia and other cities to get them into a program that meets their needs, which is a terrible thing as far as I'm concerned. But what options do we have?"

Since alcoholism programs sensitive to women's concerns still comprise only a tiny percentage of existing programs, the vast majority of women continue to be treated in facilities that fail to meet many of their most pressing needs. Many women drop out of these programs before completing treatment. The reasons they cite are varied: lack of emotional support from staff, an inability to make suitable child care arrangements, diffuse feelings of alienation and isolation, and sometimes simply an overwhelming sense that "it's not helping." Occasionally, women leave because of sexual harassment or abuse from male staff or residents. Of those who complete treatment, most studies show a significantly lower rate of recovery by alcoholic women than men, in some cases less than half the rate for men.[23] A good number of women who resume abusive drinking after leaving treatment become part of the "revolving door" syndrome. They make their way in and out of treatment programs over and over again for years to come, endlessly searching for a way out of their addiction, and endlessly failing to find it.

But how could it be otherwise? For the whole range of ways that the health system fails the alcoholic woman doesn't simply occur by chance, or even from causes that are separate and unrelated. Rather, these failures are largely the product of an unwillingness to see the alcoholic woman as she really is, and of viewing her instead through a prism of cultural myths about women that distorts both the nature of her problem and the kinds of supports and services necessary to her recovery. It is a way of seeing, ultimately, that serves the belief systems and interests of those treating the alcoholic woman far better than it serves the needs of the woman herself.

12
FREEING WOMEN

Part of me bought right into society's system for the woman. I was the nice girl, staying at home, waiting for the right man to discover me and fly me away with him to bride-beautiful land to live happily ever after. But there was this other side of me that said screw them all, this is the stupidest system and I'll go out and I'll be who I want to be and I'll raise hell and I'll be the President of the goddam United States. Stand back. I ain't getting married and living in this suburban U.S., five-kids, picket-fence world—baby, you can have it. That was the part of me that booze kept down.

Claire, 33, a teacher

I am a piece of paper
scribbled on all day.
/in between/
all those scribble lines
/little pieces/
I am all those
little pieces.

poem by Sandie Johnson, 37, written
while she was addicted to alcohol

They kept telling me I had to stop being so angry or I'd never
get better. So what was I supposed to do with 20 years of
anger—stuff it down the disposal like it was kitchen scraps?

Terry, 46, a housewife

A woman's experience with alcoholism cannot be
separated from the realities of sexism in our culture. Every
dimension of a woman's addiction—its causes, its consequences,
its subversive hidden quality, its treatment—are shaped by her
subordinate and devalued status. To a large degree, the depth of
this connection stems from the sheer pervasiveness of sexism.
Women are driven to all kinds of self-destructive escapes from
their powerlessness and their conflicted visions of themselves:
depression, compulsive eating, other drug addiction, obsessive
housekeeping, suicide.

Alcohol is only one escape among many. Women are
forced to hide not only their alcohol problems but a vast range of
other experiences and segments of themselves deemed dangerously unfeminine, from their anger to their sexual histories to their
dreams of triumph in worlds still closed to them. And when
some women finally falter under the weight of their blocked lives
and ask for help, the "treatment" they receive—not only in
alcoholism rehabilitation centers but also in mental institutions,
prisons, private psychiatrists' offices and marriage counseling
clinics—too often only wedges them more tightly into their
constricting roles. Feminist philosopher Mary Daly urges women

to dissect the word "recover" and examine the significance of its parts: re-cover. For women, its literal meaning is too frequently its actual one: Female psychic wounds are often merely covered over instead of treated at the source.

As sexism penetrates the core of women's lives, it is inevitable that it would profoundly affect their drinking problems. But sexual prejudice permeates the alcoholic experience even move deeply than many other life crises faced by women. Alcoholism is defined as a disease or illness, but it is a disease in the broadest sense, afflicting not only the body but the mind, emotions, spirit, personal ties, livelihood—in short, one's entire relationship to oneself and the world. When the acute powerlessness of the alcoholic condition is crossed with the essential powerlessness of the female condition, the outcome can only be devastating. The two conditions act upon each other, reinforcing the impotence and hopelessness of both, leaving the alcoholic woman with few resources to help her regain a grip on her life.

Sexism and alcoholism interact with particular intensity for another important reason: the grave threat posed by alcohol abuse to the sexual status quo. Women who live within the limits of their roles are sometimes rewarded by a degree of protection and approval from men that partially cushions them from the reality of their subordinate status—in fact, it often keeps them from recognizing that status. A woman's compliance wins her, among other things, economic security, reflected social status, and some protection from physical harm.* But when a woman loses control over her drinking she is no longer able to carry out the functions that buttress the sexual power system, and

*However, this is not always the case: Millions of women who have faithfully carried out their prescribed feminine duties for most of their adult lives are discarded by men who tire of them. These "displaced homemakers" are often reduced to welfare and nearly total social isolation. But women who remain within the confines of their assigned roles have a somewhat greater chance of garnering male protection than women who do not. Such women are nearly always abandoned by the men they have "betrayed."

thus she forfeits even this veneer of protection and favor. She is set adrift, the true extent of her powerlessness and expendability revealed to her.

As the foregoing chapters have demonstrated, this destructive interaction between sexism and alcoholism both intensifies the pain of a woman's alcoholic experience and almost inevitably exacerbates the alcohol problem itself. When alcoholic women are labeled "whores" and "bad mothers" for having broken with their sex roles, they are robbed of the remains of an identity already battered by the concrete consequences of their drinking problems. That this harsh stigmatization may be even more devastating than the effects of the addiction itself is suggested by a study of seventy women treated at the Johns Hopkins Hospital psychiatric center, all of whom had been involved in "deviant" behavior such as drug addiction, sexual promiscuity, or homosexuality, and all of whom had also attempted suicide. The researchers found that none of the deviant activities in and of themselves had triggered the suicide attempts, but rather the "negative public reaction to these events and activities . . . the social response to the patient's coping behavior."

The sequence of events leading to the suicide attempts were typically as follows: 1) the deviant behavior itself; 2) resulting social penalties and stigmatization which resulted in increased deviance and still stronger penalties; 3) a psychological crisis; 4) the reluctant acceptance of a new, negative identity, such as "whore" or "addict"; 5) deepening hopelessness and isolation; 6) reduced coping abilities based on the new, deviant identity, and, finally, 7) suicide attempts.[1]

This sequence is not difficult to understand in view of the severe blow dealt to a woman's identity by such stigmatization. It is not the public scorn alone that is so devastating, but also the lack of inner defenses that any "deviant" woman is likely to be able to marshal against such attacks. Many alcoholic women do attempt suicide in a desperate, final effort to forget the extent of their failures; more simply drown the knowledge of their "badness" in still greater quantities of alcohol and fearfully refuse to expose themselves to treatment. Either response renders them safely invisible to the rest of us; either, finally, is a form of sacrifice to a society that will not accept women's fallibility.

The interaction between problem drinking and women's oppressed condition exacerbates many of the concrete realities of an alcoholic woman's life as well. Alcoholism makes women even more vulnerable than usual to extreme economic deprivation; to physical abuse and rape; to the cruelties of forced separation from *and* forced caretaking of children; to men's general unwillingness to support and nurture women when women can no longer care for them and their children. None of these injustices is caused by alcoholism alone, but rather by the mediating effects of problem drinking on a woman's already devalued and dependent status. And once again, the anger and hopelessness that result are likely to only plunge a woman more deeply into the oblivion of alcohol.

The damaging interplay between sexism and alcoholism even follows those women who are finally treated for their drinking problems. As the health system is both a microcosm of the larger society and an important conveyor of its dominant values, it tends to promote oppressive views of women's "nature" and consequent needs; all women who use the health system risk the iatrogenic effects of these views. But the alcoholic woman is particularly likely to be damaged in the course of being "helped" by this system. As she is commonly assumed to have "fallen further" than most women from norms of feminine behavior, these norms may be pushed on her even more zealously than usual, and in her emotionally exhausted state, she may be less able to resist them. Further, society's patently unhealthy standards for "healthy" female behavior are likely to aggravate the conflicts about the feminine sex role that may have *contributed* to a woman's alcohol abuse in the first place.

The implications are inescapable. Every dimension of female alcoholism is inextricably linked to women's powerless social condition, and this condition is reinforced by, and in turn reinforces, their alcoholism. Clearly, then, truly significant progress in the treatment and prevention of women's alcohol problems cannot come about without a commitment to far-reaching changes in women's status in society. Many activists in the alcohol field are already well aware of this imperative, and have initiated a number of change-oriented projects with explicitly antisexist goals.

Among these wide-ranging efforts are public education programs to combat stereotypes about alcoholic women; training of health professionals to meet the practical and psychological needs of alcoholic women clients; promotion of nonsexist research; the establishment of treatment programs sensitive to women's concerns; and the development of prevention programs focusing on key conflicts and crisis in points in women's lives. All of these efforts are not only reaping immediate benefits for alcoholic women and those at risk for alcohol abuse, but are also helping to chip away at the larger social understructure that makes the reforms necessary.

Yet by themselves or even in concert, these projects cannot hope to substantially alleviate the crushing, multileveled problems facing the majority of alcoholic women, nor prevent large numbers of women from turning to alcohol abuse in the future. For all of these efforts still are being carried out within a social framework that is fundamentally oppressive to women. How can pamphlets or TV spots on women's drinking problems—or books, for that matter—appreciably lessen the stigma attached to female alcoholism, when that stigma supports values that safeguard an entire social order? How can programs to sensitize health professionals hope to significantly combat the stereotypical views of women that their own professions play a major role in creating and sustaining? How can prevention programs, however thoughtfully planned and executed, hope to effectively counteract the lifetimes of conflict, self-denial, and despair that finally drive some women to abuse alcohol? The noting of these limitations is in no way to denigrate these activist efforts; all are a crucial part of the change process and deserve strong support. But their impact will only be fully felt if they are pursued in a wider context, as part of a comprehensive movement to free all women from the social and psychological bonds that cripple them.

The larger goals that must be struggled toward in order to substantially affect female alcoholism—and other serious social problems facing women as well—go deeper than the institutional level. Changes in social structures and institutions are of course necessary, among them those affecting employment, legal rights, health care, and the sexual division of labor. But regardless of the extent of such structural reform, no thorough-going change in women's status can occur as long as men and women remain, psychologically, at the mercy of sexual stereotypes. The current sex-role system slices human nature into two dichotomous halves, attributing one half to men and the other half to women. This artificial polarizing of essentially human qualities supports a society based on male dominance, but at the price of cutting off both women and men from large segments of themselves. While women are denied the active, potent side of their natures, men are sealed off from their receptive, nurturing qualities and from the emotional vulnerability that permits real closeness to others.

Real freedom for women—and men as well—does not depend upon women becoming "more like men," but rather upon both sexes reclaiming the repressed sides of themselves and learning to respond from their fully human natures. This reintegration process is key to breaking the domination-subordination mold of male-female relationships. For only when men are no longer encased in a role that drives them to dominate others in order to validate themselves will they be able to relinquish the need to control women; likewise, only when women experience themselves as whole persons rather than the passive dependents of men will they be able to resist male attempts to limit their autonomy. Only when released from the psychic prisons of "masculinity" and "femininity" can men and women hope to truly meet as equals, with all secret agendas and manipulation put aside. And beyond specific concerns of power, the shedding of sex roles would be likely to free both sexes to be more fully themselves on many levels. A number of recent studies show that women and men who rate high on measures of masculine-feminine integration tend to be more creative, more self-confident, and more adaptable to new situations than those who more closely identify with their respective sex roles.[2]

This integration of the masculine and feminine potential within an individual is commonly referred to as *androgyny* (from *andro,* male, and *gyne,* female). In her book entitled *Androgyny: Toward a New Theory of Sexuality,* Dr. June Singer writes:

> Beyond the contest for dominance, beyond the polarization of
> *masculine* consciousness and *feminine* consciousness, lies the
> intuition that there must be something else, a further
> development in *human* consciousness . . . the androgynous
> potential is always present in each person, ready to be tapped
> as a source of energy.[3]

The concept of androgyny is an ancient one, finding expression throughout recorded history in sources as varied as the Bible, ancient Greek philosophy, the sacred traditions of primitive peoples, myths, legends, Eastern religions, and modern psychoanalysis. Its fundamental reality seems to endure despite the most strenuous attempts to bury it: The most comprehensive review of the literature to date on psychological sex differences showed that only a very few actual differences have been established, none of them indicating the major splits in consciousness that current sex roles suggest.[4] But the culturally contrived nature of these roles can be seen most clearly of all in the behavior of human beings. In the last several years, many women—and some men—have begun to break through the barriers of their sex-typed identities and substantially expand their range of responses and attitudes. These changes are occurring among too many people in too many areas of behavior to dismiss them as aberrations of women's and men's "real" natures.

Yet, despite the clear and enduring reality of androgyny, its existence has not been widely recognized. The concept of the harmonious coexistence of the masculine and feminine principles within a single individual has been particularly difficult to assimilate in Western culture. Our culture is linear and analytical in its mode of thought and tends to see differences as irreconcilable opposites rather than simply two complementary aspects of the same thing—the two sides of one coin. The validity of androgyny has also been difficult to accept for the more overriding reason that it threatens the basis of a male-controlled culture. Thus the movement of women and men toward more integrated identities will undoubtedly be a gradual, conflict-prone process, marked by confusion and anxiety as well as the rewards of emotional growth. Perhaps a fully androgynous society can never be realized; yet, it is the vision we must keep in front of us if we are serious about altering the course of women's lives.

What would progress toward such deep-seated shifts in our attitudes, in conjunction with necessary institutional changes, mean specifically for women's alcohol problems? It would not eradicate them, certainly; even a society seriously committed to human growth and freedom would engender inevitable tensions and conflicts. But when a woman developed a problem with her drinking, she would feel less compelled to hide it from the world and from herself, for she would no longer be judged by the narrow standards of femininity that now render an alcoholic woman morally contemptible. And the illness of alcoholism itself—apart from its loaded dimension for women—would probably be looked upon somewhat more tolerantly, for the culture would be less dominated by a masculine ethic that puts a premium on productivity and toughness and sneers at those who expose their vulnerability. Alcoholism might at last be accepted for the illness it is, one that both women and men could acknowledge in themselves without self-hate or guilt, and be treated for without fear of public scorn.

Almost inevitably, the process of alcoholism treatment would also change, both in goals and rates of recovery. In treatment, emphasis would be placed on helping a woman discover the aspects of herself that had somehow been denied sufficient growth and self-love, and to providing her with the support and practical tools needed to allow those parts of her to develop. That an androgynous self-concept could help alcoholic women to recover was suggested by a recent three-year study of women residents of a Washington, D.C.-area halfway house, conducted by anthropologist Joan Volpe and sociologist James Rooney. Using a modified version of the Bem androgyny scale, the researchers tested seventy women for their degree of psychological androgyny upon entering the halfway house, again one month after entry, and a third time several months later, after being judged by the halfway house staff to be significantly improved and ready to leave the program. The same test also was administered to thirty-five recovered alcoholic women who had no connection with the halfway house, but who had been able to stay sober for a year or more. The researchers found that, in general, the longer established in their sobriety the women were, the more androgynous their identities and behavior tended to be. That is, women tended to score higher on the "feminine" end of the scale upon entering treatment than at any other time, while as a group, the women who had maintained their sobriety for the longest period had also most fully integrated the masculine and feminine sides of their personalities.[5]

Although it is doubtful whether any amount of societal restructuring and realization of human potential could wipe out alcoholism entirely, the need to at least *limit* women's drinking problems has to be seriously addressed. As more than three million women currently suffer alcohol problems in the United States, and as the rate appears to be growing both among adult women and teen-age girls, the issue of prevention is a crucial one—perhaps the most crucial of all. The media have repeatedly pointed to the recent probable increase in women's alcoholism as evidence that "women's lib" actually drives *more* women to the bottle, noting that as more women become involved in male-typed life-styles, more become privy to male psychological tensions as well as to one of man's most popular forms of escape from those tensions: alcohol. This frequent and sometimes almost gleefully proffered theory smacks of a certain hostility to the women's movement that characterizes a large segment of the media, a sort of "well, you asked for it, girls!" attitude. It also betrays a lack of understanding of the prerequisite for real women's liberation described above: the expansion and ultimate dissolution of sex roles for both women and men, not the gradual transformation of women into female men. For women to aspire to the psychic imperatives of the male work ethic—the competitiveness, the lonely individualism, the emphasis on product instead of process—would only be to exchange one set of shackles for another (albeit one invested with more social power). It is true that some women have adopted certain "masculine" work habits and consequent tensions in their quest for career success, but in a culture still dominated by male values, such imitative behavior may be unavoidable—in fact, many women have to behave even more "like men" than men themselves in order to sufficiently prove their competence. But such measures, perhaps necessary in the short run, have little to do with the essence and real goals of the feminist movement.

If female alcohol problems are increasing, it is most likely not because women's liberation *has* arrived, but because it *hasn't*. Like all periods of social transition, the movement toward autonomy for women is inevitably fraught with upheaval and conflict. Many women are stranded at a juncture between the inadequacy of their old roles and resistance—both external and internal—to their struggle toward self-realization. Their efforts at personal change are frequently greeted with hostility and even panic by men who fear the demise of their own dominant status and fail to understand how they, too, are imprisoned by it. These men often refuse to support women's change efforts, either in their personal lives or through their influence on institutional structures. Consequently, many women who are struggling to forge new lives for themselves find themselves in a social environment that still binds them to their old roles; these women are doubly burdened, doubly stressed. The NORC national survey finding that women who are both married and work outside the home have among the highest rates of female alcohol abuse is testimony to the rigors of such a dual existence. Further, because of both male hostility toward feminist goals and women's own internalized injunctions to be properly "feminine," many women also suffer painful inner conflict between the safety of their old selves and the rewards of their newly emerging identities.

Recent research on the causes of female alcoholism

suggests that the kinds of conflicts many women are now embroiled in may relate quite directly to their apparently increasing rate of drinking problems. As noted in Chapter 4, several studies indicate that many women may begin abusive drinking to relieve conflicts between the consciously "feminine" side of themselves which they have been taught to wholly identify with, and less conscious "masculine" strivings which they have been trained to reject and repress. During this difficult period of social transition, when women are just beginning the process of expanding their self-concepts and are doing so in a climate that still strenuously resists such efforts, it is quite possible that such sex-role conflicts may be intensified. Moreover, the alcohol industry's campaign to encourage women's drinking through appeals to their "liberated" status may provide additional impetus to try to solve such conflicts with alcohol.

But the transitional nature of this period of heightened conflict has to be kept in mind. As women gradually become more comfortable with their new, expanded identities they are likely to experience such sex-role conflict less intensely and less frequently, and therefore ultimately have *less* need for escape into alcohol. Similarly, the alternate pattern of sex-role conflict believed to contribute to female alcohol problems, that between a consciously "masculine" identity and unacceptable, deeply internalized needs to meet "feminine" norms, is also likely to be defused as women come to acknowledge and enjoy their psychological wholeness.

It is worth noting, too, that the gradual dissolution of sex roles may well have a similar effect on the drinking problems of men. As noted earlier, one of the most prominent theories on alcoholism causation holds that men abuse alcohol in order to heighten feelings of power over others; a second widely held theory is that men drink abusively to satisfy hidden dependency needs forbidden men in adult society. Both needs—for power and for dependence—are clearly grounded in the male sex role, which is based on dominance over others and consequently cannot tolerate open expressions of dependence. But if men were permitted access to their whole selves rather than confined to the rigid requirements of "masculinity," their incessant quest for power as well as their terror of dependence would almost surely be diminished. As fully human men instead of merely masculine men, they would have less need of the compensating crutch of alcohol.

The emphasis here on the need to dismantle the sex-role system is not to suggest that sexual oppression is the only major social issue affecting women's alcohol problems. Racism, class bias, ageism, homophobia, and every other system of inequity that erodes women's power and self-esteem serve to contribute to their drinking problems, perpetuate them, and intensify their painful effects. All of these issues need immediate and serious attention. But while sexism is by no means the *only* major form of social oppression that has to be confronted in dealing with female alcoholism, the illness cannot be effectively treated or prevented *without* attacking this fundamental source of powerlessness. Not only is it the one dimension of experience that pervasively damages *all* women, cutting across all other lines of background and situation, but as alcoholism is so thickly clouded with issues of morality, sexism may well impinge on a woman's alcoholic experience more directly and deeply than most other forms of oppression she encounters. Finally—and most importantly—the ethic of power that sustains many systems of inequity in our culture is a masculine one, rooted in a sex role that equates conquest and domination with personal worth. As long as the imperatives of that male role remain in force, efforts to alleviate all forms of social oppression will meet with rigid—and powerful—resistance.

We are moving forward. In highly visible actions and in

quieter, subtler ways, more women are beginning to question the "shoulds" that have disabled them for so long, and to explore feelings and capabilities they didn't know they owned. More women are demanding control over the social and political decisions that shape their daily lives, not only in the realms of jobs and child care, but also health, criminal justice, welfare, law, education, and even religion. Consciously or unconsciously, more women are working for a society in which no group of people has the right to determine for another group its nature and its permissible behavior, a society in which the very meaning of power is transformed, so that it no longer implies domination over others, but rather the freedom to choose the terms of one's own life.

The past decade of difficult progress toward women's autonomy—and the centuries of struggle that preceded it—warn us that this goal will not be easily reached; it will continue to be a grueling process of small changes in law and consciousness, and for individual women, it will continue to entail pain and require enormous stamina. But if women—those who are alcoholic and those who are not—are to be able to truly heal themselves and go on to live authentic, freely chosen lives, it is a necessary struggle.

13

GETTING HELP FOR A DRINKING PROBLEM: A WOMAN'S GUIDE

This book is not primarily a self-help manual. Its main purpose is to awaken readers to the realities of the alcoholic woman's experience, and to show how that experience is shaped by the condition of all women's lives. It is a book that hopes to nudge readers to examine their own feelings about alcoholic women, and to spur at least some to transform their awareness into action for improved outreach, treatment, and prevention of women's alcohol problems—and for greater autonomy for all women. Yet these are future possibilities, tomorrow's goals. Meanwhile, what is she to do *now*, the woman who sits each afternoon in her darkened living room, a bottle half-emptied beside her, or who, even as she reads this book, is sipping on a mid-morning Scotch? Where does it leave you, if you have been concerned lately about your own drinking, or if you have been watching too long while a wife, sister, or friend destroys herself because she can't stop at two or three—or ten—drinks? The value of insight and concerted social action notwithstanding, there remains a need for routes to immediate help as well. What can be offered *today*, to more than three million women with alcohol problems?

This final chapter is an attempt to answer that question, both for women who need help with their drinking and for those who care about them. Among other things, this chapter discusses the symptoms of alcohol problems in women, the difficulties in deciding to get help, the most effective way to discuss a possible drinking problem with a woman you know, and various aspects of the treatment process. It also includes lists of alcoholism resources and related women's services, as well as a section on the small but growing women's alcoholism movement, with suggestions and resource listings for those who want to get involved. The chapter closes with a bibliography that includes books on women and alcohol, informational materials for activists in the alcoholism field, and "readings for survival" on a broad range of women's issues.

As Chapter 11 and other parts of this book have made clear, treatment for alcoholic women has never been a priority within our social services system. The gap between women's needs and the provision of sensitive, accessible services is enormous. Yet at the same time, there is movement afoot to bridge that gap. Slowly but determinedly, small groups of concerned people across the country—many of them recovered alcoholic women—have been working over the last decade to establish programs and support services that meet the needs of alcoholic women. There aren't enough of these kinds of programs, but they do exist and their numbers are growing.

Moreover, the alcoholism field itself is not the only potential source of help for the recovering alcoholic woman. Over the last several years, women's groups and organizations throughout the country have established a broad range of services, self-help projects, and information networks to help women gain more control over their lives. When used in conjunction with alcohol services, this women's support system can be a valuable resource for a woman who is trying to overcome a drinking problem.

In short, despite the inadequacies of our present system, help *is* available. This chapter tries to give you the information you need to find that help and make the most effective use of it.

WHAT IS ALCOHOLISM?

Nearly everyone seems to have her or his own personal definition of alcoholism, but most are fraught with myths and misconceptions that distort the real nature of the illness. According to Dr. Mark Keller of the Rutgers University Center of Alcohol Studies, an alcoholic person is "one who is unable *consistently* to choose whether he should drink or not, and who, if he drinks, is unable *consistently* to choose whether he should stop or not." In general, alcoholism has little to do with when you drink, how long you've been drinking, or even exactly how much alcohol you consume. But it has a great deal to do with how important alcohol is to you in particular situations and how seriously drinking is affecting the basic realities of your life: your health, your emotional well-being, your personal relationships, your work, and your financial situation. The more drinking is interfering with these areas of your life, the more serious is your alcohol problem.

It is also important to recognize that alcoholism is a treatable illness, as defined by the American Medical Association, the British Medical Association, and the National Institute on Alcohol Abuse and Alcoholism. It is no more a sign of weakness or moral dissipation than diabetes or German measles. And as illnesses go, it is far from uncommon. Approximately ten million Americans have drinking problems, at least a third of whom are women. It may appear to be less common than it actually is because many people—especially women—hide their alcohol abuse to protect themselves from the irrational social stigma associated with it.

DO YOU HAVE A DRINKING PROBLEM?

There is nothing easy about facing up to an alcohol problem. But painful as it is, the sooner you recognize that you are in trouble with drinking, the easier it will be to deal with the problem. Below are some questions that will help you learn how dependent you are on alcohol. This is a time to be absolutely honest with yourself—only you really know how seriously your drinking is hurting you.

1. Has someone close to you sometimes expressed concern about your drinking?
2. When faced with a problem, do you often turn to alcohol for relief?
3. Are you sometimes unable to meet home or work responsibilities because of drinking?
4. Have you ever neglected your children while drinking?
5. Have you—or anyone else—ever required medical attention as a result of your drinking?
6. Have you sometimes experienced a blackout—a total loss of memory while still awake—when drinking?
7. Have you ever come in conflict with the law in connection with your drinking?

8. Have you often failed to keep the promises you have made to yourself about controlling or cutting out your drinking?
9. Do you ever lie about how much you have been drinking, try to conceal it from others or rationalize it to yourself?
10. Do you sometimes feel guilty about your drinking?

If you have answered "yes" to three or more of the above questions, your drinking is probably affecting your life in some major ways and you should do something about it. Whether or not you are actually physically addicted to alcohol at this point is irrelevant; if drinking is interfering with any important aspects of your life, it has become a problem. And as alcoholism is a progressive illness, once a certain degree of dependence is established, one's drinking tends to get more and more out of control That means that even if you are able to limit your alcohol intake to some extent now, your drinking may well become worse over time, regardless of your attempts at self-discipline. The best time to stop drinking and seek help is now. Today.

THE DECISION TO GET HELP

Any reluctance you may feel about getting help for an alcohol problem probably has a lot to do with the way our society feels about alcoholism and alcoholic people. The myth prevails that an alcohol problem is somehow a sign of moral weakness, especially when it appears in women. As a result, you may feel that to seek help is to admit to some kind of shameful defect in yourself. But in reality, alcohol abuse is simply one way of coping—granted, an unhealthy way—with problems faced by nearly every woman at some point in her life: lack of self-esteem, family complications, the housewife's restricted and often isolated world, the working woman's pressure to compete in a male arena. When these problems become overwhelming, different women defend themselves from their pain in different ways. Some turn to psychotherapy, others to pills, and still others to a frenzied devotion to their work or outside activities. And some women turn to alcohol.

Yet even if you can come to accept your alcohol problem for what it is, there is no denying that some people will persist in their mistaken notions about the illness. There are those who not only view alcoholism as a weakness, but also, by a strange leap of logic, as a "worse" problem in women than in men. Don't let such misguided notions interfere with your decision to get treatment. Getting help for a drinking problem, and thereby giving yourself a chance to regain control of your own life, is immeasurably more important than somebody else's unrealistic expectations of you. And although some may not understand, there will be others who will respect your courage for taking steps to overcome a very human problem, and will support you all the way.

A chance for a new life, on your own terms, is the real payoff of recovery from an alcohol problem. For alcoholism treatment doesn't simply involve taking away the bottle and sending you on your way. The aim of treatment is to make you a stronger, happier, more self-aware person who doesn't *need* alcohol to function. In a treatment program sensitive to women, you will learn to understand and counteract the fears, feelings of inadequacy, tensions, and other conflicts which initially contributed to your drinking problem. A good program will also help you develop a new life plan that will correspond to your real needs and goals—not ones imposed on you by outside pressure or by your own unrealistic image of yourself.

IF A WOMAN YOU KNOW HAS A DRINKING PROBLEM

If you are reading this chapter because you suspect that a woman close to you might be in trouble with alcohol, first check out your hunch by reading the list of symptoms above. If you are sure that at least three of them apply to her, it is likely that she is having problems with her drinking. But now what? It used to be a basic tenet of alcoholism theory that the problem drinker could not possibly be reached until she had "hit bottom" and decided she needed treatment herself; until that time it was considered useless for family or friends to try to intervene. But most alcoholism specialists now believe that such a rule of thumb probably damaged more alcoholics than it helped, for it kept many from getting treatment until their physical and emotional deterioration was all but irreversible. It has since been demonstrated that actually one of the most successful ways to encourage the alcoholic to get help is through supportive confrontation by those close to her. Betty Ford, for example, ignored all signs of her own alcohol problem until her entire family sat down with her and, one by one, told her how deeply concerned they were about her drinking. Shortly afterward, she signed herself into Long Beach Naval Hospital for alcoholism and drug treatment.

Because women in particular are likely to deny an alcohol problem in themselves, the woman close to you may not even be consciously aware that she is drinking too much. Or she may suspect that she does have a problem, but is terrified of the possibility and has been furiously rationalizing her drinking for some time, both to herself and to others. In any case, your sympathetic intervention may be very important to her ability to face her alcohol problem.

This is not to say that intervening is easy. Most of us have been imbued with notions of politeness that forbid intrusions into the personal lives of others, particularly when those intrusions call attention to a problem in someone else. We are afraid of being rude, or even cruel. Yet in the long run, to confront a woman about her problem drinking is a profound and courageous act of caring. For far from attacking her, you are trying to help her free herself from a way of life that is seriously self-destructive and could eventually even kill her.

Probably the most effective time to discuss an alcohol problem with a woman you know is within a day or two of a situation in which her drinking was clearly a problem: a party where she got very drunk, a family dispute in which her drinking played a part, an alcohol-related accident. Choose a time when she is sober, both of you are in a fairly calm frame of mind, and there is an opportunity for a quiet, private conversation.

Tell her, straightforwardly and nonjudgmentally, that you are concerned about her drinking. Avoid the word alcoholism, which is not only threatening to most people but may not even be strictly accurate in her case. And take care not to adopt a lecturing, moralizing tone, for the slightest hint of condemnation in your voice or manner will be an instant turnoff. But at the same time, don't be put off by the excuses or denials which you may well receive. Be prepared to back up your concern with concrete examples of ways in which her drinking has caused problems for herself and for others, including the most recent incident. And make clear that nearby help is available.

If she is ready to deal with the problem, have ready local phone numbers and addresses where she can seek help (see pp. 262–64 for treatment resources). Offer to go with her on her initial visit to an outside source of help. And if you have already discussed the problem with other concerned family members or friends, let her know that they too can be counted on for support and assistance.

But don't be surprised if your initial attempt at intervention is unsuccessful. You are up against a powerful denial system based not only on the frightening stigma attached to alcoholism, but also on the strength of the alcohol dependence itself. Your friend or relative may well feel that she *can't* stop drinking, either physically or psychologically. Thus to ask her to stop drinking may feel to her like a life-threatening demand, regardless of the damage it is doing to her. If her initial reaction is one of extreme anger or if after some discussion she continues to deny the possibility of a problem, don't persist. Let her know that your concern stems from your caring for her, and that if she feels like talking about the subject at another time, you're always ready to discuss it. If she doesn't approach you, don't hesitate to bring up the subject again, particularly following any serious drinking-related incidents. But you can't force another person to get help for an alcohol problem, nor should you try. All you can do is offer your support and encouragement.

In the meantime, the greatest favor you can do for a woman with an alcohol problem is to begin to allow her to take responsibility for the consequences of her drinking. Out of embarrassment or a desire to "protect" the problem drinker, those close to her often expend a lot of energy making excuses for her, covering up for her mistakes, and generally extricating her from difficult situations caused by her drinking. But every time you shield a woman from the negative results of her alcohol abuse, you keep her from experiencing the effects of her problem and thereby make it easier for her to continue drinking. In effect, you are rescuing her from getting the help she needs.

THE TREATMENT PROCESS

The nature and length of treatment depend on the seriousness of a woman's alcohol problem and the kinds of resources available in her community. Treatment for severe alcoholism may include hospitalization for detoxification, followed by a long-term, intensive rehabilitation program. For a less serious drinking problem, treatment may involve a brief stay at a residential treatment center followed by participation in an alcoholism support group such as Alcoholics Anonymous or

Women for Sobriety. For those who seek help before their alcohol problem has progressed too far, outside help may be limited to attendance at alcoholism support group meetings, possibly supplemented by outpatient therapy. And as noted at the beginning of this chapter, there exists a wide variety of community resources that can be used in the treatment process, some of them designed specifically for women.

The process of recovery, then, has many dimensions and potential sources of support. The following sections describe some of the key elements of treatment, steps one can take to ensure the most effective possible care, and ways in which both alcohol and community resources can be creatively integrated into the recovery process. Addresses and further information on groups and organizations mentioned below can be found on pp. 263–69.

MEDICAL CARE

The severely alcoholic person must recover from acute intoxication and withdrawal before she can begin to change her life in more active ways. During the five- to seven-day detoxification process, which is usually carried out in a hospital or residential alcoholism facility, the patient is given medication to ensure safety and reduce discomfort, and is put on a nutritious diet supplemented with high-strength vitamins. During the same period, treatment is begun for any related health problems, such as liver cirrhosis, gastritis, malnutrition, and dehydration.

During detoxification, patients are often given Librium, Valium, or another minor tranquilizer to counteract the traumatic effects of withdrawal from alcohol. As these drugs help to ensure the safety of the withdrawal process, they are legitimately used during this period. However, apart from detoxification, some doctors put their recovering alcoholic clients—particularly women—on tranquilizers as part of the longer term treatment process. The rationale for prescribing these mood-changing drugs is that they help the newly sober person "adjust" to life without the help of alcohol. But like alcohol, some tranquilizers are also potentially addictive, and in the process of "adjustment" you may simply find yourself substituting one kind of drug dependence for another. Moreover, under the distorting haze of any mood-changing drug, it is extremely difficult to focus clearly on the issues you need to deal with in order to put your life back together. So once you become sober, avoid all mood-altering medications.

During treatment, a physician may also want to prescribe the drug disulfiram (Antabuse) to discourage you from returning to drinking. Antabuse is a very potent drug which, when taken in combination with alcohol, produces extremely painful reactions including nausea, irregular heartbeat, and a pounding headache. Because it is so powerful and its effects occasionally unpredictable, it should be taken with caution. If a doctor prescribes it, make sure he has thoroughly checked you for medical conditions that may be aggravated by Antabuse, and make clear that you want to use it only for a very limited period of time. Under no circumstances should you accept it as an *alternative* to counseling and related treatment.

THERAPY AND SUPPORT GROUPS

Virtually every kind of alcoholism treatment program includes some form of counseling to help the recovering alcoholic deal with immediate problems and learn to live more comfortably and creatively without the help of alcohol. But as this book has emphasized, the psychological needs of alcoholic women differ in some ways from those of men, both because women abuse alcohol for different reasons than men, and because many of the consequences of women's drinking are specifically related to women's societal role. For example, problem drinking women tend to struggle more with sex-role conflicts, are more subject to depression and suicide attempts, feel more degraded and ashamed of their drinking past, experience more guilt as well as ambivalence about parenthood, are more likely to have been abandoned by a spouse, and generally have lower self-esteem than alcoholic men. Obviously, these special needs must be dealt with in treatment if a woman is to recover.

If you are able to find an all-women's program or a coed program with special services for women, there is a good chance that the counseling available to you will be sensitive to your experience as a woman. However, if you find yourself in a treatment setting in which the counseling is inadequate to your needs, consider asking to start a women's group within the program, facilitated by a female counselor. Many recovering alcoholic women have found that such groups give them the opportunity to discuss issues common to women which are often difficult to talk about freely in a mixed group, such as sexuality, feelings about men, and concerns about mothering. In an all-women's group, it is also often easier to explore new behavior and roles without the fear of being put down as "unfeminine." In any case, you need—and have the right to—a space in which to freely explore the issues that matter to you. If the program does not provide that environment, consider looking for a new program. But don't abandon treatment altogether, for recovery is extremely difficult without involvement in some kind of mutual support system.

However, counseling provided by a treatment program is not the only available outlet for exploring issues related to your drinking. There are also at least two networks of voluntary, free support groups for recovering alcoholics which you can participate in during, after, or even in place of formal treatment, depending on your needs. The largest and best known of these is Alcoholics Anonymous (A.A.), which describes itself as a "worldwide fellowship of men and women who help each other to stay sober." A.A. is a huge organization, comprising thirty-two thousand local groups in ninety-two countries, and is generally recognized as one of the most effective programs in the world for helping alcoholics. There are no forms to sign, no dues to pay, no interviews to undergo; the only requirement for membership is a sincere desire to stop drinking.

Local meetings, which run every night of the week in many areas, are essentially informal, leaderless support groups in which members share experiences and encouragement in their mutual efforts to stay sober. In the process of this supportive sharing, recovering alcoholics learn that they are not alone in their struggle for sobriety and, importantly, that their alcoholism doesn't make them "bad" or "weak" people. As one woman put it: "The great thing about A.A. is that the people in it have *been there*. There is nothing you have done or felt or thought that they can't identify with. You're accepted for yourself."

Yet for all its strengths, Alcoholics Anonymous is still primarily a "male club" which some women find difficult to relate to. In 1977, women made up only twenty-eight percent of its total membership, and meetings in small towns and cities sometimes have an even more lopsided male-female ratio. Some women believe their special issues are not always dealt with adequately at meetings, or feel hesitant about bringing up certain sensitive topics at all in a primarily male group. This is a problem that seems to vary considerably from group to group. But many women who have felt uncomfortable in mixed groups have acted on their feelings by starting all-women's A.A. groups, which now number several hundred in the United States. If you join A.A. and are interested in joining a women's group, there may well be one already meeting in your area. If not, you are free to begin one yourself in accordance with A.A. guidelines.

Another potential source of support is Women for Sobriety, a fairly new national network of groups specifically geared to alcoholic women. The organization was created in 1975 by Dr. Jean Kirkpatrick, a sociologist and recovered alcoholic who felt that women were often shortchanged by traditional counseling and support systems offered to alcoholics. "Women need an organization within which they can share and solve their special problems," says Dr. Kirkpatrick. "They need an organization within which they can realize their full potential as women."

Women for Sobriety meetings focus on developing confidence in oneself as a woman and on concrete ways of coping with life stresses without recourse to alcohol. The organization's thirteen-point philosophy reflects a strongly positive vision of women's potential, embodied in such messages as: "I am a competent woman and have much to give others" and "I am responsible for myself and my sisters." Women for Sobriety now has approximately two hundred groups in all fifty states, and Dr. Kirkpatrick encourages women to form new groups. Membership is open to any woman who wants to overcome her drinking problem "through the discovery of self, gained by sharing experience, hopes, and encouragement with other women in similar circumstances."

Involvement in at least one of the above avenues of support or therapy is important to your recovery process, because they deal with your feelings and living issues in the specific context of trying to stay sober. But opportunities for emotional support are by no means limited to the resources of the alcoholism field. Once formal treatment has been completed, some women supplement their A.A. or Women for Sobriety membership with some form of psychotherapy in order to deal more intensively with certain difficult emotional issues. However, as noted in earlier chapters, therapy based on traditional psychological theory often works against women rather than in their best interests, because it tends to encourage women to adjust to limited roles and aspirations rather than to expand their visions of themselves. Fortunately, in recent years some women have begun to question the usefulness of traditional therapy and are developing new systems of emotional support.

If you decide to become involved in some form of counseling, you may want to look into feminist therapy, which is based on the concept that women's emotional problems are rooted in their limited social roles, and that to become psychologically healthy, women need to reclaim the parts of themselves that have been stifled by society. Many women psychotherapists now practice feminist therapy, both on an individual and group basis. But regardless of the kind of therapy you may choose, before making a commitment it is important to talk with your potential therapist about her/his therapeutic goals for women, as well as about attitudes toward alcoholism.

In addition to new approaches to therapy, women have also created a variety of peer support systems to help each other break free of their negative self-images and provide mutual support in solving common problems. Probably the best known of these is the consciousness-raising group, created in the early days of the women's movement as a means of freeing women from limiting, sex-typed behavior and self-images. These groups are still forming on an ongoing basis through various women's centers and organizations, and also are sometimes begun independently by groups of women interested in sharing experiences and emotional support.

But consciousness-raising groups are only one kind of mutual support system available to women. Their peer-group structure and commitment to validating women have since been adapted to a wide range of special-issue support groups for women, including those on single motherhood, divorce and widowhood, menopause, childbirth, and sexuality. Like consciousness-raising groups, support groups are sometimes begun through outside organizations, but you can also start one yourself if you know a group of women interested in exploring a common issue. You may also want to look into community-based women's groups and courses that focus on increasing self-awareness through learning new skills such as assertiveness, self-defense, meditation, or body awareness techniques. Although the specific aims of these various groups may vary considerably, they have in common the goal of helping women expand their capabilities and self-esteem. They are avenues of growth, rather than "adjustment."

TOOLS FOR LIVING

The process of putting your life back together once you are sober has many facets. At the same time that you are beginning to work on better understanding and accepting yourself, there may be a long list of complex practical matters that need attention as well. For example, you may require legal assistance to deal with a divorce or child custody case. Financial help also may be an immediate need, especially if you are living alone for the first time and have little job experience. There may be "survival skills" to master on short notice, such as basic auto repair or deciphering your first apartment lease or learning how to apply for credit. Child care and/or counseling for your children may also be a priority. And plans for the future, exciting as they may be, may also require forays into unfamiliar territory. How do you find the kind of job training you need? What is the process involved in applying to college? Where will the money come from? Sometimes you may feel that the process of beginning a new life is more than you can handle on your own.

Fortunately, there is no need to handle it by yourself, nor should you realistically be expected to. The alcoholism treatment program you participate in may be linked to community resources that can give you help in a number of areas, from job counseling and training to free legal advice to assistance in finding an apartment. In some programs, staff members will offer to accompany you in your initial dealings with various community services. However, if you don't participate in formal treatment or if your program makes only limited referrals, you can still find the kind of help you need. Many communities have women's centers and other kinds of local resource centers that provide a variety of services at a low cost, or will refer you to the specific agency that can best help you. For more information on these resource centers as well as listings of specific community organizations that may be helpful to you, see pp. 265–69.

WHERE TO GET HELP: ALCOHOLISM RESOURCES

TREATMENT PROGRAMS

A variety of community agencies can steer you to the kind of alcoholism treatment program best suited to your needs. These organizations, most of which can be found in your local phone book, include your area's council on alcoholism, Alcoholics Anonymous, your community alcoholism or mental health center, the social services or human resources department of your city or county, your county medical society, or the health office or employee assistance program in your workplace. When you contact one of these referral sources, specifically ask whether there is a women's alcoholism program in your area, or any treatment programs which include special services for women. You might also want to contact your state task force on women and alcohol, an activist organization which may keep a statewide listing of treatment programs particularly attuned to women's needs. For the address of your state task force, contact the National Council on Alcoholism (see below).

If for some reason you are unable to find a satisfactory program through any of the above channels, write to one of the following organizations for lists of treatment centers or further referral sources in your area. Most of these agencies also have free educational materials on alcohol abuse and alcoholism, available on request.

State alcohol authority
Your state capital

National Clearinghouse for Alcohol Information
Box 2345
Rockville, Maryland 20852

National Council on Alcoholism
733 Third Avenue
New York, New York 10017

SUPPORT GROUPS

Alcoholics Anonymous World Services
P.O. Box 459
Grand Central Station
New York, New York 10017

Alcoholics Anonymous headquarters can send you information on A.A. groups in your area as well as a variety of pamphlets on A.A.'s philosophy and program. However, most towns and cities have a local Alcoholics Anonymous office listed in the phone book, which can give you information on the times and places of meetings and answer any other questions you may have. This local office can also tell you whether there are any women's meetings in your area.

Al-Anon Family Group Headquarters
P.O. Box 182
Madison Square Station
New York, New York 10010

This organization sponsors groups for spouses and children of alcoholics, and also has local offices listed in the phone book.

Women for Sobriety, Inc.
P.O. Box 618
Quakertown, Pennsylvania 18951

Women for Sobriety headquarters will send you information on WFS groups in your area, and also makes available a monthly newsletter, *Sobering Thoughts,* on issues pertinent to recovering alcoholic women. If there are no groups currently meeting in your community, you will be put in touch with a regional WFS coordinator who can help you start your own group.

INFORMATIONAL MATERIALS ON WOMEN AND ALCOHOL

A.A. for the Woman and *Letter to an Alcoholic Woman,* produced by Alcoholics Anonymous. Both pamphlets discuss alcoholism in women and ways in which A.A. can be of help to problem drinking women. Available free from Alcoholics Anonymous World Services, Inc., Box 459, Grand Central Station, New York, New York 10017.

Information Packet on Women and Alcoholism, produced by the National Clearinghouse for Alcohol Information. Includes pamphlets on getting help for a drinking problem, on alcohol problems among Spanish-speaking women (written in Spanish and English), and on the fetal alcohol syndrome, as well as several popular and scholarly articles on alcohol and women. Available free from NCALI, Box 2345, Rockville, Maryland 20852.

Women and Alcoholism Kit, produced by the National Council on Alcoholism. Includes several pamphlets on the alcoholic woman, including *Danger Signals for Women Drinkers,* as well as general information in NCA. Available for $2.25 from NCA, 733 Third Avenue, New York, New York 10017.

Resources for Lesbian Alcoholics. Includes an international meeting directory for gay recovering alcoholics, a list of gay meetings of Al-Anon, and a directory of facilities and services for gay alcoholics and drug abusers (each available for $1), as well as a pamphlet entitled "The Homosexual Alcoholic" (10¢). Available from Tucker, P.O. Box 4623, Arlington, Virginia 22204.

For further readings on women and alcohol, see the bibliography starting on p. 272.

WHERE TO GET HELP: COMMUNITY RESOURCES

As noted earlier, your own community may offer a wide range of services to supplement those available from an alcoholism treatment program or support group. Many of these services have been designed specifically for women, while others are geared to the community at large. The listings below include referral sources for such services as well as specific local agencies and groups which may offer them.

LOCAL RESOURCE GUIDES

Women's Yellow Pages. In many communities, women's rights activists have compiled exhaustive resource directories on services and programs in the local area that meet a variety of women's needs. Emphasis is on nonsexist, alternative services, but usually many general community resources are listed as well. These directories are available at local women's centers, YWCAs, and some bookstores.

Community Yellow Pages. These are usually similar to women's directories in format and categories of services covered, but lack any specific emphasis on women's needs. They commonly include a mix of low-cost alternative resources and more traditionally oriented services, and are available at local bookstores and community centers.

MULTIRESOURCE AND REFERRAL CENTERS

Women's Centers. Outside of the alcoholism system, these centers may be the single most helpful source of help and information for the recovering alcoholic woman. They are community-based, often collectively run centers designed for women, by women, to meet a variety of needs in a supportive environment. The six hundred-some centers now operating in the United States vary widely in size and resources, but virtually all function at least as a referral source for a variety of women's needs, including jobs, housing, child care, therapy, health care, and legal and financial services. Many centers also sponsor their own activities, ranging from consciousness raising and other support groups to auto repair workshops and seminars on starting one's own business. Many also provide a comfortably furnished "common room" where women can simply come to talk, read, or hold community meetings on women's issues.

National Organization for Women (NOW). NOW is primarily a civil rights organization for women, concerned with employment, education, health issues, and exploring alternative roles for women. Many local chapters offer consciousness-raising groups for women (and men); workshops on such issues as sexuality, child care, and employment; and make referrals to other community services as well.

Young Women's Christian Association (YWCA). This organization, originally established as a haven for young women away from home, has broadened its scope as women's needs have changed and expanded. Most local YWCAs now offer a wide range of reasonably priced programs for women, including physical education classes, assertiveness training and other personal growth courses, and skills training for women returning to the workplace. Some Y's also operate as community women's centers, with their own hotlines or referral banks of local women's resources.

Displaced Homemakers Programs. These programs provide personal, educational and career counseling, job training and placement, and referrals to community resources for the estimated five million former homemakers in the United States who are no longer supported by their spouses and lack the training or experience to obtain adequately paying jobs. Currently, more than one hundred such programs and projects exist throughout the country, most of them operating out of women's centers, YWCAs, colleges and universities, or local social services agencies. To locate the program nearest you, write to the Displaced Homemakers Network, c/o Business and Professional Women's Foundation, 2012 Massachusetts Avenue, N.W., Washington, D.C. 20036.

Commissions on Women. These are government-supported agencies aimed at ensuring equal treatment of women in several areas, including employment, credit, housing, and domestic relations. They provide practical support in fighting "the system" as well as referrals to further sources of help.

Neighborhood Centers. These are often store-front, all-volunteer operations which try to meet some of their neighborhood's most basic needs, including sources of food, shelter, and money. They may offer a number of services and referrals in the areas of child care, housing, legal services, food coops, counseling, job training programs, health care, and financial assistance. A neighborhood center may be the best place to go for fast emergency help, particularly if you have previously had bad experiences with the bureaucratic red tape of some city and county services.

SOURCES OF SPECIFIC SERVICES

Referrals for or actual provision of all of the types of services listed below should be available from one of the multiresource centers just described. But if you need further information on a specific kind of service, one of the agencies listed below should be able to help you.

Jobs: Counseling, Training, Placement

Women's job counseling and referral centers
City or state employment service
City or county vocational rehabilitation department
City, county, or state personnel office
City manpower administration

Education

Adult education department of local school system
Admissions offices of local colleges, universities, and vocational schools
Continuing education department of local high schools and colleges

Legal Assistance

Women's legal clinics of local colleges and universities
City or county Legal Aid Society
Neighborhood, city, or county legal services agency
Division of child support enforcement of city social services department

Financial Aid, Services

County or city social services or public welfare department
Women's and community credit unions
Women's banks

Child Care: Referrals, Services

Local child care association or resource center
Extended day care program of local school system

City or county departments of social services and recreation
Churches

Emergency Housing
County or city emergency shelter
Battered women's shelter
Salvation Army

Family and Parenting Services
Family therapy services of community mental health center
Family services agency of county or city social services department
Parents Anonymous (child abuse)
Parents Without Partners

Counseling, Support, and Personal Growth Groups
Continuing education department of local colleges
Open and free universities
Women's counseling collectives
Community mental health centers

GETTING ACTIVE

Although help *is* available to the alcoholic woman, there is no denying that more effective and accessible services are urgently needed. If you are interested in working to make such services a reality, there is a movement already waiting for you. The women's alcoholism movement is essentially a loose coalition of local, state, and national groups intent on improving prevention, outreach, and treatment services to alcoholic women in the United States. On the state and local levels, where most of the activity is happening, these groups are operating on several fronts. Some are focusing on public education, producing films, putting public service announcements on radio and television, and stuffing pamphlets into supermarket racks in an effort to sensitize the public to the problem and encourage alcoholic women to seek help.

Other groups are engaged in the ambitious task of actually setting up women's alcoholism treatment programs in their own communities. Many have conducted their own systematic research on the needs of alcoholic women in their areas and have presented recommendations to local policy-makers. Still others have gone beyond city and state governments and have approached the National Institute on Alcohol Abuse and Alcoholism with demands for increased dollars and commitment to meeting women's needs.

But although there is activity afoot, in the face of the enormity of the problem, it is not nearly enough. Most of the groups working on the issue are small and unfunded, comprised of people who print pamphlets and write funding proposals on spare evenings between the demands of full-time jobs. Although commitment is high, so is frustration and turnover. There is a pressing need for more people, professional skills, and funding to be brought to the women's alcoholism movement in order for it to have real impact. If you want to get involved, below are some resources to help you get started.

ACTIVIST GROUPS AND ORGANIZATIONS

State Task Forces on Women and Alcohol. These task forces are the backbone of the women's alcoholism movement. Now operating in more than forty states, they coordinate statewide efforts to improve treatment, outreach, and prevention services to women. Some of the state task forces have spawned local chapters as well, which are looking into women's alcohol concerns in their own immediate communities. To obtain the address of the task force in your state, write to the National

Council on Alcoholism's Office on Women listed directly below. Your state task force chairwoman can tell you how you can participate on the state level as well as put you in touch with any local women's alcohol groups in your area.

Office on Women, National Council on Alcoholism, 733 Third Avenue, New York, New York 10017. The National Council on Alcoholism is the largest private alcoholism organization in the country, and its Office on Women has played a primary role in bringing the problems of alcoholic women to national attention. The Women's Office not only coordinates the activities of the state task forces, but also conducts training institutes on women and alcohol, publishes pamphlets and other informational materials, and sponsors a women's forum at NCA's annual convention.

Women's Program, National Clearinghouse for Alcohol Information, Box 2345, Rockville, Maryland 20852. The National Clearinghouse for Alcohol Information is the information arm of the federal National Institute on Alcohol Abuse and Alcoholism, and its women's program focuses on public education with an emphasis on prevention. It has produced a variety of pamphlets and special packages on women's alcohol problems, and has worked intensively with women's centers and national women's organizations on prevention and outreach projects.

National Women's Health Network, Suite 105, 2025 "I" St. N.W., Washington, D.C. 20006. This is a national membership organization of women's health groups, health professionals, and consumers which focuses on affecting federal health policy relevant to women. Its involvement in women's alcoholism issues has included efforts to secure more federal monies for women's treatment programs, recommendations to NIAAA on accreditation for alcoholism programs, and educational efforts on the fetal alcohol syndrome.

FURTHER READINGS

WOMEN AND ALCOHOL: BIOGRAPHY AND AUTOBIOGRAPHY

Allen, Chaney L. *I'm Black and I'm Sober*. CompCare, 1978.

Crawford, Linda. *In a Class by Herself*. New York: Charles Scribner's Sons, 1976.

Friedman, Myra. *Buried Alive: The Biography of Janis Joplin*. New York: William Morrow & Co., 1973.

Hall, Nancy L. *A True Story of a Drunken Mother*. Houston: Daughters, Inc., 1974.

Kirkpatrick, Jean. *Turnabout: Help for a New Life*. New York: Doubleday & Co., 1978.

Rebeta-Burditt, Joyce. *The Cracker Factory*. New York: Macmillan, 1977.

WOMEN AND ALCOHOL: READINGS FOR ACTIVISTS

Alcohol Abuse Among Women: Special Problems and Unmet Needs. U.S. Senate Hearings, September 29, 1976. (Available from Senate Documents Room, Washington, D.C. 20510).

Homiller, Jonica. *Women and Alcohol: A Guide for State and Local Decisionmakers*. Washington, D.C.: Alcohol and Drug Problems, Assn., 1977. (Available from the Council of State Authorities, ADPA, 1101 15th Street, N.W., Suite 206, Washington, D.C. 20005. Price: $7.)

Nellis, Muriel, ed. *Drugs, Alcohol and Women: A National Forum Source Book*. Washington, D.C.: National Research and Communications Associates, 1976.

Women's Project Package produced by the National Clearinghouse for Alcohol Information. Includes information and project ideas on women's alcohol concerns as well as a guidebook entitled *Alcohol Programs for Women: Issues, Strategies and Resources.* (Available free from NCALI, Box 2345, Rockville, Maryland 20852.)

READINGS FOR SURVIVAL

Making It On Your Own

Caine, Lynn. *Widow: The Personal Crisis of a Widow in America.* New York: William Morrow & Co., 1974.

Edwards, Marie and Hoover, Eleanor. *The Challenge of Being Single.* New York: J. B. Tarcher, 1974.

Hirsch, Barbara B. *Divorce: What Every Woman Needs to Know.* New York: Bantam Books, 1975.

O'Brien, Patricia. *The Woman Alone.* New York: Quadrangle, 1973.

Women in Transition, Inc. *Women in Transition: A Feminist Handbook on Separation and Divorce.* New York: Charles Scribner's Sons, 1975.

Jobs and Money

Bird, Caroline. *Everything a Woman Needs to Know to Get Paid What She's Worth.* New York: David McKay Co., 1973.

Pogrebin, Letty C. *Getting Yours.* New York: David McKay Co., 1975.

Porter, Sylvia. *Sylvia Porter's Money Book.* New York: Avon Books, 1975.

A Working Woman's Guide to Her Job Rights. Leaflet 55. [Available from Superintendent of Documents, U.S. Government Printing Office, Washington, D.C. 20402 (60¢).]

Legal Rights

Alexander, Shana. *State by State Guide to Women's Legal Rights.* Wollstonecraft, 1975.

Ross, Susan C. *The Rights of Women: An American Civil Liberties Handbook*. New York: Avon Books, 1973.

Personal Growth

Boston Women's Health Book Collective. *Our Bodies Ourselves*. New York: Simon and Schuster, 1976.

Rush, Anne Kent. *Getting Clear: Body Work for Women*. New York: Random House, and Berkeley, Ca.: Bookworks, 1973.

Seattle-King County NOW Chapter. *Woman, Assert Yourself!* New York: Harper & Row, 1974.

Children and Parenting

Boston Women's Health Book Collective. *Ourselves and Our Children*. New York: Random House, 1978.

Curtis, Jean. *Working Mothers*. New York: Doubleday, 1976.

Hope, Carol and Young, Nancy. *Momma: The Sourcebook for Single Mothers*. New York: New American Library, 1976.

Radl, Shirley. *Mother's Day is Over*. New York: Warner Books, 1974.

NOTES

CHAPTER ONE

1. Joseph J. Lawrence and Milton A. Maxwell, "Drinking and Socioeconomic Status," *Society, Culture and Drinking Patterns,* ed. D. J. Pittman and C. R. Snyder (New York: John Wiley and Sons, 1962), p. 144.

2. Muriel W. Sterne and David J. Pittman, *Drinking Patterns in the Ghetto,* vol. 2 (St. Louis, Mo.: Social Science Institute, Washington University, 1972), p. 527.

3. J. V. Rachal et al., *A National Study of Adolescent Drinking Behavior, Attitudes and Correlates* (Research Triangle Park, N.C.: Research Triangle Institute, 1975).

4. Robert W. Jones and Alice R. Helrich, "Treatment of Alcoholism by Physicians in Private Practice: A National Survey," *Quarterly Journal of Studies on Alcoholism,* 33 (1972), pp. 117–131.

5. U.S. Senate, Subcommittee on Alcoholism and Narcotics of the Committee on Labor and Public Welfare, Hearings on "Alcohol Abuse Among Women: Special Problems and Unmet Needs," 94th Congress, 2nd sess., 1976, p. 16 (hereafter cited as U.S. Senate Hearings).

6. Marc A. Schuckit and Elizabeth R. Morrissey, "Alcoholism in Women: Some Clinical and Social Perspectives with an Emphasis on Possible Subtypes," *Alcohol Problems in Women and Children,* ed. M. Greenblatt and M. A. Schuckit (New York: Grune and Stratton, 1976), pp. 5–36.

7. Patricia Kent, *An American Woman and Alcohol* (New York: Holt Rinehart and Winston, 1967), p. 45.

8. Simone de Beauvoir, *The Second Sex,* trans. and ed. H. M. Parshley (New York: Bantam Books, 1968), p. 447.

9. U.S. Senate Hearings, p. 18.

10. Edith S. Gomberg, "Women and Alcoholism," *Women in Therapy,* ed. V. Franks and V. Burtle (New York: Brunner/Mazel, 1974), p. 177.

11. Marc A. Schuckit, "Sexual Disturbance in the Woman Alcoholic," *Medical Aspects of Human Sexuality,* 6 (1972), p. 44.

12. "Is This Your Problem?" *Woman Magazine,* 15 June 1974, p. 42.

13. Erik Erikson, "Inner and Outer Space: Reflections on Womanhood," *Daedalus,* 93 (1974), p. 586.

14. Bruno Bettelheim, "The Commitment Required of a Woman Entering a Scientific Profession in Present-Day American Society," *Women in the Scientific Professions: The M.I.T. Symposium on American Women in Science and Engineering,* ed. J. A. Mattfeld and C. G. Van Aken (Cambridge, Mass.: M.I.T. Press, 1965), p. 15.

15. Phyllis Chesler, *Women and Madness* (New York: Avon Books, 1972), p. 278.

CHAPTER TWO

1. C. B. Avery, ed. *Greek Mythology and Legend* (New York: Appleton-Century-Crofts, Meredith Corp., 1972).

2. Robert Graves, *The Greek Myths,* vol. 1 (New York: George Braziller, 1959).

3. Martin P. Nilsson, *The Dionysiac Mysteries of the Hellenistic and Roman Age* (New York: Arno Press, 1975).

4. Dionysius of Halicarnassus (c. 25 B.C.), *The Roman Antiquities*, vol. 1, trans. E. Cary (Cambridge, Mass.: Harvard University Press, 1937), pp. 381ff.

5. Valerius Maximus, *Facta et Dicta Memorabilia*, book 6, from French trans. of T. C. E. Baudement (Paris, 1850), p. 274.

6. Geoffrey Chaucer, "The Canterbury Tales," *The Portable Chaucer*, ed. T. Morrison (New York: Viking Press, 1949).

7. M. D. George, *London Life in the 18th Century* (New York: Capricorn, 1965), p. 26.

8. Rebecca H. Warner and Henry L. Rosett, "The Effects of Drinking on Offspring: A Historical Survey of the American and British Literature," *Journal of Studies on Alcohol*, 36 (1975), p. 1396.

9. T. G. Coffey, "Beer Street, Gin Lane: Some Views of 18th Century Drinking," *Quarterly Journal of Studies on Alcohol*, 27 (1966), p. 671.

10. Henry Fielding, "An Enquiry into the Causes of the Late Increase of Robbers, with Some Proposals for Remedying this Growing Evil" (London: A. Millar, 1751), pp. 9–10.

11. Mark Lender, "Drunkenness as an Offense in Early New England: A Study of 'Puritan' Attitudes," *Quarterly Journal of Studies on Alcohol*, 34 (1973), pp. 354–355.

12. Andrew Sinclair, *Era of Excess: A Social History of the Prohibition Movement* (New York: Harper and Row, 1964), p. 59.

13. M.E.J. Kelley, "Women and the Drink Problem," *Catholic World*, 69 (1899), p. 679.

14. Agnes Sparks, "Alcoholism in Women," *Medico-Legal Journal*, 15 (1897), p. 219.

15. Ben Barker-Benfield, "Sexual Surgery in Late Nineteenth Century America," *International Journal of Health Services*, 5 (1975), pp. 279–288.

16. Andrew Sinclair, *The Better Half: The Emancipation of the American Woman* (New York: Harper and Row, 1965), p. 222.

17. Ibid., p. 224.

18. Sinclair, *Era of Excess*, p. 407.

19. Walter R. Cuskey and T. Premkumar with Lois Sigel, "Survey of Opiate Addiction Among Females in the United States Between 1850 and 1970," *Public Health Reviews*, 1 (1972), p. 11.

20. Horatio C. Wood, "Facts About Nostrums," *Popular Science,* 68 (1906), p. 531.

21. George Creel, "Suffering Women," *Harper's Weekly,* 9 January 1915, p. 28.

22. Cuskey, "Survey of Opiate Addiction Among Females," p. 12.

23. Margaret C. Banning, "Lit Ladies," *Harper's Monthly,* 160 (1930), p. 161.

24. Ibid., p. 163.

25. Sinclair, *Era of Excess,* p. 287.

26. J. Kobler, *Ardent Spirits* (New York: G.P. Putnam's Sons, 1973), p. 238.

27. Walter Davenport, "Sisters Under the Skinful," *Colliers,* 11 September 1926, p. 18.

28. Kobler, *Ardent Spirits,* p. 339.

29. "On Girls Learning to Drink," *The Literary Digest,* 7 January 1933, p. 20.

30. George Gallup, *The Gallup Poll: Nationwide Drinking Audits* (Princeton, N.J.: American Institute of Public Opinion, 1939, 1974, 1977, 1978).

CHAPTER THREE

1. Bernice Rosenbaum, "Married Women Alcoholics at the Washingtonian Hospital," *Quarterly Journal of Studies on Alcohol,* 19 (1958), pp. 79–89.

2. B. Karpman, *The Alcoholic Woman,* 2nd ed. (New York: Lancer, 1972).

3. Paul C. Whitehead and Roberta G. Ferrence, "Women and Children Last: Implications of Trends in Consumption for Women and Young People," *Alcohol Problems in Women and Children,* ed. M. Greenblatt and M.A. Schuckit (New York: Grune and Stratton, 1976), pp. 163–192.

4. David J. Hanson, "Drinking Attitudes and Behaviors Among College Students," *Journal of Alcohol and Drug Education,* 19 (1974), pp. 6–14.

5. Henry Wechsler, "Epidemiology of Male/Female Drinking" (Paper presented at NIAAA Workshop on Alcoholism and Alcohol Abuse Among Women, Jekyll Island, Ga., April 2–5, 1978), p. 17.

6. San Mateo County, California, Department of Public Health and Welfare, "Student Drug Use Surveys, San Mateo County, California: 1968–1974," mimeographed (1974).

7. Bureau of Labor Statistics, *Employment in Perspective: Working Women* (Washington, D.C.: U.S. Department of Labor, 1978).

8. Clark Gavin, ed. *The Wine Marketing Handbook: 1977* (New York: Gavin-Jobson Associates, 1977), p. 92.

9. Clark Gavin, ed. *The Liquor Handbook: 1977* (New York: Gavin-Jobson Associates, 1977), p. 114.

10. Ibid., p. 30

11. Gavin, *Wine Marketing Handbook,* p. 17.

12. *Executive Newsletter: The Original Newsletter of the Beer, Wine and Spirits Industries,* 24 March 1978, p. 1.

13. Gavin, *Liquor Handbook,* p. 111.

14. Ibid., p. 30.

15. Bureau of the Census, *Statistical Abstract of the United States, 1977* (Washington, D.C.: U.S. Department of Commerce, 1977), p. 431.

16. Ibid., pp. 845–847.

17. Kaye M. Fillmore, "Drinking and Problem Drinking in Early Adulthood and Middle Age; An Exploratory 20-Year Follow-up Study," *Quarterly Journal of Studies on Alcohol,* 35 (1974), pp. 819–840.

18. Judy F. Coakley and Sandie Johnson, *Alcohol Abuse and Alcoholism in the United States: Selected Recent Prevalence Estimates,* working paper no. 1 (Rockville, Md.: National Institute on Alcohol Abuse and Alcoholism, 1977).

19. Robert W. Jones and Alice R. Helrich, "Treatment of Alcoholism by Physicians in Private Practice: A National Survey," *Quarterly Journal of Studies on Alcoholism,* 33 (1972), pp. 117–131.

20. Marc A. Schuckit and Elizabeth R. Morrissey, "Alcoholism in Women: Some Clinical and Social Perspectives with an Emphasis on Possible Subtypes," *Alcohol Problems in Women and Children,* ed. M. Greenblatt and M. A. Schuckit (New York: Grune and Stratton, 1976), pp. 5–35.

21. Marvin A. Block, "Women Alcoholics," *Alcoholism: Its Facets and Phases* (New York: John Day, 1965), p. 158.

22. Mark Keller and Carol Gurioli, *Statistics on Consumption of Alcohol and on Alcoholism, 1976 Edition* (New Brunswick, N.J.: Journal of Studies on Alcohol, 1976), p. 14.

23. John L. Norris, "Analysis of the 1977 Survey of the Membership of Alcoholics Anonymous" (Paper presented at Thirty-second International Congress on Alcoholism and Drug Dependence, Warsaw, Poland, Sept. 3–8, 1978), p. 16 (hereafter cited as "Analysis of 1977 Survey of AA").

24. Max Gunther, "Female Alcoholism: The Drinker in the Pantry," *Today's Health*, 53 (1975), p. 16.

25. Norris, "Analysis of 1977 Survey of AA," p. 16.

26. Laurence A. Senseman, "The Housewife's Secret Illness: How to Recognize the Female Alcoholic," *Rhode Island Medical Journal*, 49 (1966), p. 40.

27. Paula Johnson, *Sex Differences in Drinking Practices* (Report to National Institute on Alcohol Abuse and Alcoholism, U.S. Department of Health, Education and Welfare, Contract no. ADM-281-76-0020, April 1978).

CHAPTER FOUR

1. Donald Goodwin et al., "Alcohol Problems in Adoptees Raised Apart from Alcoholic Biological Parents," *Archives of General Psychiatry*, 28 (1973), pp. 238–243.

2. Edith S. Gomberg, "Alcoholism in Women," in *Social Aspects of Alcoholism*, ed. Benjamin Kissin and Henri Begleiter (New York: Plenum Press, 1976), p. 127.

3. Margaret Mead, *Male and Female* (New York: Dell Publishing Co., 1949), pp. 416–417.

4. William McCord and Joan McCord with J. Gudeman, *Origins of Alcoholism* (Stanford: Stanford University Press, 1960).

5. David C. McClelland et al., *The Drinking Man* (New York: Free Press, 1972).

6. McCord, *Origins of Alcoholism*, p. 162.

7. Georgio Lolli, "Alcohol and the American Woman," in *Social Drinking*, ed. G. Lolli (New York: Collier, 1960), p. 260.

8. McClelland, *The Drinking Man*, p. 296.

9. Sharon C. Wilsnack, "The Effects of Social Drinking on Women's Fantasy," *Journal of Personality*, 42 (1974), pp. 43–61.

10. Sharon G. Wilsnack, "Sex Role Identity in Female Alcoholism," *Journal of Abnormal Psychology*, 82 (1973), pp. 253–261.

11. Sharon C. Wilsnack, "The Impact of Sex Roles on Women's Alcohol Use and Abuse," in *Alcoholism Problems in Women and*

Children, ed. Milton Greenblatt and Marc Schuckit (New York: Grune and Stratton, 1976), pp. 37–63.

12. Frederick B. Parker, "Sex-Role Adjustment in Women Alcoholics," *Quarterly Journal of Studies on Alcohol,* 33 (1972), pp. 647–657.

13. Inge Broverman et al., "Sex Role Stereotypes and Clinical Judgments of Mental Health," *Journal of Consulting and Clinical Psychology,* 34 (1970), pp. 1–7.

14. Marc A. Schuckit, "The Alcoholic Woman: A Literature Review," *Psychiatry in Medicine,* 3 (1972), pp. 37–43.

15. Mary C. Jones, "Personality Antecedents and Correlates of Drinking Patterns in Women," *Journal of Consulting and Clinical Psychology,* 36 (1971), pp. 61–69.

16. Walter R. Gove and Terry R. Herb, "Stress and Mental Illness Among the Young: A Comparison of the Sexes," *Social Forces,* 53 (1974), pp. 256–265.

17. Jones, "Personality Antecedents," pp. 67–68.

18. Edith S. Gomberg, "Women and Alcoholism," *Women in Therapy,* ed. V. Franks and V. Burtle (New York: Brunner/Mazel, 1974), p. 177.

19. Edith S. Gomberg, "Risk Factors Related to Alcohol Problems Among Women: Proneness and Vulnerability" (Paper presented at the NIAAA Workshop on Alcoholism and Alcohol Abuse Among Women, Jekyll Island, Ga., April 2–5, 1978), p. 18.

20. Myrna M. Weissman and Gerald L. Klerman, "Sex Differences and the Epidemiology of Depression," *Archives of General Psychiatry,* 34 (1977), pp. 98–111.

21. Lenore Radloff, "Sex Differences in Helplessness, With Implications for Depression," *Career Development and Counseling of Women,* ed. L.S. Hansen and R.S. Rapoza (New York: Charles Thomas, 1978).

22. Joan Curlee, "Alcoholism and the 'Empty Nest,' " *Bulletin of the Menninger Clinic,* 33 (1969), pp. 166–167.

23. Wilsnack, "The Impact of Sex Roles," p. 47.

24. Pauline Bart, "Depression in Middle Aged Women," *Women in Sexist Society,* ed. Vivian Gornick and Barbara K. Moran (New York: Basic Books, 1971), p. 169.

25. Alice Rossi, "Family Development in a Changing World," *American Journal of Psychiatry,* 128 (1972), p. 1058.

CHAPTER FIVE

1. Paula Johnson, *Sex Differences in Drinking Practices* (Report to National Institute on Alcohol Abuse and Alcoholism, U.S. Department of Health, Education and Welfare, Contract no. ADM-281-76-0020, April 1978), p. 15.

2. Leonard S. Brahen, "Housewife Drug Abuse," *Journal of Drug Education,* 3 (1973), pp. 13–24.

3. Lawrence S. Linn and Milton S. Davis, "The Use of Psychotherapeutic Drugs by Middle-Aged Women," *Journal of Health and Social Behavior,* 12 (1971), pp. 331–340.

CHAPTER SIX

1. Bureau of Labor Statistics, *Employment and Earnings* (Washington, D.C.: U. S. Department of Labor, 1979).

2. U.S. Department of Labor, Bureau of Labor Statistics (Unpublished data, Washington, D.C., 1978).

3. Bureau of Labor Statistics, *Employment and Earnings.*

4. Bureau of the Census, *Current Population Reports,* series P60, no. 116 (Washington, D.C.: U.S. Department of Commerce, 1977).

5. "Women-Headed Households Growing Rapidly," *Dollars and Sense,* 37 (May–June, 1978), pp. 14–15.

6. Louise Kapp Howe, *Pink Collar Workers* (New York: Avon Books, 1977), p. 11.

7. Paula Johnson, *Sex Differences in Drinking Practices* (Report to National Institute on Alcohol Abuse and Alcoholism, U.S. Department of Health, Education and Welfare, Contract no. ADM-281-76-0020, April 1978), p. 33.

8. Margaret Wilmore, *NIAAA Alcoholism Treatment Services for Women* (Report to National Institute on Alcohol Abuse and Alcoholism, U.S. Department of Health, Education and Welfare, Sept. 29, 1977), p. 2.

9. Interview with Sheila Salcedo, Coordinator, Employee Assistance Program, New York City Off-Track Betting Corp., New York City, March 1978.

10. Karen Zuckerman, "Women and Alcohol" (Paper presented at Rochester Institute of Technology, Rochester, N.Y., June 8, 1976), p. 7.

CHAPTER SEVEN

1. Paula Johnson, *Sex Differences in Drinking Practices* (Report to National Institute on Alcohol Abuse and Alcoholism, U.S. Department of Health, Education and Welfare, Contract no. ADM-281-76-0020, April 1978), p. 15.

2. Metropolitan Life Insurance Co., "Mortality from Alcoholism," *Statistical Bulletin*, 58 (1977), pp. 2–5.

3. H.J. Malin and N.E. Munch with L.D. Archer, "A National Surveillance System for Alcoholism and Alcohol Abuse" (Paper presented at Thirty-second International Congress on Alcoholism and Drug Dependence, Warsaw, Poland, Sept. 3–8, 1978), pp. 9–10.

4. Johnson, *Sex Differences*, p. 13.

5. Women's Bureau, *Minority Women Workers: A Statistical Overview* (Washington, D.C.: U.S. Department of Labor, 1977).

6. Office of Health Resources Opportunity, *Health of the Disadvantaged* (Washington, D.C.: U.S. Department of Health, Education and Welfare, 1977), p. 2.

7. National Institute on Alcohol Abuse and Alcoholism Advisory Council, "Minutes of Advisory Council Meeting," 23 May 1977, p. 2.

8. Muriel W. Sterne and David J. Pittman, *Drinking Patterns in the Ghetto*, vol. 2 (St. Louis, Mo.: Social Science Institute, Washington University, 1972), p. 527.

CHAPTER EIGHT

1. J. V. Rachal et al., *A National Study of Adolescent Drinking Behavior, Attitudes and Correlates* (Research Triangle Park, N.C.: Research Triangle Institute, 1975).

2. Henry Wechsler, "Epidemiology and Male/Female Drinking" (Paper presented at NIAAA Workshop on Alcoholism and Alcohol Abuse Among Women, Jekyll Island, Ga., April 2–5, 1978), p. 21.

3. Mark Keller and Carol Gurioli, *Statistics on Consumption of Alcohol and on Alcoholism, 1976 Edition* (New Brunswick, N.J.: Journal of Studies on Alcohol, 1976), p. 4.

4. Lee H. Bowker, *Drug Use Among American Women, Old and*

Young: Sexual Oppression and Other Themes (San Francisco: R. & E. Research Associates, 1977).

5. Richard W. Wilsnack and Sharon C. Wilsnack, "Sex Roles and Drinking Among Adolescent Girls" (Unpublished paper, July 1977).

6. Richard Jessor and Roderick S. Carman with Peter H. Grossman, "Expectations of Need Satisfaction and Drinking Patterns of College Students," *Quarterly Journal of Studies on Alcoholism,* 29 (1968), pp. 101–116.

CHAPTER NINE

1. Marcel T. Saghir et al., "Homosexuality IV: Psychiatric Disorders and Disability in the Female Homosexual," *American Journal of Psychiatry,* 127 (1970), pp. 147–154.

2. Muriel W. Sterne and David J. Pittman, *Drinking Patterns in the Ghetto,* vol. 2 (St. Louis, Mo.: Social Science Institute, Washington University, 1972), p. 585.

3. Lillene H. Fifield and J. David Latham with Christopher Philips, "Alcoholism in the Gay Community: The Price of Alienation, Isolation and Oppression" (Los Angeles: Gay Community Services Center, 1977), p. 3.

4. L. J. Lohrenz et al., "Alcohol Abuse in Several Midwestern Gay Communities" (Unpublished paper, 1976).

5. Alan P. Bell and Martin S. Weinberg, *Homosexualities: A Study of Diversity Among Men and Women* (New York: Simon and Schuster, 1978).

6. Saghir, "Homosexuality," p. 154.

7. Brenda Weathers, "Alcoholism and the Lesbian Community" (Unpublished paper, Los Angeles, Ca., 1976), p. 4.

8. Fifield, "Alcoholism in the Gay Community," pp. 11–12.

9. Ibid., p. 2.

10. Ibid., pp. 16–17.

11. Ibid., p. 18.

12. Weathers, "Alcoholism and the Lesbian Community," pp. 5–6.

CHAPTER TEN

1. Howard M. Bahr and Gerald R. Garrett, *Women Alone: The Disaffiliation of Urban Females* (Lexington, Mass.: D.C. Heath and Co., 1976), p. 135.
2. Gerald R. Garrett and Howard M. Bahr, "Women on Skid Row," *Quarterly Journal of Studies on Alcohol,* 34 (1973), p. 1232.
3. Ibid., p. 1240.
4. Bahr and Garrett, *Women Alone,* pp. 136–137.

CHAPTER ELEVEN

1. Jane E. James, "Symptoms of Alcoholism in Women: A Preliminary Survey of A.A. Members," *Journal of Studies on Alcohol,* 36 (1975), p. 1567.
2. Robert W. Jones and Alice R. Helrich, "Treatment of Alcoholism by Physicians in Private Practice: A National Survey," *Quarterly Journal of Studies on Alcoholism,* 33 (1972), pp. 117–131.
3. LeClair Bissell and Robert W. Jones, "The Alcoholic Physician: A Survey," *American Journal of Psychiatry,* 133 (1976), p. 1142.
4. Phyllis Chesler, *Women and Madness* (New York: Avon Books, 1972).
5. Marilyn W. Johnson, "Physicians' View on Alcoholism With Special Reference to Alcoholism in Women," *Nebraska State Medical Journal,* 50 (1965), p. 380.
6. Herbert I. Abelson et al., *National Survey on Drug Abuse: 1977,* vol. 1 (Rockville, Md.: National Institute on Drug Abuse, U.S. Department of Health, Education and Welfare, 1977), p. 102.
7. John L. Norris, "Analysis of the 1977 Survey of the Membership of Alcoholics Anonymous" (Paper presented at the Thirty-second International Congress on Alcoholism and Drug Dependence, Warsaw, Poland, Sept. 3–8, 1978), p. 20.
8. Luise K. Forseth, "A Survey of Minnesotas' Halfway Houses for the Chemically Dependent" (Unpublished paper, 1976), p. 9.
9. Ingrid Waldron, "Increased Prescribing of Valium, Librium and Other Drugs: An Example of the Influence of Economic and Social

Factors on the Practice of Medicine," *International Journal of Health Sciences*, 7 (1977), p. 55.

10. Jane Prather and Linda S. Fidell, "Sex Differences in the Content and Style of Medical Advertisements," *Social Science and Medicine*, 9 (1975), pp. 23–26.

11. Christine McRee and Billie F. Corder with Thomas Haizlip, "Psychiatrists' Responses to Sexual Bias in Pharmaceutical Advertising," *American Journal of Psychiatry*, 131 (1974), p. 1274.

12. Association of Halfway House Alcoholism Programs of North America, "Statistical Survey of Full Member Halfway House Alcoholism Programs" (St. Paul, Minn.: 1976), pp. 6–7.

13. Cheryl Gillen et al., "Report on Survey of Eighty-Eight New York State Outpatient, Detoxification, Halfway House and Rehabilitation Facilities" (New York: Committee on Women and Alcoholism in New York State, 1977), p. 1.

14. Edith S. Gomberg, "Women and Alcoholism," in *Women in Therapy*, ed. V. Franks and V. Burtle (New York: Brunner/Mazel, 1974), p. 183.

15. Johnson, "Physicians' Views on Alcoholism," p. 380.

16. Stephen J. Levy and Kathleen M. Doyle, "Attitudes Toward Women in a Drug Treatment Program," *Journal of Drug Issues*, 4 (1974), p. 430.

17. Inge Broverman et al., "Sex Role Stereotypes and Clinical Judgments of Mental Health," *Journal of Consulting and Clinical Psychology*, 34 (1970), pp. 1–7.

18. Ardelle M. Schultz, "Women and Addiction" (Paper presented to Ohio Bureau of Drug Abuse, Cleveland, Oh., June 17, 1974), pp. 23–24.

19. National Institute on Alcohol Abuse and Alcoholism, U.S. Department of Health, Education and Welfare, *Women in Treatment for Alcoholism in NIAAA Funded Facilities*, 1977 (Rockville, Md.: 1978), p. 8.

20. Levy and Doyle, "Attitudes Toward Women in a Drug Treatment Program," p. 431.

21. Marian Sandmaier, "Women Helping Women: Opening the Door to Treatment," *Alcohol Health and Research World*, 2 (1977), pp. 17–23.

22. New York City Department of Mental Health and Mental

Retardation Services, *Mental Health, Mental Retardation and Alcoholism Services, 1976–1980 Plan* (New York: 1976), p. 299.

23. David A. Pemberton, "A Comparison of the Outcome of Treatment in Female and Male Alcoholics," *British Journal of Psychiatry*, 133 (1967), pp. 367–373.

CHAPTER TWELVE

1. Ronald W. Maris, "Deviance as Therapy: The Paradox of the Self-Destructive Female," *Journal of Health and Social Behavior*, 12 (1971), pp. 122–123.

2. Donnie M. Hoffman and Linda S. Fidell, "Characteristics of Androgynous, Undifferentiated, Masculine and Feminine Middle-Class Women" (Paper presented at the 1977 annual meeting of the American Psychological Association).

3. June Singer, *Androgyny: Toward a New Theory of Sexuality* (New York: Anchor Press/Doubleday, 1976), pp. 24, 35.

4. Eleanor Maccoby and C. Jacklin, *The Psychology of Sex Differences* (Stanford, Ca.: Stanford University Press, 1974).

5. Joan Volpe and James Rooney, *The Halfway House Experience for Alcoholic Women* (Final Report to National Institute on Alcohol Abuse and Alcoholism, U.S. Department of Health, Education and Welfare, Research Grant no. R01-AAO-3185, 1979).

INDEX